PLAYS AND POEMS:

BY

GEORGE H. BOKER.

IN TWO VOLUMES.

VOL. II.

BOSTON:
TICKNOR AND FIELDS.
M DCCC LVI.

STEREOTYPED BY
HOBART & ROBBINS,
New England Type and Stereotype Foundery,
BOSTON.

CONTENTS OF VOLUME II.

PLAYS.

POEMS.

THE BETROTHAL:

A PLAY.

DRAMATIS PERSONÆ.

Marquis di Tiburzzi, ...	*A decayed nobleman.*
Count Juranio, ...	*A wealthy nobleman.*
Salvatore, ...	*His kinsman.*
Marsio, ...	*A wealthy merchant.*
Pietro Rogo, ...	*His friend.*
Pulti, ...	*Servant to Marsio.*
Costanza, ...	*Daughter to the Marquis.*
Filippia, ...	*Her cousin.*
Marchioness di Tiburzzi, ...	*Mother to Costanza.*

A Priest, a Notary, Guests, Servants, &c.

Scene, Tuscany.

THE BETROTHAL.

ACT I.

SCENE I. *An Apartment in the* MARQUIS DI TIBURZZI'S *Castle.*
Enter the MARQUIS *and* MARCHIONESS DI TIBURZZI.

Marquis. WHY urge forever Marsio's rich estate?
Wealth is not sovereign. Should his money sprout,
And yield a thousand-fold, it could not change
Its master's nature. In the glare of gold
Unnumbered blemishes oft come to light,
That had been better hidden in beggar's rags.
Marchioness. What faults has he?
Marq. It matters not.
March. Why not?
Marq. If I dislike the man, the end is gained
Without a summing of antipathies.
March. But should Costanza love him?
Marq. Bless me, madam!
Am I an oracle? Your questions reach
Beyond my thinking.
March. Stranger things have been.
The maids of Greece, for all their dainty tastes,
Gambolled with Satyrs. Men can never know

The shifting fancies of a woman's heart.
Some love the outer, some the inner man,
And some the garniture which fortune gives;
Some love to rule, others to be enslaved;
Some love for pity, some affect the bold;
Some on entreaty, others from sheer spite
And sturdy opposition, will consume
With three-fold fire. This slender bodkin's point
Is ample basis for a woman's love.
Marq. Not for Costanza's. Do not wrong our daughter
With empty fables, nor impute to her
The melting weakness of all womankind.
If she should love — Poh! poh! I squander breath;
The thought is monstrous.
March. Pray, what see you, sir,
In Signore Marsio — think him what you may —
To banish him beyond the pale of love?
He is not handsome! Well, and what of that?
These girls have apes for playthings. Cannot talk?
She 'll slit his tongue, and busy her for hours
With her new human magpie. Here 's a husband
To banish Maltese cats and singing-birds!
What if she love?
Marq. Her love would sanctify
More vice than Marsio's little soul can hold. —
But this is idle.
March. Now, what do you mean?
First, Marsio's blemishes; next, your dislikes;
Then, Marsio's vices, and his little soul!
Why do you hate him?
Marq. Hate is not the word:

I would not choose him for my daughter's husband.
First, his mean birth. —

March. Ho! pause we at his birth.
Did his low birth beget his character?
I hold you, sir, he is so nobly minded
That he will pick an empress for his dam,
If you give choice.

Marq. Like still engenders like:
'T is nature's law. The rugged mountain horse
Breeds not the silk-skinned barb; the shaggy cur
Litters no fine-limbed greyhounds. It may take
Whole ages of ancestral blood, to crown
A long-drawn race with one true gentleman.
Think you his peddling stock can shape a mate
For her whose fathers, at great Cæsar's voice,
Out-flew the conquering eagles?

March. There it is!
Cæsar and all his legions! We have stood
A hungry siege from him for many a day.
Would he had strangled at his birth,
With all his captains!

Marq. Why this argument?
I have heard ten thousand, in my time, yet never
Knew one wry notion straightened by them all.
What would you?

March. Why not ask me that before
The matter smothered in the argument?

Marq. Speak; I attend you.

March. Should Costanza's eyes
Have found some merit, unobserved by you,
In Signore Marsio — should it so have wrought
Upon her woman's fancy as to gain,

In Cæsar's spite, that precious heart of hers —
Would you oppose her choice?

Marq. Oppose her choice
Why, you amaze me. Have you seen good grounds
For such a question?

March. I have seen enough.
I have observed kind looks from Marsio's eyes
By echoing blushes answered from her cheeks;
I have — Lord, Lord! what have I not observed? —
Sufficient to have bred a plague of love,
If love were catching.

Marq. This is very strange.

March. No; 't is as old as Adam. Maids will love,
And fathers will not see it. From these signs,
Knowing our daughter's happiness might hang
Upon your voice, I would forestall her grief,
By timely checks, ere love has grown a habit;
Or, should you wish, confirm her doubting heart
By your full sanction.

Marq. Wonderful indeed!
She fancy Marsio! Had I been asked,
I 'd said she shunned him.

March. No unusual trick
Of love-sick girls. — But here Costanza comes.
Leave her to me — nay; if you question her,
You 'll scorch her words in blushes.

Marq. As you will
You are wrong, believe me. She has ever borne
So plain a heart to me, so dutiful,
So zealous to fulfil my wish as never
To question of its justice — yet such acts
Performing not with the cold hand of duty,

But with the fiery eagerness of love —
That I shall feel some twinge of jealousy,
If she has ousted me from my fair seat,
Henceforth a stranger's, without common notice.
Question, but do not vex her. I would rather
Your keen suspicion had o'ershot its mark,
Than that my daughter should have wasted love
Upon this — this —

March. Noble, thrice noble man;
Half deified by her subliming love!

Marq. I have no heart for jesting. [*Exit.*]

March. Nor for acting:
Your feeble nature shifts the deed on me.

(*Enter* COSTANZA.)

Costanza. Where went my father?

March. To concoct some scheme
About a penny-worth of musty bread.
It takes more work, to live this starving way,
Than would be used in earning us a fortune.
But we are noble, very noble, daughter;
We have some centuries of rich, proud blood,
On which we live, and therefore need not labor.
We feed, like fleshy men, upon our fat,—
Self-eating cannibals.

Cos. Fasting has its mirth,
Feasting its sorrow.

March. Ay, ay; much the mirth
We see the death's head grinning.

Cos. True, my mother;
Death has a whisper in the maddest mirth
Of us poor mortals.

March. You are gloomy, child.

Cos. No more than usual. 'T is a gloomy thing

To see a father, so deserving love,
Bowed with a load of vulgar, petty cares —
Too mean to tax the housewife of a hind —
That nip and pinch him into actual life,
Giving his aching mind no dreaming pause
'Twixt day and day.

March. Of all disgusting things
Commend me to our old, familiar friend,
Proud poverty.

Cos. Would I could lighten it!

March. And so you can.

Cos. I! how?

March. I trow, my daughter,
You 'll be no victim, no burnt-offering,
No chattel, traded for your father's peace:
No; let us starve, drown, hang — why, what care you?
You have a heart, forsooth, a virgin heart,
Not to be hung on matrimonial shambles!
In faith, you are right.

Cos. What is your purpose, mother?

March. There 's Signore Marsio; do you fancy him?

Cos. I never weighed my feelings for him.

March. No?
But he loves you.

Cos. For that I owe him thanks.

March. Now — do you mark me? — should you marry him,
We are rich at once.

Cos. That never crossed my mind.

March. It has ours.

Cos. "Ours"?

March. Your father's and my own.
Cos. My father spoke of this?
March. Just ere he left.
Cos. Does he desire me to wed Marsio?
March. You know your father far too well for that.
He would not have you wed for his sake only;
Would not persuade you, press you, and so forth.
With such spasmodic eagerness, with such
A trembling lip, and clutching of the hands,
He says these things, that I, who know his ways,
With half a thought can fathom his desire.
Cos. Which is?—
March. That we should want no longer.
Cos. How!
Wed Marsio?
March. Not unless with your consent.
Well, would you try it? Tell your father, then,
You love rich Marsio, whose countless wealth
Can bribe his sorrow, ease his shaking mind,
And make his days lapse calmly to their end—
Marsio, whose golden finger puts to flight
Duns, bailiffs, tradesmen, all the brood of want,
And makes a jest of every former grief
To talk of in foul weather. Nay, my child;
Breathe not a word of this: say simply thus—
I love good Marsio; I would be his wife.
You 'll see the issue.
Cos. Signore Marsio stands
Far better with my father than I thought.
Doubtless there is some good in Marsio—
In Marsio—in Marsio—
March. Well, well!
Why do you dwell upon his name?

Cos. There seems
A strangeness in it, I ne'er marked before.
March. You will attempt this little loving ruse?
Cos. Mother, I dare not tamper with the love
My father bears me.
March. Poh! 't is but a trial.
You need not marry Marsio, for all.
Cos. This I will say: if to my father's mind
Marsio appear a proper husband for me,
And Signore Marsio should incline to me,
I will accept him.
March. Bravely spoken, child!
I know you do this for your father's sake;
And 't is a beautiful, most saint-like act,
On which the angels smile. May Heaven reward you!
Then, in Italy, marrying is one thing,
Loving is another.
Cos. What did you say?
March. You will find out ere long. But, hark, Costanza;
If you are resolute, let every action,
Which falls beneath your father's eyes, appear
Full of kind thoughts for Signore Marsio.
Cos. I feel but kindly towards him. O, my mother,
If he, or any man — a clown — a fool —
More hideous than the nightmare, crueller than
The ragged tooth of famine —
March. Tut, tut! daughter,
Marsio is none of these.
Cos. I hope not, madam.
Doubtless, I 'll learn to love him very soon.
It seems to me, duty would tutor love,

At the first moment my poor father smiled.
Marsio must know the terms.
March. What need of that?
When did love ever chaffer about terms?
I 'll tell him, if 't will ease you.
Cos. Let us go.
My father's word must sanction this high treason
Against the sweet dominion of god Love.—
You see I am merry, mother; am I not?
March. Yes; very merry.
Cos. As we go along,
Give me a catalogue of all our ills.
Tell o'er my father's sufferings; then rehearse
The royal qualities of Marsio's gold.
How do you think my father's face would look
With one bright smile upon it? Do you know,
'T is a long, dreary age since I beheld
What you might call a smile upon his face?
I need to hear these things. Think you this marriage
Would be no sin against my better nature?
March. Heaven counsels filial love.
Cos. Yes; you shall feast,
And wear gay clothes, and build our shattered house,
And brush the cobwebs from our ancestry,—
That seem to suffer like decay with us,—
And there shall be no name in Italy
Prouder than the Tiburzzi! Did you think,
When you first saw me lying in my cradle,
An impotent, cross bantling, that one day
Your poor Costanza could do all these things?

I know you did not — ha, ha! (*Laughing.*) Woe is
me!
Tears are close neighbors to such mirth as mine.
[*Exeunt.*]

SCENE II.

Another Apartment in the Castle. Enter MARSIO.

Marsio. If I know money — Heaven knows I
should —
They must come to it. Needy, needy, say you?
I have known the needy murder for a ducat:
Lo! here are millions; and but for a name.
A very ancient, very noble name,
I grant; but somewhat damaged in the keeping. —
Easily patched, however, easily patched with gold.
Join Marsio's riches to Tiburzzi's name,
And who can stand against them? But the name,
Ungilt and naked, is an empty noise,
Which Marsio's gold — Marsio's hard, solid gold —
As well can purchase in the daily market
Where parents vend their marriageable wares.
Why should I doubt? There's nothing like a heart
To chaffer for. I never bought a heart.
Men say I want one. Ha, ha! how they lie!
[*Laughing.*]
'T is a great rock on which all commerce wrecks.
There is no rival, no keen moneyed man,
To weigh his scrapings 'gainst my topmost bid;
So says the Marchioness — O, pardon me —
Our mother, I should say; though ne'ertheless
A marchioness for all that, Costanza dear. —

Conny, and Con, and Stanza, when you please me,
Besides a hundred other sweet, pet names,
To come up on occasion. Ha! our mother!
And all one splendor with a blaze of smiles!

(*Enter the* MARCHIONESS.)

I guess your meaning.
Marchioness. Hist! the Marquis comes.
Show no surprise; one doubt may mar the whole.
Hear, ere you speak.
Mar. I am all ears, no tongue.

(*Enter the* MARQUIS.)

Marquis. Welcome, friend Marsio!
Mar. "Friend Marsio!"
Well spoken, friend Tiburzzi! (*Aside.*) Gracious sir,
Your proud addition to my humble name —
March. Stoop not too low, or you may never rise.
[*Apart to* MARSIO.]
Mar. — My deeds shall ratify.
March. Turned just in time.
[*Aside.*]
Marq. Frankness is best —
Mar. The coin of honesty!
March. For Heaven s sake, peace! Art talking for a wager? [*Apart to* MARSIO.]
Marq. Signore, it seems my daughter and yourself,
Unknown to me — and therein much I blame you —
Have leagued your hearts —
Mar. What! she —
March. O, silence, silence!
[*Apart to* MARSIO.]

Marq. You would excuse her, signore, with such reasons
As, to the partial wits of lovers, seem
Both law and right; on me they fall full coldly.
That love, which breeds such ecstasy in you,
To me is breach of trust. But let that pass.
Mar. Against your word —
Marq. Do not deceive yourself;
Hearts will make way against ten thousand words.
Mar. Are you so wilful? Forward, then. [*Aside.*]
March. You see,
My lord but seeks our daughter's happiness.
Marq. Yes; take her, sir. No foolish whim of mine
Shall stand 'twixt heart and heart.
Mar. "'Twixt heart and heart!"
What does he mean? Well, I will swallow all. [*Aside.*]
Your frank approval stifles my poor thanks.
Let me repay your frankness with its equal.
No man, who is your friend, has wanted eyes
To see how, day by day, that ancient wealth,
Which once so proudly propped your mighty name,
Has slipped beneath the thing it should support;
Till all the glories of this noble house
Seem tottering down to ruin and oblivion. —
Nay, do not chafe; I cannot choose but know it.
Marq. "Know it, know it!" the very beggars know it,
And, with unbegging laughter, pass me by!
My name 's the jest of all this mocking land. —
The blind, dumb, deaf, conceive it! Idiots, jays,
Parrots, have wit to say, "Poor, poor Tiburzzi!"

Mar. I would not ape them.
Marq. O, 't is nothing new:
Heaven makes us feel our chastenings commonly.
Of all realities, the reallest thing —
Of all heart-sickening, spirit-killing things —
That can unnerve, unsex, and bring to naught
The proudest purposes of stubborn strength,
Making brawn Hercules a whining baby —
The very top and crown is poverty!
It feeds on hope, it glories in despair,
It saps the brave foundations of the will,
It turns our simple faith to blasphemy,
It gnaws its way into the very spirit,
And with a weary siege starves out the soul,
Sending to judgment that bright denizen
So changed in hue, so fallen from its estate,
That Heaven, in the poor, warped, and shivering thing,
Can scarcely recognize its handiwork!
Mar. My purse shall aid you. Use it, without stint,
In common with me.
Marq. Pshaw! I need it not.
I and my wants have grown such intimates
That 't would seem strange to part us. Prisoned men
Have wept at parting from their old, dull cells:
So custom, I doubt not, may reconcile
A father to an unconfiding child.
I can take naught of him. [*Aside. Walks apart.*]
March. Urge him no more:
His mind is troubled with an idle fancy
About Costanza's want of trust in him.

He has scarce patience, now, to speak with her:
But he will change, next moon. [*Apart to* MARSIO.]
Marq. Pray treat her well,
Pray treat her well, good signore Marsio:
One sin makes not a sinner. She is worth it; —
Yes, yes, although she 'd not confide in me.
But then, you know, we fathers have no vows
Like you hot lovers; have no skill, to show
The depths and heights of customary feeling,
With high-spiced words. Love grows a gray-beard in us,
And lacks the prattle of the wingéd boy.
Pray treat her well.
Mar. I 'll have no other care.
A precious store ne'er wants a zealous ward.
Marq. Let not that promise rust.
March. Our daughter waits.
Signore, go on before. What, what, so tardy!
Does your love use a herald?
Mar. By your leave, then. [*Exit.*]
March. Stands it not as I said?
Marq. Is she my daughter?
March. If she is mine.
Marq. That strain I cannot doubt:
There the blood cries.
March. If it amuses you,
Pray rail away. There 's many an out-door saint
Blows off his wolfish humors at his wife,
And paces forth a lamb.
Marq. Love Marsio? — No!
What, sell herself? — pah! pah! Come, let us in.
This shivering on the brink is worse than drowning.

I 'll link these lovers. When the knot is tied,
The galling process of the action stops,
And I may rub my fretted hands at ease.
I 'll not be tortured. — Marry, marry shall they;
And sooner than they think! Still waiting, madam?
Heavens! what a new Tiburzzi fortune sends!
[*Exeunt.*]

SCENE III.

Another Apartment in the Castle. Enter COSTANZA *and* FILIPPIA.

Filippia. Would I wed Marsio? Would I wed the —
Costanza. There!
Your common phrases have sufficient strength,
Without appealing to another world.
Fil. Would I wed Marsio? (*Laughing.*) Why, 't is something new
To hear you jesting, cousin! Would I wed
A man who ever thrusts his money forth
As his best quality? — a man who feels
No inward stir of man's nobility,
But, like the poor ass with his golden freight,
Is worth just what he carries? Then he has
A wicked, subtle, and consuming devil,
Pent in the corners of his red-rimmed eyes,
That 's always dodging, like a serpent's tongue,
Angry but fearful.
Cos. What a character!
Fil. 'T is Marsio to an eye-lash.

Cos. Your wild tongue
Ever outruns your stricter meaning, cousin.
I shall wed Marsio.
Fil. What a woful sigh!
That is the tone Gonsalvo gave me, when,
Tearing his tattered ruff — worn for the nonce —
He cried, "I shall drink poison!" But he did not.
Cos. But I will.
Fil. Drink poison?
Cos. No; wed Marsio.
Fil. The poison in another shape.
Cos. Fie! fie!
Are quibbling jests the best advice you give?
Fil. 'T was jest chase jest. You are not serious?
Cos. Indeed I am.
Fil. Then here 's a weeping matter.
Cos. Marsio has made an offer for my hand,
Which I intend accepting.
Fil. O, you shall not,
You shall not, by my faith!
Cos. By mine I shall.
Fil. I hate him, hate him!
Cos. I 'm not jealous of you.
Fil. Who 's jesting, now?
Cos. You 've taught me your own tongue.
Fil. I see through this. You marry that base wretch —
That sallow, spider-legged, bow-shouldered wretch —
That man of money — that great human purse —
That — that —
Cos. Hie forward, forward, cousin dear!
I would not have you keep such humors to yourself;
They might breed inward danger.

Fil. Out upon you!
Your father's wants have driven you to this end.
You should not dare — I say, you should not dare,
If famine wrestled with us throat to throat —
Offer the holiest portion of your nature
To this gold calf. 'T will have a grievous answer,
One day, Costanza; for 't is mortal sin
To strike at the dim instincts of the heart.
Why are you weeping? Cousin, dear Costanza,
The sun shines upon nothing that I love
As I love you. That 's generous; smile again. —
But, lo! the gentle lover! lo! sweet Marsio!
Dragging his fingers o'er the entrance wall
Like a belated school-boy!

Cos. Cousin, cousin!

Fil. He sees you —blushes! Ay: by my faith, blushes,
Through all his leathern skin, from ear to chin!
Come, that is cheering! Marsio can blush.

Cos. Do leave, Filippia.

Fil. I! I dare not leave.
Look to your trade, Costanza. Push him sharply.
He 'll get the better of you. I 'll be witness;
And if he slip one tittle, we will close
Upon him roundly. Tell him hearts are dear
This season; the supply of maiden hearts
Has dwindled down; he may have widows' cheaper;
Old maidens' for the asking. Money 's plenty,
And begs for usury. Nay, mark these things;
He 'll trick you else. We must protect our interest.

Cos. Have done! have done!

(*Enter* MARSIO.)

Good welcome, sir!

Marsio. I thank you.
A fair day, lady!
Fil. Dare the knave say that,
With such a falling-weather face? Perhaps,
Some day, he'll find I'm not invisible,—
The ill-bred cur! [*Aside.*]
Mar. May we converse alone?
Fil. Better and better! He has seen my ears;
I'll show my tongue, next. [*Aside. Seats herself apart.*]
Cos. Signore Marsio—
Mar. Yes, lady, yes.—I have a mortal dread
Of girls and babies. [*Aside.*]
Cos. You would speak with me?
Mar. Ay; if I could. [*Aside.*] Has not your mother—Pshaw!
I came to lay my fortune at your feet;
And I will hold it doubled fifty times,
If you bestow one smile upon the act.
Fil. Prolific smile! [*Aside.*]
Cos. Sir, if my simple smile—
Fil. Or my compounded laughter, shout on shout. [*Aside.*]
Cos. This is deceit. [*Aside.*]
Mar. O, horror, what a strait!
Never a word! Her silence will upset me.
Would she might fall to cursing! [*Aside.*]
Fil. Conny, dear,
A million, Conny; 'tis well worth a million.
Mar. What means yon lady?
Fil. You shall see, anon. [*Aside.*]
Cos. 'T would pose my cousin, signore Marsio,
To show a meaning in one half she says.
Mar. Your servant, lady. [*Bowing.*]

Fil. Of the latest date. [*Curtseying.*]
Mar. Here 's my excuse. [*Pointing to* COSTANZA.]
Fil. A fair excuse, indeed:
I know no fairer, sir.
Mar. I said not so:
You might teach schoolmen, if you knew yourself.
Fil. Well done! We get on bravely. [*Aside.*]
Mar. Gentle lady,
Our business waits. [*To* COSTANZA.]
Fil. There the mart speaks again. [*Aside.*]
Cos. Has not my mother told you of the terms
On which I listen to your suit?
Mar. She has —
O, golden chance! here comes the Marchioness!
I'd have gone mad, ere long. [*Aside.*]

(*Enter the* MARQUIS *and* MARCHIONESS.)

Marquis. Daughter Costanza,
Do you love signore Marsio?
Cos. I hope
To love him better, sir.
Marchioness. Well said, well said!
Love 's but a baby, Hymen is a boy;
He grows apace in wedlock. — Well said, daughter!
This coyness is the privilege of maids:
Do not compel her to a public blush.

[*Apart to the* MARQUIS, *who walks up the stage, gloomily.*]

Cos. How sad my father seems!
March. 'T is very natural;
He parts from you; but it is like the parting
Of a young twig, that, when it sunders, adds
A vigorous life to the old parent tree.
Think of that, daughter.

Cos. But the twig will wither. —
So be it, though, if it revive the tree.
Marq. You would wed signore Marsio?
Cos. I will wed,
With your approval, signore Marsio.
Mar. It irks me much that you must bare your heart; —
Both irks and pleases.
March. Are these questions decent?
[*Apart to the* MARQUIS.]
Fil. She changes words, and never answers straight.
She's mad for misery. There's something wrong.
If I but dared — I will — (*Aside.*) My lord, my lord —
Marq. She has declared it. Take her, signore, take her!
And may she never want the duteous love
A wife should show a husband! May she lean,
In an unbroken confidence, upon
The upright manhood she has found in you;
And may you never know what bitterness
Burns in the silent chambers of a heart
That loves, yet cannot trust! God bless you, child! —
Yea, give your husband all you held from me!
[*Aside.*]

ACT II.

SCENE I. *The Park of the* MARQUIS DI TIBURZZI. *Enter* JURANIO *and* SALVATORE.

Juranio. WHOSE grounds are these?
Salvatore. The Marquis di Tiburzzi's —
A sorry sequel to an ancient stock,
Whose wide dominion once outstretched our sight.
Alas! for him, poor man, malicious fortune
Threw all the choicest of her random smiles
Upon the wrong end of his famous race,
And now mocks him with what his fathers were.
Ju. A pretty place! Some heritage of beauty
Yet harbors here. Mark how the clustered blossoms
Star the dark back-ground of yon shady wood.
Sal. O! yes; but mark how jealous avarice
Has shorn the chiefest saplings to the root.
Ju. Yet spared us every flower. Praise be to Heaven!
Their beauty is not marketable. See,
A living bower, a bower of growing vines,
All carpeted with last year's fallen leaves!
Sal. A thrifty thought! The very dead are used.
That hint was stolen from Egypt, where they burn
Their spicy ancestors. 'T were a proud thing,
To sit down at a fire of Ptolemies,
With Cleopatra for a back-log.
Ju. Ugh!

You would put out the harmony of heaven
With your great sprawling jokes. The hand of taste,
Making best use of few materials,
Is here.

Sal. The hand of woman.

Ju. Worse and worse!
I'll fly you, shortly.

Sal. 'T would confess your devil,
To fly at holy names. Why do you shun
These dainty blossoms of humanity
With such stern care? — So ho! run, run for life!
There go two maids — two full-blown, dangerous maids —
Hide you, sir modesty!

Ju. You know them maids?

Sal. I take them so on credit.

Ju. Save you, save you!
Good lady-broker, you will one day fail
From such long credits.

Sal. See, they make this way.
Here comes the goddess of your living bower.

Ju. Which one?

Sal. The shorter.

Ju. No; the taller one.

Sal. How know you that?

Ju. I trace her little fingers
In the soft curvings of each vine.

Sal. Ho! ho! (*Laughing.*)

Ju. I'll bet my Arab — saddle, spurs, and all —
Against your empty laugh, those cunning girls
Are plotting to ensnare some luckless man:
I see such malice in your small one's eyes.

Sal. Done!

Ju. Done! — Come hide.
Sal. A mere excuse for running,
You arrant fly-frock!
Ju. Here, behind the bower.
[*They secrete themselves.*]

(*Enter* Costanza *and* Filippia.)

Costanza. Press me no more; my motives are my own.
You grant me judgment?
Filippia. More than you grant me.
You have some cloudy fancy in your brain,
That needs but airing,— some weak, flimsy notion,
That common reason would dry up at once.
Cos. You rate me poorly, cousin.
Fil. There again!
You would be off. Stick to the text, Costanza.
Do you love Marsio?
Cos. Would I wed him else?
Fil. You dare not answer strictly.
Cos. Why then ask?
Fil. I know you do not. 'T is not in your nature
To fall so meanly. O! be warned in time.
The twin-born heart to whom you owe allegiance,
To whom, perforce, you must surrender love,
Will track you out at last. How fearful, then,
To perish piecemeal with a smothered passion,
Or — I will not repeat it: 't was a story
Old at the flood.
Cos. Here I dare answer strictly.
If you will not allow me Marsio,
At least, I love no other.
Fil. But you will —

Nay, never raise your brows — you will, I say,
Fall in a frenzy of outrageous love
With some stern, mulish creature, like yourself,
Who swears he 'll wed the blackest blackamoor,
And will — that will he! — though the heavens should fall!
Tell me, Costanza, — tell me, darling cousin, —
What are your motives in this strange affair?
Cos. Then will you cease your torments?
Fil. Ay; and vow
To keep good counsel.
Cos. Nor by word or deed
Again oppose my purpose?
Fil. Yes, to that;
But 't is a bitter contract.
Cos. Let us walk:
The story is a long one. [*They walk up the stage.*]
Ju. Salvatore,
This eavesdropping is scarcely honorable.
Sal. What a fine moral sense! Just as you lose
The last faint whisper of their pretty talk,
Up starts indignant honor.
Ju. Ah! her voice
Held honor spell-bound. Did you mark, with me,
How the low music trickled from her lips?
All heaven was listening to her, why not we?
Sal. Which one set heaven agog?
Ju. The taller one.
Sal. The small one spoke the more.
Ju. More, but less valued.
The other's phrases served to bind together,
As baser metal solders sovereign gold,
The broken links of her harmonious thoughts.

Sal. Zounds! are you mad?
Ju. I know not what I am:
I am something I was not an hour ago.
Sal. Unhappy idiot!
Ju. See, see, she walks!
Sal. A wonderful exploit!
Ju. I must address her.
Sal. Fellow, there are two. To my unbiassed eyes,
The smaller is the fairer. Let us leave,
As partial penance for our vulgar fault.
Will you not come?
Ju. No; I must speak to her.
Sal. That were ill-bred.
Ju. I 'll frame new codes of manners.
Fair lady, by your leave — [*Advancing to* COSTANZA.]
Sal. Nay, be not startled.
'T is but a simple kinsman of my own,
A poor brain-darkened lunatic; but harmless,
Quite harmless to a lady. Pray you know him;
The Count Juranio — once a wiser man.
[JURANIO *bows.*]
Ju. And here his cousin, signore Salvatore,
[SALVATORE *bows.*]
A world-wide jester, a professed buffoon;
The globe 's his bauble, all mankind his mark;
Each word of his a jest, or meant for such.
A cunning ferret after doubtful phrases,
A subtle reasoner upon groundless proofs,
A deep inquirer into shallowness,
A dangerous friend, a harmless enemy;
His own best jest, oftener laughed at than with.

Weigh well your words, give him no cavilling point,
And you are safe.

Fil. Two weighty characters!

Cos. What mean you, gentlemen? — You should be such
By dress, if not by manners.

Ju. We — I — I —
What would we, Salvatore?

Sal. We would know
The way to town.

Fil. Why, all the steeples stare
Above yon hill.

Sal. Ah! yes.— True — true, indeed —
I see — What would we, Count Juranio?
There is an awful mystery here, which I
Would fain explain, if we might meet again.
[*Apart to* FILIPPIA.]

Fil. A mystery! How, meet me? I cannot tell
But I may often ramble hereabout.
[*Apart to* SALVATORE.]

Sal. Our ways are doubtful: odder things have been
Than two chance meetings. [*Apart to* FILIPPIA.]

Ju. Has my tongue strayed off? [*Aside.*]
Lady, from that small spring, the human heart,
Arise a thousand swelling impulses,
Each one a mystery to the sober brain:
'T were vain to ask why we do thus and thus,
Why crush that good intent, and rear this wrong,
While the poor reason, that would fain inquire,
Is impotent to rule. 'T was such an impulse
Drove me to what I did; which, being done,

I forge no false excuse, but simply beg
Your gentlest censure.
Cos. Sir, a fault confessed
Pardons itself one half. I will not grudge
A full forgiveness, if you ask it of me.
Ju. I do, most humbly. It is not my wont
To sue for breach of manners.
Sal. That I swear!
He was the flower of distant etiquette
To all things feminine.
Cos. Nor are my manners
Of the sour, formal cast that freezes back
The generous feelings of o'erflowing nature,
And bars the way between our hearts and lips;
Nor — nor — Indeed I know not what I say —
I talk at random. Pray you, leave me, sir:
You trifle with me.
Ju. Lady, are you just?
Cos. O, heaven! I am not; neither to myself,
Nor those who own my duty. Say no more;
But leave me, leave me!
Ju. I obey; how sadly!
May we not meet once more?
Cos. No; never, never!
[*Exit with* FILIPPIA.]
Sal. Gods! we are all mad together!
Ju. "Never, never!"
Sal. You lost your Arab.
Ju. Did I? — "Never, never!"
Sal. Ay; but you did.
Ju. 'T is granted. — "Never, never!"
[*Exit.* SALVATORE *following him amazedly.*]

SCENE II.

The House of Marsio. *Enter* Marsio.

Marsio. Where I had purposed to court, beg, and bribe —
To out-scheme Machiavelli, and so tug
Against the disadvantages of birth and rank,
That, by sheer strength and resolute force of will,
I hoped to barely conquer — they at once
Thrust the fair prize in my astonished arms,
Blow all my crafty net-works to the wind,
And half undo me with sheer wonderment.
They say she loves me. — Hum! I 'll think of that:
It looks suspicious. — Nonsense, Marsio!
Hold up thy head! Did they not, upon 'Change,
Marvel at thy advancement? Ah! did not
That sneering beggar, Volio, who can boast
Some half-score drops of gentle blood —
Who never condescended — bless his stars! —
To speak with thee; — did not that ragged wretch —
Ha! ha! I watched him from behind a pillar,
Close, very close, as 't was rehearsed to him —
Did not even he turn blue with choking envy?
Swore 't was a lying scandal; but no less
Bowed his majestic forehead to his belt
When next we met? Lord bless us! and he spoke,
So sweetly spoke, in such a winning whisper,
Of the "dear Marquis," of the "dear Marchioness;
Hoped the fair lady of my heart was well;
When would my marriage be?" And then he took

So grave and formal a farewell of me! —
The devil claw him!

(*Enter* PIETRO ROGO.)

How now, Master Rogo?
Rogo. So! How now, Master Marsio? Men have said
Your grand betrothal has upset your brains: —
By heaven! I think so. "Master Rogo," sooth!
Why, yesterday 't was "Good friend Pietro;"
And "Kinsman Pietro;" and "Pietro,
I have a secret for you!" Out upon you!
I thought to hear some folly, but your style
Out-fools conceit!
Mar. I prithee be not rude;
Nor so presume on former fellowship —
Rogo. Where are your wits?
Mar. Cease your blunt manner, sir!
Rogo. What?
Mar. Cease, I say!
Rogo. The world is full of marvels;
I myself can dream some stretch of wonder,
And they say poets, and such-like madmen, can,
By some shrewd knack, make that appear as truth
Which really is not; but roll all the poets,
All my wild dreams, all the earth's prodigies,
In one huge mass, and Marsio makes them tame.
Mar. Good Master Rogo —
Rogo. Pietro is my name.
No man shall master me.
Mar. Pietro, then;
Since yesterday, as you observe, a change
Has come across me. Yesterday we met

As Marsio, the merchant, and his friend:
To-day I represent the last great branch
Of the Tiburzzi; and as such expect
That due observance of my rank and person
Which it is but my duty to demand,
And is as much your duty to bestow.

Rogo. You thrice-dyed fool! With the Tiburzzi's daughter,
Did you receive the blood of all the race?
Their gentle culture, their refined politeness,
Which wins, but never asks, a man's respect?
I tell you, Marsio, you have climbed a tower,
To make your shameless folly further seen.
Come, come, be ruled.

Mar. Begone, sir! Leave my house!
I wear a sword.

Rogo. A lucky thought, my lord,—
My bold Tiburzzi! By the devil's beard,
I 'll try your lordship's hand at noble arts!
When we get through with this, we 'll run a tilt.
Draw!

Mar. Will you leave me?

Rogo. Draw, my noble sir,
Or I will thresh your noble lordship's shins
With a good Milan blade. The devil take me,
If I endure your airs! I 'll make a hole
To let discretion in you. Draw, you oaf!

[*They fight.* ROGO *drives* MARSIO *round the stage.*]

Your lordship gives, gives to this vulgar man?—
That 's charitable! [MARSIO *is disarmed.*]
Now, sir, were it not
For the huge sin of surfeiting the devil,
With such a lump of folly, I would let

Your windy soul out of some ugly gash. —
Nay, you 're not off yet. Promise me to be
My old, dear friend, Marsio of yesterday,
Or I will send that semblance of my friend,
Into whose body you have falsely crept,
To sup black Pluto! — Swear! or, on my life,
Your shrift is short!

Mar. Come, come, friend Pietro.

Rogo. You are improving. Swear it!

Mar. Well, I swear.

Rogo. Never to be a lord to me?

Mar. No, never.

Rogo. Ever to listen to my wholesome counsel,
Though it be rugged as the road to heaven;
And to receive it, if your candid judgment
Can bring no cause against it?

Mar. Yes, and yes.
Take your cursed rapier from my throat!

Rogo. 'T was blessed
To your salvation, most ungrateful man.
Go up, old Milan: when you are sunned again,
May you be umpire in as good a cause!
Now of this marriage; is the rumor true?

Mar. Ay; have you aught to say?

Rogo. Against the fact,
Nothing. — Though, in this easy-jogging land,
Marriage seems quite superfluous to me: —
And the same cause which makes a single state
Endurable, should scare us from a wedding.
Well, let that go. You are a wealthy man,
And must have lineal heirs — either your own,
Or seeming so — undoubtedly, your wife's —
To squander your slow millions in a day.

Mar. Are the sour sneers of an old sapless miser
What you call counsel?

Rogo. Patience, patience, friend.
Who is the maid?

Mar. Had my heart rhetoric,
'T would answer in fit phrases.

Rogo. Bless my soul!
He 's metamorphosed to a first-class lover!
You have a tongue, perchance?

Mar. The fair Costanza —
Costanza di Tiburzzi is the name —

Rogo. They doused her with at baptism. Fair, you say?

Mar. Fair as — as —

Rogo. What?

Mar. As any thing you choose.
Her charms outsoar my fancy; fly your own:
Come, Pietro.

Rogo. Ecstatic driveller! Fair?
I like not fair. The ugly ones are best:
They bear the patent of their chastity
In their brown skins, in their green, filmy eyes,
Their clawish hands, their broad, earth-flattening feet,
Their crooked ankles and their camel backs.
Without temptation, there can be no sin;
But where the fruit is jolly, and hangs out
As a ripe challenge to all passers by,
Heaven only knows who tastes, who handles it,
And who goes harmless past!

Mar. Pietro Rogo,
Is there one subject under the mad moon
Too weak to found an argument upon?

I 'll venture, with your talents, you can prove,
Against all comers, that incontinence
Is but a wide benevolence ; that murder —
Under the million given circumstances
With which your nimble wit shall hedge it in —
Is a humane achievement ; theft, an instinct ;
Cheating, a thrifty thoughtfulness of self;
And so forth, on through all the deadly sins.
Poh ! poh ! what stuff you talk !

Rogo. Back to our subject.
Costanza di Tiburzzi should be daughter
To an old dwindled noble of that name :
Is it not so ?

Mar. It is.

Rogo. They want your wealth.

Mar. And they shall have it ! Our long-shadowed name
Shall blaze, with a new light, through Italy.

Rogo. O, ho ! "our name !" My sword crawls in its scabbard.
Friend, you have not one generous aim in this ;
Your own huge pride awakes this forward zeal :
But you 'll learn wisdom through humility.

Mar. How, raven, how ?

Rogo. A hundred little things
Shall make you gnaw your fingers to the quick.
You 'll haply blunder at the first grand feast :
At which Lord So-and-so will titter, titter ;
And Lady Somebody will simper, simper ;
And sly Count Nobody, a noted wit,
Will wink and wink ; while some bluff honest duke
Howls out his laughter. Then our father wriggles,
And stares straight through a six-foot granite wall ;

Our mother blushes, and talks violently
About the price of spaniels to her neighbors;
Our bride hangs down her head — perchance a tear,
Like a full dew-drop, gathers on her cheek,
And drowns out its carnations.

Mar. I will hire
The world's opinion till my manners mend.
Life is but one long lesson.

Rogo. Ah! I fear
Your lesson will be paid for in rude coin.
Now hear me, Marsio; if you are horn-mad,
Wed some fresh country girl, some honest thing,
Too big a fool to be a lady sinner —
Too proud of you to think you aught but perfect —
Too ignorant to know your faults of breeding —
One every way inferior to yourself —
And I will chime in with your marriage-bell.

Mar. You waste your wisdom, Pietro; I'll wed
No other than Costanza. [PULTI *sings within.*]

Rogo. Hark! here comes
Our merry gossip, Pulti. Let us ask
A fool's advice. Babies and naturals
Speak, sometimes, by a kind of inspiration.

Mar. You will not condescend? —

Rogo. 'Sblood! he's a man!
I have no princely notions, like your own,
To pull me from my fellows.

(*Enter* PULTI, *singing.*)

Pulti. The devil wriggled,
The devil squealed,
The devil gave a shout;

But Saint Dunstan he
Held on stoutly,
And put the fiend to rout.

Mar. Stop your din!
That villain has one long, unending song
About a certain devil, who has seen
More sad adventures than the Golden Legend
Recounts of all its saints.
Pul. Hem, hem, hem, hem!
Mar. What do you hem at?
Pul. I have seen in churches,
When the dull preacher would not hem himself,
The congregation would hem for him.
Rogo. True.
What thinks your wisdom of your master's marriage?
Pul. Lord! sir, I seldom think; it spoils my talking.
I scorn your thoughts; the stealthy, spectral things
Smell of the church-yard, and of heaven and hell —
And bygone happiness, and present pain —
And barren futures filled with new-made graves —
And baby-hopes nipped in our nursing arms —
Of all that 's dreary, and of naught that 's bright.
They are huge stoppers for a flowing mouth,
That still by strangling.
Rogo. Have you naught to say?
Pul. I 'll race my tongue with any man's. I say,
My master will be wiser than he 's rich.
Rogo. A goodly store of wisdom, that! How, boy?
Pul. When he has gathered in his bursting brains

All the fantastic humors of a woman,
He 'll have more thoughts than ducats.

Rogo. Marsio, mark:
The knave 's a prophet. What is wedlock like?

Pul. Much like sin's journey after happiness.
We start upon it with a merry heart,
Proceed upon it with a sober one,
And end —

Rogo. Ah! yes; where end we?

Pul. Not at all:
We stumble in our graves.

Rogo. A gloomy thought.

Pul. 'T is not a thought. I lit upon the fact
By seeing, and not thinking. For your thinkers
Go stumbling headlong in with all the rest,
Thinking of all save death.

Rogo. Sage doctor Pulti,
You shall teach me your doctrines.

Pul. I will, sir,
In one short rule. — Keep your eyes ever open.

Mar. Have you not done? For Pulti will reply
Till doomsday break. 'T is not his wonted mood;
He 's oftener gay than sad.

Pul. 'T is a sad thought —
Note, signore Rogo, thinking makes one sad —
To weigh two losses with a single gain.

Rogo. Your wit outshoots me.

Pul. With a feeble shaft.
I, by this marrying, must lose a master;
My poor, poor master — who may comfort him? —
Must lose a servant! — Such a servant, sir! —
So sober — when you keep his wine away;
So sweetly tempered — when you do not cross him;

So grave and seemly — when there 's naught to laugh at;
So frugal -- when you give him naught to spend;
So every way perfection — where you grow not
The carnal apple to assail his Adam.
I have lived on these conditions, many a day,
The best of slaves.

Rogo. But where 's your single gain?

Pul. Nay, 't is but half a one: master and man
Share it between them. — 'T is an untried mistress —
A vast, dim, shadowy, uncertain fear,
That may be saint or devil.

Mar. Pulti! — dog!
Saddle my horses!

Pul. For the beggar's ride.

Mar. Dare you presume so far upon my kindness,
You coarse-grained knave?

Pul. Not I; I never trespass
On such unstable ground.

Rogo. Where do you ride?

Mar. Where should a lover ride?

Rogo. O, pause at once.
All things cry out against this unmeet match:
Blood, rank, and breeding, fortune, friends, and tastes,
In rigid opposition stand between.
You cannot mould these opposites to one;
Force them together, and earth's primal chaos
Were harmony to their eternal jar.

Mar. You could not move me, had you Tully's tongue;
Prop heaven with virgin gold, you could not buy me;

Summon the damned, with all their terrors on,
You could not daunt me! — To the horses, Pulti!

Pul. I am going, sir. [*Sings.*]

These horns were worn,
Ere you were born,
The grinning devil said;
Then take no care,
But proudly wear —

Mar. You know this cudgel, sirrah?

Pul. Thank you; we 've often met before. His name
Is oak; his mother was an acorn. See,
I know the family from end to end.
You need not introduce us, signore. [*Exit.*]

Mar. Rogo,
The aims of my existence have been few,
Yet, in the service of the thing I sought,
I have offered up my health, my life, my soul.
He must be rash, or confident, who stands
Between a zealot and his single mark. —
My horses, Pulti! — I have set my heart
Upon this marriage; let heaven frown or smile,
Till I am blasted into nothingness,
I will pursue it as if heaven were not! —
My horses, knave!

Pulti. (*Without.*) Here, sir. Ho! Lucifer.

Rogo. I 'll try to cross you for your own advantage,
If honest means may prosper.

Mar. Well, push on!
Choose your own weapons, fight as you think fit;
But, Pietro Rogo, when we are at the tug —
When the blood boils, and timid conscience flies —

When what opposes, with a friendly front,
Is not distinguished from an enemy —
Then call for mercy to the prayer-stunned saints,
And hope an age of miracles may come,
But not to Marsio! — My horses wait. [*Exeunt.*]

SCENE III.

A Room in the Castle of the MARQUIS DI TIBURZZI. COSTANZA *and* FILIPPIA.

Filippia. Saw him before?
Costanza. Yes; — only once before.
Fil. But where, and how?
Cos. Can you not call to mind
The day our duke was welcomed by the people?
Fil. As well as yesterday.
Cos. Indeed, indeed!
It seems a weary age since then, to me.
Among the nobles, who rode nigh the duke,
Was one who, in all noble qualities
Of port and majesty, rode there supreme:
Clad in black velvet, for his father's death;
Yet wearing a long plume of ostrich white,
As a fit emblem of the general joy.
Fil. Lord! you know all about him!
Cos. Yes — why — yes. —
Surely the people talked of him alone.
Fil I was beside you, yet I heard them not.
Well, well, go on.
Cos. It chanced a beggar's child,
A pretty boy — one of those nimble imps

That live by miracles 't wixt horses' feet,
And under carriage-wheels — became entangled
In the unusual press ; shrieked out for help ;
Then, suddenly, was still for very fear.
The whole crowd held its breath, and one great
heart
Beat through it all. Now there arose a cry :
Yet while the silly people did but scream,
Down from his charger leaped the cavalier,
Dashed in the throng, and, ere I cried God bless
him,
The boy was laughing in his mother's arms !
Fil. Now, I recall some little scene like that.
Cos. 'T was a great scene ! The duke stretched
out his hand ;
And, glorious in his dimmed and miry suit,
The hero mounted lightly on his horse.
Some nobles laughed, some sneered, some looked
askance ;
But all the people raised a mighty shout ;
And the great sun, bursting a heavy cloud,
Shone round Juranio like a halo !
Fil. Brave !
Yet, cousin, I saw not one half that you did.
I heard a child scream ; heard some voices call ;
Saw a man quickly leap down from his horse ;
Heard a faint murmur ; then the show went on. —
About the sun and halo I know nothing.
Cos. 'T was many a day ere I forgot the Count ;
And when we met this morn, a sudden thrill
Of the old feeling stirred my memory,
And brought me back that moving scene again, —
Which much confused me.

Fil. Ah! "Which much confused you!"
Take my word, cousin, our heroic Count,
When he caught up the beggar's little boy,
Caught up a certain lady's heart, I wot of. —
But I approve it.
Cos. What do you approve?
Fil. The catching up of fair Costanza's heart.
Cos. I beg you, cousin, not to break your jests
Upon so grave a subject. Had my mother
O'erheard your heedless nonsense, this would be
A stormy day for me.
Fil. I have a secret —
Nay, a surmise, which I have made a secret —
That casts a fearful shadow. —
Cos. I am listening.
Fil. I fear to speak; knowing the steadfast love
You cherish towards your parents.
Cos. Dear Filippia,
My marriage has perplexed you sadly. Speak;
For it must be your subject. I absolve you
From your hard promises. Come, come, give tongue;
Draw off your rancor to the very dregs:
Ill words, well-purposed, have no mischief in them.
Fil. Has not your mother an o'er-anxious care
About this marriage?
Cos. Is it not a duty
She owes my father?
Fil. But your father looks
So sad and moody! Then he never speaks.
There 's something in his silence.
Cos. It reveals
The wishes that lie nearest to his heart.
He fears his choice has swayed my inclination;

And that I marry signore Marsio
More from a sense of duty than from love:
So he withholds his counsel, leaving me
My own conclusion.

Fil. Doubtless that might be.
I could unfold such things. — The saints forgive me!
Love, gratitude — owed, if not well repaid —
O! why do you cry out so loud against me?
She took me when a child, a helpless orphan —
When no one else would keep me — when my kin
Hawked me about, with a sour charity,
From one hand to another; — reared me so
That the most jealous eye could not detect
Wherein my training differed from her own,
Her own dear child, Costanza's; for whose sake —
But what affection pardons treachery?

Cos. Filippia, darling, pray be plain!

Fil. No, no;
I cannot, dare not. I have said too much.
Your mother's smile will be a long reproach
To me, who should deserve, above all others,
The never-ending smile she suns me in.
I have had thoughts, base, base, degrading thoughts,
But I will kill them, if I perish with them —
Which, but to speak, would make yon old Tiburzzi
Leap up and shudder in their frames; would shake
This ancient roof-tree on my wicked head,
And hide my shame in ruins! It were just.
Believe me not, Costanza; scorn my hints;
Cling to your mother — she is worth your love.
I, I — O, vile! — nay, do not pity me —
Am the most faithless of a high-souled race!

Cos. What mean you ? Speak ! — You do not love me. Speak ! —
What is this mystery ? Speak !
Fil. No ; never more.
We must all wreck together ; I am dumb.

ACT III.

SCENE I. *The Park of the* MARQUIS DI TIBURZZI. *Enter* JURANIO.

Juranio. HAIL! once again, thou blooming vine-clad bower!
How long is it since the fair mistress' hand
Curled thy soft tendrils to this artful flow,
Moulding the straggling wildness of thy humors
Into such harmony? By your leave, rose.
[*Plucks a rose.*]
These crumpled features tell some dainty hand
Has pressed into the cramped and knotted bud,
To force its backward nature into flower.
Say, have you told her, treacherous confidant —
For you are full of whispering winds, that tell
To me, a late companion, many a tale
Of the gray East, where all your kindred speak
The lover's low, close language — have you told
How oft your leafy screen has covered me,
While she, the mistress of us both, swept by,
Sad, but majestic? Wherefore is she sad?
My tongue runs tripping, but my heart is lead.
O, Count Juranio, what a fool art thou,
To waste thy manhood on a maid who cares
No atom for thy countship! To lie hidden,
Hour after hour, upon the dank, rough ground,
Merely to catch the glimmer of a girl —
A girl who casts the pearl of her affection

Before that swinish usurer, Marsio!
By heaven, 't is villanous! And were it not —
So much her seeming gives report the lie —
That I believe this marriage forced upon her,
By the parental usage of our land,
I 'd fly her as infectious. What, what! she
To prop a selfish dotard's crumbling house
With the untimely ruins of her youth!
To spin a few thin moments for his age
Out of her heart's blood! Suffer worse than death,
That one old man may crawl down to his grave
With a stuffed pocket! By the blessed saints,
Blood has no claim upon her! She is mad,
To nurse the childish folly of old age
To such portentous bigness! Ha! once more
Hide love and me, my sweet confederate!
[*Goes behind the bower.*]

(*Enter* COSTANZA.)

Costanza. Fit season for my visit. It was morn
When first I met him; every leaf and flower
Looked up and opened to increasing day;
Nature spread wide her arms, in liberal joy,
Yielding her flushing bosom to the sun.
Even as a tardy flower, my heart unclosed
To revel in his presence; even as
Rejoicing nature, my whole quickening frame
Glowed into new existence. While the sun
Plunges in haste behind yon western clouds,
To course dun night around his broad domain,
The leaves and flowers may weep themselves to rest;
Nature may cross her placid arms in sleep,
And dream of morn beneath the merry stars;
But, ah! to me there is no tearful rest,

No quiet sleep, no dream of happiness,
No star of comfort. In the middle heaven,
Yet veiled and ominous, burns my sun of love,
Never to set again.

Ju. Hold your peace, winds!
Silence, ye fluttering leaves, that I may hear her!
[*Aside.*]

Cos. Juranio—

Ju. My name! [*Aside.*]

Cos. Juranio,
'T is weak, 't is wicked, to maintain my grief
On thoughts of thee. For thought breeds love, and love
Redoubles grief, and grieving multiplies
Both thought and love, in an unending round.
O! had we met one little day before,
Ere fate could mock me with the double pain
Of what I am, of what I might have been!
I know thou lov'st me—

Ju. (*Advancing.*) Hadst thou been inspired,
Thy words could not be truer.

Cos. Ha!—O, shame!
Juranio—Count Juranio!—

Ju. Hear me, love!

Cos. Begone, begone, sir!

Ju. Hear me, dear Costanza! [*Kneels.*]

Cos. By what new license do you use that title?

Ju. By the allowance of your lips.

(PIETRO ROGO *crosses the back of the scene, observing* COSTANZA *and* JURANIO, *significantly.*)

Cos. How low,
How far beneath my honest scorn, you seem,
Poor Count Juranio! Will you not arise?—

The place is public. Or do you intend
To crown your treachery with my dishonor?

Ju. A day of marvels! (*Rises.*) But a minute since —
The words even now are echoing in my heart —
I heard you — if a man may credit sense —
I heard you, lady —

Cos. Crop the guilty ears
That were abettors to their lord's disgrace!
Is it your custom, Count, to play the listener?
Our former meeting was in some such way
As this wherewith you honor me.

Ju. Coquette!

Cos. Signore!

Ju. I heard enough to settle such a name
On all the seed of Eve.

Cos. Redoubted cynic!
Where has your manhood fled, that you employ
Knowledge so basely found, so weakly used,
Upon a lady? What I may have said
In lavish fancy, granted truth compact,
Stands by the favor of your merit only:
After this paltry act — this poor attempt
To scare me to confession, by arraying
My private thoughts against my open words —
How rank you your own merit? Had you been
The generous man I one time held you for,
My thoughts had sunk, as rain-drops into sand,
To cool, but not to quicken. Leave me, sir!

Ju. Costanza di Tiburzzi, ere I go,
Listen. I love you with a single heart.
I do confess much folly in the deeds
To which love drew me. Hidden by yon bower —

While peeping buds unfolded into flowers —
While infant leaves uncurled their tiny scrolls,
And, full-grown, basked them in the mellow sun —
While all creation was an active hymn
Of ceaseless labor to approving God —
I have stood idly, though the dear time sped,
Waiting to catch the faintest glimpse of you.
Then, happy with that treasure of my sense,
Have hied me home, to fill my waking thoughts
With growing fancies; or, through fleeting night,
Made my dreams golden with the memory
Of what had blessed my day. I cover nothing:
I have no skill nor wish to circumvent you.
You know the mystery of my presence here;
You know the secret of my love, — ah! yes,
You knew it ere I spoke it. You can lift,
By confirmation of your former words,
A sinking heart to rapture. Speak, O, speak!
My fate hangs on your mercy!

Cos. Have you heard
No rumor of my marriage?

Ju. Yes; a rumor, —
A baseless rumor.

Cos. Ere another week,
That rumor and my fate will be but one.

Ju. Is there no hope?

Cos. I chose my portion, sir.
And must abide the issue.

Ju. Dear Costanza,
Did you but know the energy, the power,
Which I might use to sway your destiny;
To foil a wretch —

Cos. Hold! Do you counsel me

To scheme against my honor? Farewell, sir!
I know not by what weakness I have staid
To hear — Kind Heaven, some strength!
[*Aside. Exit hastily.*]

Ju. Stay, lady, stay! —
What, shall I follow? — Gods! I 'll drown this feeling!
Follow, forsooth, to glut her cruelty,
To make myself the plaything of a girl, —
I, Count Juranio, follow like a spaniel,
And on a cold scent too! Is this thing love?
I ween 't is more like hate — sound, manly hate.
Cold, cruel, heartless jilt! Yes, she was cold —
Cold, very cold. Love is not self-possessed.
But was she cruel? I cannot call her cruel.
I hope not heartless. Yet she loves me not.
Nay, she was very sparing of my feelings.
I broke upon her rudely — startled her;
At such a time too. Yet she loves me not.
Ah! yes; at such a time! while every word
Lightened the freight of her o'erburdened heart.
'T was rash in me — thoughtless: I should respect
Maiden reserve. She likes not sudden passion.
In faith, nor do I. Reason should confirm
Our hearts' emotions, ere we give them way.
Perhaps she loves me yet! I 'll swear she does;
Or sovereign Love is but a gilded toy!

(*Enter* Salvatore.)

Salvatore. Ho! there, Juranio!
Ju. Signore Marsio —
Sal. My name is Salvatore, please you.
Ju. So!

But let him stand aside; I cannot answer
Where love may drive me.

Sal. Can you answer me?
Deaf man! — Juranio! Are you dumb too? Here,
Let us talk with our fingers.

Ju. Salvatore,
I 've met her, spoken with her!

Sal. So have I.

Ju. What said she?

Sal. Little. In my breathing-times,
She edged a word in.

Ju. What had you to say?

Sal. O! nothing plainly; I 've not come to that.
But, here and there, I tumbled in a hint,
Like love astray, which she may ponder on.

Ju. You love her?

Sal. Ay, sir; she is not preserved;
I was not poaching; she is open game.

Ju. How did she take it?

Sal. Kindly, very kindly.

Ju. Villain! — traitor! [*Seizes him.*]

Sal. Lord love the man! Let go!
Is she the only she within the realm?
I have another she, to whom your she
Is only cousin.

Ju. Miserable jester!

Sal. No; I am serious. O, thou dear Filippia,
Couldst thou but hear this shabby creature sneer
At us, and at love's majesty! Base, vile,
Soulless Juranio!

Ju. On this very spot,
Hidden behind yon bower, I heard her own
Such feelings for me — ah! such rapturous feelings

Of maiden innocence! My beggar heart
Was rich at once, as if the heavens rained love!

Sal. Heard whom?

Ju. Costanza — why, Costanza, surely.

Sal. I pray you do not gall me, kinsman, thus.
I am rashly jealous, deadly quarrelsome;
I'll fight you for a feather.

Ju. While the words
Still tingled in my ears, upon this spot,
This very spot, — see where her little feet
Have nestled in the grass, — I heard her say
She could not love me, never would be mine,
And, worse than all, would marry Marsio!

Sal. Worms gnaw the fellow! All Filippia said
Was "Marsio, and Marsio," and "Cousin,
Poor, poor Costanza!" And now you begin!
Think you the heathen means to wed them both?
What is this Marsio?

Ju. A wealthy merchant,
Or usurer, or some such sorry thing,
Picked by the Marquis for his daughter's bed:
A slow, sure matrimonial poison, used
To fatten purses, — death to flesh and blood.

Sal. I understand. We must be rid of him.

Ju. But how?

Sal. Quite simply — [*Musing.*]

Ju. How?

Sal. Why break my thoughts?
I quarrelled, fought him, was just burying him,
By an unfailing plan; but you destroyed it.

(*Enter* PULTI, *singing.*)

The devil looked down,
With a curse and a frown,
  And to the young witch he said,
'Ods blood! I 'd far rather
Quell hell in hot weather,
  Than govern one headstrong maid!

Ju. Whence comes that devilish song?
Sal. From yonder knave.
Come hither, nightingale.
Pulti. You called me, signore?
Sal. Ay, warbler, unperch. What is the news in hell?
Pul. The devil has a surfeit of light fools,
And sends for solid food; I 'll pass you by.
Sal. Now, by his tongue, the bird 's a woodpecker.
Pul. And rapping on your poll.
Sal. His tongue 's a foil:
He foins and parries like a mountebank.
Whom do you serve?
Pul. Myself most faithfully,
To answer strictly; but I give, sometimes,
To answer more at large, slack services
To Signore Marsio.
Sal. That name again!
How many Marsios are there?
Pul. One at present.
He gets to breeding shortly; there 'll be more.
Ju. Are you purveying for a cudgelling?
Pul. Heaven knows. What means the gentleman?

Sal. Scarce nothing:
His thoughts are hardly fantasies just now.
How do you like your service?
Pul. Why, so far
As one may thrive on musty wine, thin diet,
Most scanty wages —
Sal. What a churlish wretch,
To treat so brave a fellow to such fare!
Pul. Signore, you wrong him. I 'm as well supplied
With work as bees are; I 've more blows than Winter;
Oaths thick as stars; frowns bountiful as sunlight:
I am called up early, like an April violet;
Sent to bed tardily, like a waning moon;
I am railed and sneered at like Heaven's providence;
Outraged like modest nature —
Sal. So! boy, so!
Is Marsio honest?
Pul. Passably, so far;
But then, you know, the devil has a say,
Sooner or later, in the best of lives.
Sal. Would you change masters?
Pul. Ay, with Satan's dog.
But that is hopeless; wit 's uncurrent coin;
Men drop me sooner than they take me up.
Sal. Serve me.
Pul. I 'm yours. Now, farewell, Marsio!
I 'll leave my rags as keepsakes.
Sal. Not so fast.
My service is peculiar; but its wages
Out-go your dreams. A fortnight I desire
You watch o'er Marsio, note his slightest act,

Become more zealous, more familiar with him;
Let naught escape you. When the time is fair,
You 'll run to me, and make a full report.
I have suspicions of this Marsio's truth,
From certain hints a shrewd-brained lady dropped;
And should I catch him — (*Aside.*) Can we not agree?
Pul. How! I play spy!
Sal. Are you a Christian man?
Pul. Yes; of the latest make.
Sal. Then hearken, man!
If Marsio 's honest, you can say no ill;
If he is false, 't is nothing but plain duty
To fright his brother sinners with his sins.
Make him hell's scare-crow; for example, brother,
Is your best governor of coward man.
There is a pithy sermon, preached for you,
Upon the mote and beam text. After this
Short fortnight's service, life is all your own.
Pul. I 'll do it. But forgive me, if I think
Your promise better than your argument.
Sal. The knave is apt. [*Aside.*]
Ju. Kinsman, 't is treacherous
To set a spy upon your enemy:
You lower to his level.
Sal. Well, sir saint,
E'en leave the schemer to his wicked schemes.
Wash your hands, Pilate! I can bear the sin.
Remember — What 's your name?
Pul. Pulti, good master.
Sal. Remember, Pulti.
Pul. Ay, sir; have no doubts.
This wretch, this crooked beast, this Marsio,
Must be — What, what? I 'm working in the dark.

Sal. That saves the sin.

Pul. I am not tender-minded.
I have the knack of talking sins to naught,
With your best casuists. Use your pleasure, master.

(*Sings.*) Quoth the fiend, I was born
On a Friday morn,
My fall out of heaven was Friday,
On a Friday the reign
From my kingdom was ta'en ; —
The curse of the seven was Friday!

To-day is Friday, sir.

Sal. That 's the tune, bird!
Time wears, Juranio.

Ju. Why, let it wear!
Would you clog time? Put wings upon his feet:
Each passing day 's a drop of precious balm
To wounded hearts. Alas! what empty talk!
Time will but add another, deeper pain,
The curse of memory; a dreary waste
Of blasted life, stretching from now to death!

Sal. You and your love make up the universe!

Ju. Then leave me to my world. I would not talk;
I wish no comfort, no companionship,
No mocking hope, no fruitless sympathy.

Sal. Ugh! what a wintry heart! I hope yet. — Come! [*Exeunt.*]

SCENE II.

The House of MARSIO. *Enter* MARSIO *and* PIETRO ROGO.

Marsio. You saw her, said you? Do you know Costanza?

Rogo. Do I know you?

Mar. I cannot credit it.

Rogo. You would not credit it.

Mar. Upon his knees?

Rogo. As fine a looking fellow as you 'll meet.
A Court-gallant, a man of her own tribe,
A new Adonis, who strings women's hearts
On mournful osiers, like an angler's fish.
Trust me, a dangerous youth, with broad, white brows,
That buzz with sonnets, and such lady-traps,
Like two great bee-hives. There I saw him down,
Down on his knees. — 'T would pose you, Marsio,
To spring your chalky joints.

Mar. Pshaw! Pietro,
Your trick is barefaced.

Rogo. Trick, trick! — How? pray how?

Mar. You 'd make me jealous.

Rogo. By the blessed Virgin,
I swear I spoke the truth!

Mar. If it be so,
I 'll crush Tiburzzi, daughter, wife, and all,
Into the dust! Look you, friend Pietro,
I hold these beggars in my open hand.
Here, here — I have been provident for slips —
This little parchment covers all their worth

Down to a lira. Only let them blench,
And they shall pray for Purgatory. 'Sblood!
Trick me! — use me! — make me security
For a cracked daughter!
Rogo. Who 's to blame but you?
Mar. Enough of that. I 'll watch her, Pietro —
Nay; are you serious?
Rogo. On my soul, I am!
Mar. I 'll tax her with it. Will you not confront her?
Rogo. That were base usage.
Mar. Furies! what care I?
She 'd make a stale of me before we 're coupled!
Rogo. Mend your own botching.
Mar. Marry, that I will!
And yet I 'll wed her, spite of her and you.
Rogo. That frets me little.
Mar. O! I know your drift!
You have bred a crooked notion in your brain,
That still keeps twisting. You would shape the end
Of the disastrous prophecy you made,
Merely to be called prophet. Look you, look you,
Martyrs are fashioned of such holy stuff!
Rogo. Your rage defeats your judgment. I would guard,
Not govern you.
Mar. Come, let us to the Park.
Perchance we 'll meet these billing doves again:
And if we do, Tiburzzi's crazy house
Shall rattle in his ears as if doom's trump
Clamored against it! We will say no more.
I 'll see her, Pietro. — A word ends all.

[*Exeunt.*]

SCENE III.

The Park of the MARQUIS. *Enter* FILIPPIA *and* SALVATORE.

Salvator. By Cupid's beard, I love you hugely, lady!
Filippia. By that same oath, I doubt it strangely, signore!
Sal. Try me by all love's ordeals; if I fail
In any point of doctrine, faith, or duty,
Protest me arrant.
Fil. Fairly challenged, sir.
I have a test.
Sal. O! name it, name a thousand!
Fil. You are acquainted with my cousin's fate,
With her betrothal to one Marsio?
Sal. Gods! I know nothing else!
Fil. Fie! restive lover!
Sal. Between Juranio and you, my knowledge,
My precious knowledge — scraped by hard degrees —
Bids fair to be ingulfed in that one fact.
Fil. Be patient. Would you win?
Sal. On any terms.
I might stand Marsio's name some ten times more;
Costanza's some two-score. — But do be brief;
My reason totters when you mention them.
Fil. We 'll drop their titles. If you foil this marriage,
My hand is yours; ay, and the largest piece
Of a most grateful heart.

(*Enter, behind,* MARSIO *and* PIETRO ROGO, *observing them.*)

Sal. But should I fail?

Fil. Were mankind merged in one, and you that one,
I vow I would not —
Sal. Hist! swear not; 't is wicked.
What if you broke your oath? 'T were perjury;
A deadly sin. I swear by saving rules,
That take the peril from a broken vow:
Let me do all the swearing.
Fil. I am firm.
I err in asking this; but, having erred,
I 'll have my wish to lull my conscience with.
Sal. I merely sought to guard against mischance. [*Kneels.*]
Here, on my knee, I swear —

(MARSIO *and* ROGO *advance.*)

Marsio. Hem!
Sal. Zounds! who 's this? [*Starting up.*]
Mar. He is used to kneeling. This pair, Pietro,
And your old eyes, have cozened you.
Rogo. No, no;
Yon doting couple, and the pair I saw,
Are no more like than geese and swans. This Park
Must breed such creatures.
Fil. Marsio himself!
Sal. You fellow, there! — Sirrah! — you thieving clown,
I 'll have you whipped for poaching!
Mar. Sir!
Sal. You trespass:
You are intruding upon private grounds.
Mar. They should be private, if you often use them.

Sal. How, dog?

Mar. Sir!

Sal. Quite at your command, sir. — Draw!
Here is a pretty piece of level sod;
This lady is my second; there stands yours.
Draw, draw! [*Draws.*]

Fil. Do not forget yourself! [*Apart to* SALVATORE.]

Sal. Not I.
This were a speedy way to settle all.
[*Apart to* FILIPPIA.]
I wait you, sir. [*To* MARSIO.]

Mar. I do not wish to kill you.
Put up your sword. I would advise you, friend,
To find as safe a scabbard for your tongue.

Rogo. 'Sblood! do you bear that Court-fly's impudence?
Hark you, sir; signore Marsio is my friend,
My next of kin; might I supply his place? [*Draws.*]

Sal. Most charmingly. One of the family
Is something toward. [*To* FILIPPIA.]

Fil. Have you no respect,
No feeling for a woman?

Mar. Shame upon you!
I 'll cut the first man down who makes a pass.
Put up, good Pietro. This cause is mine:
He is no friend who takes it off my hands.
Make no excuse. [*To* SALVATORE.]

Sal. O! never fear for me.

Mar. I pardon you, unasked. The gentleman
Has the infirmity of wrath. Alas!
Heaven made him so, for mortals to forgive.

Sal. We 'll settle, one day.

Fil. Come, come, signore Firebrand;
I wish a valiant escort home.

Sal. Dear lady,
Forgive my rudeness.

Fil. No; I praise your zeal.
This bold beginning is a happy presage.
[*Exit with* SALVATORE.]

Mar. Ha! ha! ha! ha! — You would gull Marsio, ha? [*Laughing.*]
Know you that man? 'T is signore Salvatore,
The foremost swordsman in all Italy.
Your life would last two passes, and no more,
Before his blade. When I crave suicide,
I 'll take my quarrel up again. Go, Rogo.

Rogo. 'Sdeath! no: here I 'll abide him.

Mar. Mad as a March wind!
Is there no other way to tame wild bulls
Than butting at them with a pair of horns?
Meet him with his own weapons! Where 's revenge —
Where 's honor, satisfaction, and all that —
When you are wriggling half-way up a rapier,
Your heart pinned to your back? I have a way
To make his bilbo harmless as a rush;
I have an airy weapon that can stab,
Without a wound; yet make our satin signore
Grovel for life. I 'm master of that blade,
And he is not: I 'll use it, Pietro.

Rogo. Keep to your own dark pathway, leave me mine —
Nay, sir; I will not go!

Mar. Pish! headstrong man!
I am walking towards the Castle, I shall meet him,—

With the most lowly reverence of my cap, —
If you persist, I 'll lead him round this place.
I say you shall not fight! 't would ruin me.
Now, dear friend Pietro. —

Rogo. O! well, to please you.
The sun must rise to-morrow.

Mar. Are you sure
These two were not the pair seen yester eve?

Rogo. I swear it, by Saint Peter! She alone,
Lady Costanza — 'sblood! I know her well —
Was the divinity; the worshipper
I never saw before. Within an hour
You shall know all about him.

Mar. At my house
Meet me, anon. I 'll bring her secret to you.
Lady Costanza has an open heart,
And I will tax it.

Rogo. Do not trip yourself.
You have a dangerous ignorance of rank,
And the refinements of its ticklish honor.
I fear some blunder.

Mar. 'T is the quickest way;
I cannot sleep until the fact stand clear.

[*Exit* ROGO.]

As for our heady signore of the blade,
Let him look well to his economy;
To whom he credits, what he owes, what holds —
To what he eats, what drinks, what physic takes —
To how he sleeps, and how he goes abroad;
Let him beware dark nights, and crooked lanes —
Smooth billet-doux, and angry challenges;
For, by the wrath to come, a sudden death
Might lurk in any of them! Let him watch:

He opened credit with a punctual firm ;
We must break quits ere long ! Here lies my path.
[*Exit.*]

SCENE IV.

A Room in the Castle of the MARQUIS. *Enter the* MARQUIS *and* MARCHIONESS DI TIBURZZI.

Marchioness. 'T is the perversity of woman, sir,
A subtle fiend forever creeping in
Between a young maid and her interest.
Our girls are spoiled. The women of this age
Are infants from the crib down to the grave, —
Weak, mindless children, full of baby whims —
All smiles, all tears ; but he is weather-wise
Who can predict their changing humors surely.
Ah ! for the Roman matrons, the strong moulds
In whom the hero race was cast of yore ! —
What, not bite at the Romans ? — sad indeed !
[*Aside.*]

Marquis. Our daughter's grief is deeper than a whim ;
And now her gloom seems doubling. Oft of late
I have seen her slyly wiping tears away.
If I observe her — for I cannot help
The old love rising sometimes in my eyes —
At once she makes such frantic starts at mirth —
The dreary ghost of bygone merriment —
The dismal echo, when the sound has died —
The laughing lip, but not the laughing heart —
That I cannot but wonder at a state
So nigh to frenzy.

March. She has lost your love.

Marq. Can it be that? She shall have all my love;
Yes; I will double its best outward show.
I have been cruel. . It may be that, indeed.—
But she has Marsio's love, for which she bartered,
Most wittingly, most calmly, my regard.
I can forgive her that, too. My old age
Is over-greedy, to presume her youth
Should cramp its action to my selfish bounds.
What arrogance! I had a father once,
And loved him dearly; but a little maid
Stole me and all my duty. Right, Costanza!—
She 's right, I say!
March. I did not question it.
Marq. I grant you, madam, natural love is pure,
Holy, and calm, and fixed unalterably;
Yet there is something in that other love,
With all its turbulence and fiery passion—
Its frenzies verging into bitterness—
Its sudden heats, and sudden shivering chills—
A mystery, and a far-fading feeling,
So wraps this fruitful union of two hearts,
That I can rather think its hidden start
To be from some great viewless source above,
Than from the many, obvious, natural springs
Which rise around us in our wonted paths.
What think you, wife?
March. Sir, sir, I raise no question.
Two passions in yourself hold this debate.
Marq. Two struggling passions cause Costanza's grief:
Her love for Marsio jars her love for me.
March. You 're in a desperate way, sir, if you hope,

With the small pack of human faculties,
To hunt down girlish freaks.

Marq. Freaks, madam, freaks!

March. My plot works cross-grained. (*Aside.*)
Could you trust Costanza —
Ah! how he winces! — (*Aside.*) You might condescend —

(*Enter a Servant.*)

Well?

Servant. Signore Marsio. [*Exit.*]

(*Enter* MARSIO.)

Marq. Fair day to you!

Marsio. Thank you, my lord. Your daughter? where is she?

Marq. Out in the Park.

Mar. What business draws her there?

Marq. Her love of nature.

Mar. Nature! — Human nature?

Marq. No; heaven's and earth's. Sunshine, and air, and flowers,
Have stronger charms, for the full pulse of youth,
Than the gray walls which chill age cowers in,
Through dread of sun-strokes, draughts, and sickening scents.

Mar. Sunshine, and air, and flowers! Fine things, no doubt!
Is she oft out for sunshine, air, and flowers?

Marq. Yes; every hour. I cannot keep her in.
She seems to draw some comfort from the breath
Of these bland May-days.

Mar. The old man is frank. [*Aside.*]
Have you much company? — I ask you this
Because I seek acquaintance with your friends.

Marq. Friends! I have none.—How your thoughts skip about!—
Besides yourself, and my large family
Of well-known creditors, no one, save those
Whom it scarce shelters, comes beneath this roof.
Mar. No one?
Marq. No one.
Mar. 'T is sad.
Marq. Custom has made
What troubled me at first, an easy loss.
Mar. But, then, your Park has many charms,
Even for the dainty relish of your daughter,
And her fair cousin — I must not slip her:
But now I met her with a cavalier.
Marq. How now! Filippia with a cavalier!
I am her guardian; but 't is news to me. —
Wife, wife, Filippia with a cavalier!
March. Well, well, what harm? This is no nunnery:
She is full-aged. Her own sharp-cornered wit
Is her best guardian.
Marq. I must look to this.
Mar. 'T is said — but with what truth I'll not avouch —
Your daughter has another cavalier.
These cousins hunt in couples.
Marq. Fairly said!
You would excuse Filippia. Ha! ha! sir; [*Laughing.*]
By the sly twinkle of your eye, I judge
You are the other cavalier.
Mar. 'Sdeath! no!
I have no taste for sunshine, air, and flowers;
'Ods blood! I hate them!

Marq. You are strangely moved.

Mar. Moved strangely, sir, by a most strange device.
'T were better, till I 'm fairly bound, at least —
Until my honor cannot 'scape her pranks —
That she — Costanza, sir, — your daughter, sir, —
Showed more regard to common decency!

March. What is all this?

Marq. Our sweet son, Marsio,
Gives us an inkling of his filial love!

Mar. Ne'er sneer at me, sir, — never sneer at me!

Marq. I am talking to this lady.

March. Pray be calm. [*Apart to* MARSIO.]
If signore Marsio has been well informed,
He has just cause to take offence.

Marq. Gods! madam —

March. Here comes Costanza: she can set us right.

Marq. No; she can set you wrong, — can show how basely
You slander purity!

(*Enter* COSTANZA.)

March. You have been walking?

Costanza. Yes. — Good-day, signore Marsio!

March. Alone?

Cos. O, no! O, no! There was one little bird
Followed me strangely on, from tree to tree,
Measuring his lagging flight by my slow steps,
As if he sought to keep me company;
And when I paused a moment, he would hop,
In open view, upon the nearest spray,
And pour into my ears such moving notes —
So melancholy, yet so sweet withal —

That I scarce knew whether to stop and hear,
Or to pass on, and end his melody.
Mar. Sunshine, and air, and flowers! and now a bird! —
Pish! do they take me for a fool? [*Aside.*]
March. Costanza,
Had you no other company?
Cos. None, mother.
Mar. Bah! how she feathers us! I'll pluck your bird. [*Aside.*]
Lady Costanza.
Cos. Signore Marsio.
Mar. I am a candid man — a little rough,
Perchance, sometimes, yet meaning honestly.
I never steal upon my enemy,
But march straight to him, pounding all my drums.
Marq. Your enemy!
Cos. Must I be rated one? [*Laughing.*]
Mar. I hope not, lady. But this busy world
Buzzed ugly sounds — unlike your pretty bird's —
Into my ears, as I walked hither.
Marq. Well!
Would you out-stare each other?
Mar. Bluntly, then:
'T is said — I hope without foundation, lady —
A bird is not the only company
Of your long walks and pauses in the Park.
One gossip winks, and swells his windy cheeks,
As I go by; then gluts his brother's ears
With a low, stealthy tale, told in fierce whispers, —
Of how you wander with a cavalier,
Pensive and silent, treading down the flowers,
That glitter so amid the dark-green grass,

As if you really cared not to blot out
God's handiwork. Another has a tale,
Fetched through a multitude of serving-men —
But all truth 's truth, he will go bail for that —
Of how this self-same cavalier was seen
Upon his knees to you — to you! At this
The whole fraternity smile forth a sigh,
And pity poor, dull Marsio. Lady mine,
I loathe man's pity! Is there aught in this?
Whom saw you yesterday? — the day before?
You do not answer.

Cos. First, sir, by what right
Do you advance the question?

March. Answer, child.
You are betrothed: he has a right from that.

Marq. He has not, madam; nor will I permit
My daughter to be catechised.

Mar. (*Aside.*) Ho! ho!
I 'll tame you shortly.

Cos. Signore Marsio,
Do not misjudge me. Till my wedding-day,
My erring acts will fall on me alone.
When I do aught to peril my fair name —
Which, now, I hold you have no check upon —
I shall be first to show it, and absolve you
From all your obligations. Until then,
I am the proper guardian of my conduct.

Marq. Well spoken, daughter!

March. You maintain her folly.

Mar. You 'll not deny it?

March. 'T is but a word, love —
Nay, for your mother's sake.

Marq. For my sake, peace!

Cos. Neither will I deny it, nor affirm it.
Mar. You dare not, dare not!
Cos. Signore Marsio!—
Mar. By heaven! I credit—
Cos. Listen to me, sir.
Our marriage contract is not ratified;
Tear it, I beg you. I have no desire
To hold you to it, if you doubt my truth.
Marq. Ay, ay! tear up the parchment.
Mar. No, no, no!
What, would you bait me?—Look, Tiburzzi, look
The galled beast turn not on you! I have here—
No, no; I have at home, in safest hands—
That which shall beggar you. I hold your debts—
All that heaven left your miserable name—
Under my mercy! Yes, I bought them up
For half-price, sir—your credit has run low—
By the sweet saints, I'll use them!
March. Patience, signore!
Mar. I am all patience, when I am well used.
March. You see our situation.
[*Apart to the* MARQUIS.]
Marq. We are toiled,
Trammelled, betrayed, by this damned usurer!
The Duke shall hear me.
Mar. Ah! the Duke, the Duke!
Above the Duke sits Justice, robed in law,
His mistress and the state's. Best pray to heaven:
They say its tardy mercy 's sure at last.
Marq. Graceless blasphemer! Here to heaven I cry,—
The gray-haired father of this child, ensnared

By arts beneath the cunning of a thief, —
Against a heartless villain!

Cos. O, be calm!
No harm shall touch you. Signore Marsio,
I will abide the contract.

Marq. You shall not!
What, do you love him yet? You never did:
'T was feigned, to save me.

Cos. As much as ever.

Marq. My curses drag you down to his base level! —

Cos. My father — O, my father! God forgive you;
You 've made my father mad! Come hither, sir.
Walk with me — help him, mother — with Costanza.
Nay, lean on me. Your little daughter, father, —
Only a child. Here is the same poor head
You used to bless so. I will tell you all:
I cannot here. That 's kind. Now come with me.
You should respect him, signore Marsio.
I hold you to the contract.

[*Exit the* MARQUIS, *supported by* COSTANZA *and the* MARCHIONESS.]

Mar. Well for you. —
The devil broil you all! O, yes, my lord,
Whisper your daughter, lower upon your wife;
I 'll mate you yet, for all your starving pride;
Ay, and I 'll find your lover, lady mine.
You have him, yes, you have him, to console
Your wretched wifehood. Should he see the day
Whereon I wed you — if he be not off,
Even at this moment, to the antipodes —
May I be wed and buried in one hour!
'Ods love! fool me — fool Marsio! — Ha! ha!

[*Exit, laughing.*]

ACT IV.

SCENE I. *The House of* Marsio. Marsio *and* Pietro Rogo

Marsio. Juranio — Count Juranio — who is he?
Rogo. The people's darling, the nobility's
Envy and general pattern, the good Duke's
Prime favorite and most familiar friend.
You will encounter no one, high or low,
Who speaks not well of him.
Mar. Rich?
Rogo. Marvellously;
He beggars you.
Mar. Hum! Handsome?
Rogo. Love-sick girls,
In dreams, bedeck the object of their thoughts
With no such beauty as our mere calm sense
Must render him perforce.
Mar. Pietro Rogo,
I am not handsome.
Rogo. Ho! ho! — Why no, no! [*Laughing.*]
Neither outside nor in.
Mar. I do not see
The justice of it, Pietro. Why chance
Crowds this man's clay into Apollo's mould,
Yet scrapes the fair, plump flesh from my lank fingers,
From my gaunt, bony arms, from my crook'd legs —
Scoops out my narrow chest — from every part,

Where usage orders, steals my buxom matter,
To pile it in one lump upon my back;
Making me hideous with the very stuff
She uses to create a paragon.
Why this should be, I say, amazes me,
And gravels reason. Well, to kick at fate
Is but a laming trick. My reptile form,
At least, contains the reptile's cunning. Now,
There is some justice there. Perhaps your Count,
For all his beauty, lacks the use of it.
Has this fair shape a mind?
Rogo. We'll see anon.
The people give him out as full perfection.
What said your lady-love?
Mar. Ah! there's the doubt;
I cannot fathom her.
Rogo. Nor ever will.
When you believe you touch the lowest depths
Of women's hearts, there's something still beneath,
You wot not of.
Mar. Tush! Pietro: I tell you
I hold my friend Tiburzzi in a leash,
To come and go as I may whistle him.
Rogo. How bears he that?
Mar. He struggled for a while;
But when I hinted what a time they pass
Who tug their lives out at a galley's oar,
Neither for gain nor pleasure; how to row
Even a shallop, without any aim,
Would be a sad thing; and described a hulk
As something bulkier than Costanza's shoe;
When, to all this, I hinted doubtful fears

Of his dear daughter's fate, if he were gone,
He grew a rival for the meekest dove.

Rogo. You are a villain, Marsio.

Mar. I know it:
I'm what is called a villain by a world
That sees its huge face in my little glass.
'T is false! I am no villain. I am one
Who must achieve what my heart prompts me to,
Or be no more forever. I'm as well
As any man who works his purposes,
Despite his fears.

Rogo. For all your interview,
You still are doubtful. Why not give her up?
I would far rather wed a Magdalen
Than a suspected woman. Doubts and fears
Make up full half the substance of our ills.

Mar. I'll solve my doubts before the wedding-day.
If she prove true, I gain a trusty wife;
If she do not — why, even as I said,
Tiburzzi rows a galley. I will have
My wife or my revenge. Gods! Pietro,
The girl looks chaste.

Rogo. Looks chaste! — O, save us! — looks!
Yet that might cozen one. I often gaze
Upon a piece of ruined womanhood
With strange, blind feelings — a blank wonderment
That one so fair, so chaste, to outward show,
Must by the cautious intellect be held
As mere corruption. There's a fearful jar
Betwixt the heart and brain upon this theme.

Mar. I have an ordeal for her. It may be
That Count Juranio knelt and prayed to her,

As sinners do to the shut ear of heaven,
With bootless zeal.

Rogo. Yes; even that might be.

Mar. You are lenient to-day.

Rogo. Low-spirited,
Dyspeptic.

Mar. Ah! Here is my little plan.
Tiburzzi dare refuse me nothing: I
Will bring together the enamored Count
And his fair idol; — yea, I will cast in
His friend, fierce signore Salvatore. Thus
His Countship shall have scope, unbounded room;
Tempted by love on one side, on the other
Urged up by valor. I will throw Costanza
And the sweet Count, ablaze 'twixt love and wrath,
Into incessant contact, while I watch
The play my puppets make. — Ha, Pietro?

Rogo. Blast your dark plots! But reason splits on you;
You'll have your way.

Mar. That will I. Come with me.
I'll take you to Tiburzzi's house. Perchance
He'll hold me better for my company. —
Ha, Pietro?

Rogo. Ha, Marsio! Sneer, sneer!
I will not go.

Mar. You fear Tiburzzi?

Rogo. No!
Curse your Tiburzzi! Would you take me there,
As a set off to your own awkwardness?

Mar. Ho! ho! well thought! [*Laughing.*]

Rogo. I'll meet you in the Park.

Let me have notice when this pretty plot,
Against your own repose, is toward.

Mar. Yes.

Rogo. You'll rue your plotting. Crime has its degrees;
Wade in its shallows, and you drown at last.

Mar. Lord, Pietro! what a good man you are! [*Laughing.*]

Rogo. I'll have the laugh upon you shortly, sir,
If I know aught of woman.

Mar. That would be
A bitter laugh for old Tiburzzi. No;
It must end well. Costanza will prove true;
My test will school her virtue, not destroy it;
And Count Juranio —

Rogo. Well, well, what of him?
I partly love the boy, men speak so fairly.

Mar. Why, so do I. But he must feel his trespass;
Know what it is to woo a man's betrothed.
That were a moral lesson, fitly taught
For his soul's health. But lightly, Pietro —
I will but check him with a father's hand —
Quite lightly, Pietro. Ha, ha! poor boy, [*Laughing.*]
He will not need correction more than once.
Come, come, to business! Love has played wild tricks
With my neglected balances, of late. [*Exeunt.*]

SCENE II.

The House of JURANIO. *Enter* JURANIO *and* SALVATORE.

Salvatore. Cheer up, Juranio! Do not hug your grief;
All that is lovable in you is wasting
Before its sickly drought. Remember, man,
You are supported by a deity.
The blind brat, Love, despite his want of eyes,
Will find you out a way to win at last.
Trust your own idol. Shame upon despair!

Juranio. You talk, to cheer me, with a cheerless heart;
Between your words, your face is sad as mine.
Salves for a mortal wound, drugs for the dead,
Hopes for the hopeless!

Sal. Every thought 's astray.
Why, all things are merely as we behold them,
Taking such qualities as we bestow.
One only looks at the bright side of things;
And he 's your gull, the prey of all mankind.
Another gloats upon the darker side,
Pleasing himself with self-inflicted pain;
And he 's your misanthrope. Another scans
Both bright and dark, with a calm, equal eye;
Lo! your philosopher. But then — now mark —
Comes up the happy soul who looks at nothing,
Yet turns whatever is to present pleasure;
Tastes Fiascone in thin Pavian wine;
Wallows in down upon a bed of straw;
Smells roses in a swine-yard; hears sweet tones
From the harsh, grating rasps of puffing smiths;

Beholds the sunshine glorify the flower,
And change all nature to one merry hue,
Beneath the duskest sky of bare December.
Here 's your true liver, kinsman mine! A man
Who neither fools, nor frowns, nor calculates,
But dreams away this aching thing called life:
Make him your model. If your lady frown,
Why, look up one who smiles.

Ju. Dear Salvatore,
'T is but a vain attempt to reason down
Our smallest feeling. The mind's snow may lie
A dreary winter on the torpid heart,
Yet never kill it. Slack the rigor once,
And, like a violet that leans its cheek
In mockery against some melting drift,
Up springs the heart, more fruitful for its rest.

(*Enter* PULTI, *singing.*)

Pulti. So the devil was wroth
At the gentlemen both,
Though no one could fathom his matters;
And he dashed around hell,
Like a dog tailed with bell,
And tore all his dwelling to tatters!

Sal. Well, Pulti, well?

Pul. Signore, it is not well.
I am beaten to a cripple; I must leave;
I cannot stand your service longer.

Sal. Why?

Pul. Marsio is mad. Would you could see him now!
He foams and rages round his frighted house

Like a bear newly caged. He 's full of curses,
Full of dire threats against some hapless foes;
And every time he passes me — O Lord! —
My humble manner seems to prick him so —
He takes compassion on his enemies,
And deals me half their vengeance. See me, sir!
I am basted like a piece of English beef:
I had just strength to crawl here, and no more.

Sal. Who has enraged him?

Pul. That I cannot tell.
Two gentlemen, I judge, by what I hear:
By what I feel, I judge these gentlemen
Must bear a striking likeness to myself.

Sal. Can he suspect?

Ju. What is there to suspect?
The length that I can enter in his thoughts
Would be a comfort to him. As for you,
Doubtless he has forgotten you ere met:
These merchants have no care for points of honor.

Sal. But—

(*Enter a Servant.*)

Servant. Signore Marsio.

Sal. What, what?

Pul. The devil!
O, could I clamber to the frozen moon,
And cut away my ladder!

Ju. How is this?

Sal. What said you, sirrah?

Serv. Signore Marsio waits.

Ju. Admit him. [*Exit Servant.*]

Pul. O, I beg you, sir —

Sal. Here, Pulti,
Into this room.

Pul. Avaunt! A priest, a priest! [*Exit.*]

Sal. What can this mean?

Ju. Marsio will tell us that.

(*Enter* MARSIO.)

Marsio. Am I intrusive?

Ju. O no; welcome, sir!

Mar. A good-day to you, signore Salvatore!
We have met once before.

Sal. Good-day to you!
He claims acquaintance on strange introductions.
[*Aside.*]

Mar. You wonder at my coming, gentlemen.
I am but agent for my lord, the Marquis.
He honors my betrothal to his daughter
With a small feast to-night. We want but guests.
Knowing a sadly-broken intercourse
Had once existed 'twixt your name and his,
I volunteered to bear my lord's respects
And humble wishes to you. May we hope?

Sal. Why, signore —

Ju. We will come.

Sal. How, Count?

Ju. We'll come.
I rage with thirst; the sweet I cannot taste,
I'll drain the bitter to the very lees,
And she shall see it! [*Aside.*]

Mar. Further, gentlemen —
Though I am trenching on fair courtesy —
Could you not pass the day — 't is early yet —
With the good Marquis? So preparing you,

By slow degrees of interchanged regard,
For more familiar greetings at the feast.
I push your kindness ; but my lord's content,
And a desire for your unfrozen ease,
Is my sole object.

Ju. Yes ! by all the gods !

Mar. Ha ! why this energy ? (*Aside.*) You shame my thanks
By more than noble courtesy. Farewell !
Within an hour my horses will be round.

Ju. Expect to meet us.

Mar. Lo ! the trap is set.
Look how you tread, my courtly innocents,
Or Herod's bloody day shall come again !

[*Aside. Exit.*]

Sal. A strange request: I think him honest, though.

Ju. I care not what he be.

Sal. The saints protect us !
You 're roaring drunk with love and jealousy,
Blind and incapable.

Ju. I 'd reach the worst.
To be forever baited by my passions
Is more than I can bear. My hopes and fears
Tear me to pieces. I am man enough
To toss despair into the grave of love ;
But these sweet tortures of insidious hope
Oppose no front to armèd fortitude.

Sal. Now you talk sanely. When you come to blows —
To strangling passion, burying despair,
And setting up a commonwealth of reason —

My heart fights with you. You shall have your way.
Ho! for Tiburzzi!

(*Reënter* PULTI.)

Pulti. Signore Salvatore, [*Sings.*]

O! pray what said the devil,
With his cloven tongue of evil,
As he drew his hoof under his gown?
Why, to them he said sweetly,
Sweet gentlemen, I greet ye!
But he wished they might hang, starve, and drown.

Sal. Whate'er he wished, he spoke us fairly, Pulti.

Pul. I heard it all. Beware of Marsio!
You know him not, as I do. I suspect
You are the gentlemen who woke his wrath.

Ju. Pish! how?

Pul. Do we not often fall to hating
For the same cause we mostly fall to loving —
Simply, for none at all? Perhaps your cloak
Is of a hateful dye in Marsio's eyes;
You grow moustaches, but he loathes a beard;
Your dress is much too dandified; your hat
Worn too much on one side; your cheeks
Hint of the roses, and he scorns a rose;
Your hair is raven black, — "Out upon black!"
Says Marsio; "black hairs thatch empty heads."
Here is enough to raise a riot, sirs,
And overturn a state. Why will you go?
I am sure he means you ill.

Sal. Why think you so?

Pul. I cannot tell ; I have no reason for it ;
My mind jumped to that end.
Ju. We waste time, kinsman.
Pul. O ! do not, do not go !
Ju. Peace, sirrah, peace !
Pul. I have more interest in you, gentlemen,
Than your best gold can buy. You are the first,
For many a weary day, who 've made me feel
The simple worth and dignity of man.
I 've hidden my heart under outrageous mirth —
O, heaven ! how sad it beat there ! — till my jests
Became a natural language. I have lived
To sneer, and to be beaten ; all content
If my poor wit were sharper than the blows.
I love you for your kindness. — Hear me, sirs —
I 'd rather see this fair world torn to shreds,
Than harm befall you.
Ju. I respect your grief;
And were my life not centred in this thing,
Your single wish should sway me. Salvatore —
What, you hold off !
Sal. You know for whom I do it.
Pul. If Marsio escape my eyes to-day,
May I want eyes to see him on the morrow ! [*Aside.*]
Ju. I 'll go alone. You cannot balk me thus.
Were Marsio the devil Pulti sings,
I would confront him. Ere the night set in,
I shall be free ; or — Down, ye maddening hopes !
O ! were your whispers certain prophecy ! [*Exeunt.*]

SCENE III.

A Room in the Castle of the MARQUIS. *Enter* COSTANZA *and* FILIPPIA.

Filippia. After this treatment of your father, too?
Costanza. Yes, yes. Each act which sinks him in my mind,
Binds me more closely to him. I but think
Of my poor father, feeble, heart-sick, dying,
With nothing but the mercy of this man
Between him and the galleys. Gracious heaven!
Marsio dared threaten him with even that,
While all the glory of the setting sun
Looked on him through the windows! Do men think
That this vast theatre of their wickedness —
With its brave lights of sun, and moon, and stars —
Its shifting scenes, from Spring around to Winter —
Its moving canopies of cloudy blue —
Is crowded with a spiritual audience,
Keeping mute watch upon our lightest acts?
Fil. Ah me! I know not. Musing minds, like yours,
Ask questions without answers. Save my eyes!
Are these things phantoms?

(*Enter* MARSIO, JURANIO, *and* SALVATORE.)

Marsio. Good-day, ladies! — How!
Are we infringing on your privacy?
Pray, what disturbs you? Nay, we will withdraw.
Cos. Stay, signore: you mistake us.

Mar. By your leave,
I bring two friends of mine, or rather guests —
Guests for the present, friends henceforth I hope —
To share our feast to-night. Receive them kindly;
For they deserve no less. Let me present,
Lady Costanza, Count Juranio.
Cos. Sir, we have met before. —
Mar. Ah! so indeed?
A chance acquaintance, doubtless. As my friend,
He asks a double share of your regard.
Mistress Filippia, signore Salvatore:
I pray you know him.
Fil. Do not jeer at me!
You know we 've met before. I will not stand
To be a butt for your dull, headless jokes!
Mar. Gently, my little lady, gently now!
Do I o'erstrain good breeding? Have you had
A formal introduction to my friend?
Salvatore. 'Sblood, signore Marsio —
Mar. Banish all restraint.
Swear if you list, dear Salvatore, swear!
The ladies will forgive you, for my sake.
Hang on no ceremonious usages.
I beg you 'll know each other. Laugh, dance, sing;
Open all avenues to fellowship;
For, by my hopes of wedded bliss, old Time
Shall make oblation of this day, at least,
To rouse the gods of genial jollity!
Where hide the old folk? Let us seek them.— What,
You laggards! — Forward, to the stretching Park!
Stone walls cramp action. Lead my lady forth,
Good Count Juranio. Why, you stand amazed;
Dismal as death! Cannot a man be gay,

Without your wonder? Count, conduct your charge
I give you a safe escort, lady mine.
Now, Salvatore, buckle sweet Filippia
Under your strong right-arm. I 'll follow you,
With nothing but my mirth for company.

Sal. Can Marsio be mad? [*Apart to* FILIPPIA.]

Fil. Heaven only knows!
My heart is fluttering at a fearful rate.
[*Apart to* SALVATORE.]

[*Exeunt* COSTANZA *and* JURANIO, FILIPPIA *and* SALVATORE.]

Mar. So, well done, now! Lord! how they fall to talking!
My presence must have been a chill upon them.
Bless us! Filippia 's all alive with speech;
Arms and hands going — how she brings them down! —
Clinching some sentence, through and through, with truth.
And now she darts her head and curving neck,
Like an affronted swan. Ha! quiet yet,
Costanza, pensive still! And your fine Count
Striding as at a funeral! Why is this?
Where 's your love-rhetoric? Heaven speed ye all!
The twigs you tread are limed. Join wits with me!
Who is the fooler now? who are the fooled? [*Exit.*]

SCENE IV.

The Park. *Enter* COSTANZA *and* JURANIO.

Costanza. Where are our friends?

Juranio. They have deserted us.

Cos. Let us return to them. — Why came you here?

Ju. To be a guest at your betrothal-feast.

Cos. But was that kindly done?

Ju. I cannot say:
One, more or less, can make small difference.

Cos. Sir, you dissemble with me.

Ju. Do I, lady?
Who taught the lesson?

Cos. Is it manly in you
To seek so poor a victory over me?
Perchance, you thought to see my features pale,
My eyes swim blindly, and my limbs give way,
When you approached me first. — You did not, sir!
Perchance you think when, at the festival,
They toast my union with Marsio,
To see me falter, nay, to faint outright —
A crowning triumph for your vanity. —
You shall not, sir! O! Count Juranio,
This is unworthy a less man than you!

Ju. As you behold it; but you wrong me much.
Why have you ever held me in contempt?
Why have you sought the motives of my acts
Among the lowest heaven allows the base?
Why have you turned my honest love aside
With irony? I never wronged you, lady,—
No, by my soul, neither in word nor thought!
I never wished to tempt you into ill,
With the bare modest offering of my love.
Why do you fly a gentleman's regard,
And fix you on this loveless Marsio?

Cos. These are strange questions, Count Juranio.
After to-day, our paths lie far apart;

Pledge me your honor ne'er to see me more,
And I will answer. — Nay; my fate is fixed.

Ju. You will not understand me: your ill thoughts
Stretch to futurity, and hint at things
Beyond my heart's conception. I would rather,
Far rather, know your holy chastity
Were pining in a dungeon — dying — dead —
Than clasp your blighted beauty in my arms,
With Helen's charms joined to it!

Cos. Gentle sir,
You misconceive me. I would spare the pangs,
The fearful struggles, which our love —

Ju. "Our love!"

Cos. Ay, ay! I love you, love you, love you!
I tell it to you with a breaking heart:
I must speak once, though ruin follow it.
A little while, and this still agony
Shall vanish from existence; yes, the sod
Will rest as quietly above my grave
As o'er a yearling infant's.

Ju. Happiness!
Costanza, dearest,— turn not from me now:
I am all yours. O! I have loved you long:
I'll spend my life in telling you how much.
Do not allow cold fancies to tread down
These buds of joyous promise. There is naught
Between us and the fulness of our hopes,
Save feeble Marsio.

Cos. A giant!

Ju. No;
A very pigmy. Dearest, do not shun me.

Cos. I pray you, Count, remove your hands from me —

My father's life hangs on my constancy —
Away, sir, I am sacred !
Ju. Spurned again !
Do you act thus to torture me ? O ! answer !
Is cruelty your practice, grief your sport ?
You walk in mystery ; every deed is blank
And purposeless to me.
Cos. Forbear, forbear !
You should not taunt me thus. My destiny
Tramples on love, and overrules my life.
O ! tempt me not !
Ju. Explain, explain yourself.
I would not think unworthily of you.
Cos. You know my father's poverty —
Ju. Yes, yes ;
And to enrich him — for his sake alone —
Am I not right ? — you marry Marsio.
Cos. Quite right. But my betrothal was performed
Ere — ere —
Ju. You loved me. But what hinders now ?
Cos. My father's debts were large, strewn here and there,
The wide accumulation of old dues
Gathered for ages round our sinking house.
Marsio knew this, and bought the scattered claims
For a bare trifle ; though the full amount
Would beggar a state's revenue to pay.
He held these debts — alas ! that I can say it
Of one to whom I must be linked for life ! —
Above my father's helpless head, and swore
Either to wed me, or to send my father —
Think of it, signore, an infirm old man,

Full of ancestral pride and gentle thoughts —
Yes, to send him — chained, coupled, mixed with thieves —
Even to the galleys!

Ju. The outrageous wretch!
I'll bury him in gold!

Cos. Too late, too late!
Though you held all the Indies in your fee.
Upon the threat — from which no prayers could move him —
I promised Marsio, most solemnly,
To keep my marriage-plight.

Ju. Alas! I mourn
More for your fate than for the loss of you.

(*Enter, behind,* MARSIO *and* PIETRO ROGO, *observing them.*)

Is there no way? Yes, yes; the Duke —

Cos. The Duke!
The holy Pope, himself, is naught to me
Before my promise.

Ju. Lady, do but think
Of the long life of weary misery
That lies before you.

Cos. I have thought of that.
Will you attend the feast now?

Ju. I am bound,
Almost by oath, to Marsio.

Cos. Indeed! —

Ju. After the feast — O heaven! have mercy on me!
I cannot, cannot yield you. Chance, nay, heaven
Has thrown me in your way to succor you.
I slighted women till the day we met:

Each feeling which love's prodigals spread out,
In lavish wastefulness, upon your sex,
I have stored up to tender you alone.
Shall all be lost? Ah! lady — [*Kneels.*]
Cos. Count, be strong!
Life 's but an atom of eternity.
Ju. But love makes life immortal.
Cos. 'T is in vain;
You must not strive to weaken my resolve.
Farewell!
Ju. So be it, then. (*Rising.*) Yet, ere you go,
Leave some remembrance — ay, that golden cross
Is a fit emblem of my martyred love.
Cos. No, no; forget me. It were weakness, sir,
To pamper memory with a toy like this.
Yet when a thought of me will come to you,
Judge me not harshly — as of one who died,
Rich in rare gifts, bequeathing you no part —
But as a poor, poor friend, who, dying, left
All she possessed, her blessing. — May God bless
you! [*Exit.*]
Ju. O! fate! what I have lost!
Rogo. How think you now?
Marsio. That Count Juranio is my best of friends.
He proved my wife the soul of constancy.
I 'll love him from this day. Why, Pietro,
I do not see you laughing at me — ha!
Rogo. Be quiet, man; my laugh may come at last.
Juranio will make a famous friend,
After your marriage. Just the youth, I think,
To show your lady to a masquerade —
To hand her shawl — to read her fiery poems —

To dance with her — and do all other things
Which you are slow at. — Ha ! friend Marsio ?
Mar. Poor fellow ! Pietro, I almost fear
The hapless youth will pine himself to death
Ere I am married — though I 'll stir for him —
I fear so, Pietro. Why, look you now,
He has a dying face ; so strangely pale !
Doubtless, there is some fatal sickness nigh,
Which this sad interview has hastened on.
Poor, crest-fallen lover ! Let us speak to him.
[*They advance.*]
Ho ! Count Juranio ! What, you are alone !
Where has the lady gone I charged you with ?
O ! faithless guardian ! On my honor, Count,
I 'll never trust her to your care again. —
Would you, friend Pietro ?
Ju. She just departed.
Some duty called her to the castle.
Mar. Ah !
Some duty past persuasion ; or no doubt —
So high I value sweet Costanza's charms —
You 'd have detained her. — Ha ! Count ? Now, a youth,
Of your fair person, should have ample power
To hold a restive maiden.
Rogo. How he rubs him ! [*Aside.*]
Ju. I did not urge her stay.
Mar. Indeed ! Well, well,
You lack my feelings ; — but I cannot hope
That all the world will look through lovers' eyes.
Here 's signore Salvatore, and alone !
Fair maids are in discredit. Save you, sir !

(*Enter* SALVATORE.)

Salvatore. A moment with my kinsman.
Mar. Ask a thousand.
[JURANIO *and* SALVATORE *talk apart.*]
Rogo. The devil take me, if you have a heart!
I would not worry these poor boys so much,
To sway the dukedom.
Mar. Yes, I have a heart—
A heart which these poor boys would trample on,
Did I not wear a head to second it.
Even now they scheme to compass me.
See, the plot opens.
Sal. Signore Marsio,
You are a merchant, traffic is your trade,
You look on all things under heaven as worth
Just so much money.—
Mar. Mark you, Pietro,
Here 's the ideal merchant. Well said, signore;
A golden measure is a certain thing
To gauge the world with.
Sal. Hold you anything
You have not measured with this golden rule?
Have you aught priceless?
Mar. Nothing—let me think.
No; there is naught I know of.
Sal. Frankly, then;
What is Costanza's value?
Mar. Ha! ha! ha! [*Laughing.*]
You are the maddest dog in Christendom!
Perchance, you are serious? Signore, if you are?—
Rogo. Zounds! Marsio, you are a mean, tame fool,
To brook this insolence! [*Apart to* MARSIO.]

Mar. Bear with me, friend. [*Apart to* Rogo.]
Sal. My words were plain enough.
Mar. Well — let me see —
I should receive — I put her low to you —
At least ten million ducats. I will give
A warranty for kindness, soundness, age ; —
She has no tricks,— you may put trust in her.
Is this fair dealing, Pietro ?
Rogo. Pshaw! pshaw!
Sal. You jest with me.
Mar. Faith, I am serious.
Ten million is a serious thing. I wish
To fit some argosies. Ten million ducats!
Within a year I 'd nearly double them.
I want ten million.
Ju. Take them, in heaven's name!
I still shall have my little villa left
Among the vineyards.
Mar. But I want that villa.
Can you not throw it in ?
Ju. Most gladly, signore,
Yet be your debtor. I have arms to work.
Mar. Now, should I wish a limb or so ? —
Sal. Take mine;
Leave my trunk bare. One limb of mine is worth
All yonder puny fellow's.
Mar. Ha! ha! ha! [*Laughing.*]
Could you unbowel earth of all its gold —
Cover the globe with vineyards, and sow villas
Thicker than sands upon the roaring beach,
Amid the vine-sticks — were mankind unlimbed,
The whole race at my mercy — these would make
No atom of the sum I hold her at!
'Sblood! will you flout me ?

Sal. Well, well, I have lost.
Mar. Ay, lost — How lost?
Sal. Forgive the liberty.
I made a sportive wager with the Count,
That I could purchase anything you owned:
He named your lady. — As I live, Juranio,
You scarcely used me fairly.
Mar. Ah! a jest.
Sal. A jest that lifts a trader's character
Above my former thinking.
Mar. Pietro,
If I should put this jesting home again,
They could not murmur?
Rogo. No, forsooth.
Sal. No, no;
'T is give and take.
Mar. Why, signore Salvatore,
I half believed you meant it. Well done, faith!
How did you keep your countenance? 'T was rare!
Costanza must know this. So, merry men,
On, to the castle! Count Juranio,
You played well too. You must feel lively, Count,
With such a flood of spirits.
Sal. Curse the brute!
He cuts Juranio with a two-edged sword. [*Aside.*]
Mar. Now forward, sirs! We must break even yet.
I'll plan some joke; but, when 't is working hard,
You must not flinch, if it be something rude.
Forward, mad boys! We are all jesters now:
For want of bells, we 'll shake our empty heads!
[*Exeunt, on one side,* MARSIO, JURANIO, *and* SALVATORE; *on the other,* PIETRO ROGO.]

ACT V.

SCENE I. *The House of* Marsio. *Enter* Marsio.

Marsio. Kneel to Costanza, — test her constancy!
There 's something in me mutinies at that:
But she shall have full vengeance. Kneel to her!
As if I were not. Have I fallen so low
That this fine gentleman, this courtly scum,
Scorns to regard me? Traffic for her, too!
As if I kept my lady on my shelves,
To wait a market. On my life, you 'll find
My heart boils sometimes, and the reek is death
To such as stir it! She shall be revenged!
[*Draws forth a vial.*]
Now, trembling liquid, who, to look at thee —
At thy pale, sickly aspect — at thy bulk,
Cowering to nothing in thy crystal house —
Would think that thou couldst give so brave a fall
To his befeathered Countship? What, canst thou
Stiffen the strong steel sinews of yon man
Who wields the sword so featly? As I live,
I doubt thee, mainly! Come, one sturdy shake,
To rouse thy courage. Ha! my little fellow,
How thou dost caper! Thou hast spirit, yet.
But how to face thee with thy enemies?
'T would fix suspicion on me, to be seen
Hanging around their cups. Now, could I bribe
Some fool among the servants — but whom, but whom?

Curse on my negligence! I should have thought—
There 's Pulti — Pulti —

(*Enter* PULTI.)

Pulti. At your elbow, sir,
Quoth sin unto the devil.

Mar. Merry dog!
What brought you back?

Pul. You left so hastily,
I thought I might be wanted.

Mar. Faithful heart!
Here is a trifle for you. By my soul,
Your love deserves it richly, Pulti. [*Gives a purse.*]

Pul. Well,
It makes him so much poorer. [*Aside.*]

Mar. Pulti —

Pul. Signore.

Mar. You love your master, Pulti?

Pul. That I do!
I 'd swim through burning brimstone for my master—
Good signore Salvatore! [*Aside.*]

Mar. Bravely said!
Now, had your master two unresting foes —
Dogging his footsteps — crossing his fair plans —
Marring his hopes — turning his sweetest cup,
Ere it were tasted, to cruel bitterness —
Pursuing him with most vindictive hate —
Ever hot-footed on his way of life,
Beating its quiet path to choking dust;
Until your heart-sick master — note me, Pulti —
Longed for the grave to hide him from their wrath;
What would you do, brave, noble fellow, ha?

Pul. Cut them to slivers!

Mar. Famous! Rashly bold,

A little over-bold, however. No ;
You 'd take this vial, hidden in your sleeve —
Thus, Pulti, thus — and when the wine went round,
You 'd slyly drop five drops — no more nor less —
In each one's cup — ha ! Pulti ? And, next day,
This vast machine of earth would tumble on,
As if these dreadful bullies ne'er had been. —
Would you not, Pulti ?

Pul. Yes, indeed. I 'll swear —
Tell me some fearful oath to swear it by.

Mar. Poh ! poh ! These bugbear oaths are chil dren's toys,
Mere scare-crow buckram, to the big-souled men
Who do such mighty deeds. But you would say —
All quietly, in silent, breathless words —
My master and myself are in one boat,
And sink or swim together. — Would you not ?

Pul. I would be cautious.

Mar. Doubtless, my wise boy !
Prudence and courage make a powerful yoke
To tug along the world.

Pul. I take you, sir —
As rats are taken. — O ! I slander rats. [*Aside.*]

Mar. But will you do it ?

Pul. By this hand, I will.

Mar. I love to shake an honest comrade's hand.
There 's more gold, Pulti — millions, millions, boy —
And you shall share it. You shall revel out
A prince's ransom ; live a gentleman,
And kick work to the devil. Hey ! my trump !

Pul. Who are these enemies ?

Mar. You long to see
The villains drink each other's healths ?

Pul. Ha! ha! [*Laughing.*]
O! bless me, you are droll!
Mar. These are our foes —
Yours, Pulti, and my own — that velvet Count,
That clothes-pin, modish Count Juranio,
And signore Salvatore, carte and tierce,
The ruffian, with his beaver on one side,
Who swaggers through the world, and pushes all
That do not please him in the kennel. 'Sblood!
'T were no great harm to cut such fools adrift;
'T would save some lace a sunning, and give steel
A holy rest.
Pul. Lord! how you draw them, sir!
Those very men have troubled me a deal.
Give me some ratsbane.
Mar. Just before the feast,
I'll slip it in your hand. Be faithful, Pulti;
There's no such gold as mine.
Pul. Have faith in me.
May heaven forsake me, when I leave my master!
Mar. Bring out the horses. I must back again:
My absence will be noted.
Pul. Bless you, bless you! —
I find it in my heart to bless you, sir,
That you employed no one but me for this. [*Exit.*]
Mar. The knave's a God-send! Who had ever thought
That little, crooked Marsio could wake
So warm a feeling in the breast of man?
Why, what a cat's-paw for my dangerous nut
The ready villain is! I never deemed
The monstrous wretch was crammed so full of sin:
He poisons at a hint. Heaven save you, Count!

My fiery lover, we will cool your blood:
Heaven save you, too, bold signore Salvatore!
My dashing swordsman, we will break your guard.
Heaven save you both together, gentlemen!
I 'll bow you to your graves to-morrow morn!
[*Exit.*]

SCENE II.

An Apartment in the Castle of the MARQUIS. *Enter* SALVATORE *and* PULTI, *meeting.*

Pulti. Stand back! I'm Marsio's chief poisoner!
[*Sings.*]

Quoth the devil, I 'll mix
Both the Acheron and Styx,
To brew them a deadly potation —

Lord! I 'm too gay to sing.
Salvatore. Why, Pulti, Pulti!
Pul. Unearthed, at last! The fox has broken ground,
And I am holding to his brush — ho! ho!
[*Laughing.*]
Saint Dunstan's tongs were mercy to this hand.
O! but I have him!
Sal. Pulti, are you crazed?
Pul. Half mad with joy. Here is his precious plot —
Sal. Whose plot?
Pul. Why, Marsio's. What other fiend
Could shape one like it? Had you seen me, sir,
Just playing with him, like a well-hooked fish;
I gave him all my line.
Sal. Now for the plot.

Pul. Then tremble! Signore Marsio — Ho! ho!
[*Laughing.*]
The devil catch me! I must laugh it out.
Well, signore Marsio has hired me, me —
Me, me — his Pulti — do you understand? —
To poison you and Count Juranio.
Sal. Ha! — Where, and how?
Pul. O! at the feast to-night.
Sal. In meat or wine?
Pul. In wine. The merry ape
Would see you two pledging each other's healths;
Just for the joke's sake. Do you take it?
Sal. Yes:
How the sky brightens after Marsio's thunder!
Bless his invention! I will match his coin.
Some paper, quickly.
Pul. Here, sir. [*Showing paper, on a table.*]
Sal. Let me think.
Now, school of Padua, help thy dullest scholar
To mix a draught for Marsio. 'Ods blood!
I have not practised physic for so long,
That I scarce recollect the crooked things
Which stand for drachms and scruples.
Pul. Never care
For scruples, only call the drachms to mind:
I long to dose him.
Sal. Ah! I have it now:
It all comes back together. (*Writes.*) Here we are;
Signed, Doctor Salvatore. Pulti, run —
Ask for the next apothecary — run!
Our time is short. [*Gives a paper.*]
Pul. Here is a full receipt
For all your poundings, master Marsio!

Sal. You 'll throw the drug in Marsio's cup. Fly, fly!
But where 's his poison? You must get me that.
Pul. As soon as Marsio puts it in my hands.
Sal. Enough — away! [*Exit* PULTI, *singing.*]

Quoth the man to the devil,
Thou spirit of evil,
Foul poison is brewed from fair peaches;
A curse on your vowings!
Your scrapings and bowings,
Like poison may lurk in fair speeches.

Sal. Bright Cupid and dark Death
Join hands, in an unnatural fellowship,
Like morn and midnight at the northern pole;
But I can see a pathway, green with hope,
Beneath the twilight.

(*Enter the* MARQUIS DI TIBURZZI.)

Marquis. Can you spare a moment?
Sal. Your question wrongs me: I would gladly spend
A lifetime in your service.
Marq. I believe you:
Although men's tongues too oft outnoise their deeds,
And gain in clamor what they lose in aim.
When you approached me for my niece's hand,
I saw in you such manly qualities
As led me to receive you, not alone
As her best suitor, but as my best friend.
You are a man of action, I am not;
You are a man of hopeful vigor; cares

Soon dried my leaves of early promise up,
And age puts forth no more. Sir, I am old,
Feeble, and hopeless; I would have a friend.
Sal. Confide in me.
Marq. I need your confidence —
Not for myself; these gray hairs warn me oft
That I shall drop into my barren grave
Ere many seasons; but my daughter lives,
To blossom o'er my ruins, or to wither.
God only knows.
Sal. To blossom, bear, and yield,
In holy sunshine!
Marq. And you know her fate,—
Her vile betrothal to this Marsio?
Sal. Did you not make it?
Marq. No! they juggled me.
Her — Well, well, signore, I 'd not think of that.
Now, I would break the bond; but Marsio
Holds my ancestral debts, and threatens me
With whips and galleys. I could bear them all,
If that would free Costanza.
Sal. Let me add
Another misery, then break the whole.
Your daughter loves Juranio.
Marq. Gracious heaven!
Woe piles on woe! Had I a choice of men,
I would have picked him for her.
Sal. Rightly too,
You would have picked the flower. Your simple word,
To follow, without flaw, what I design,
Shall free Costanza, wed her to the Count,
And ransom you.

Marq. You mock me.
Sal. Mock you!
No, no; I 'll show you what I rest upon.
Marq. You seem a sober man.
Sal. To Marsio
I am fate's deputy. Crime gives a hold
Which rivets the transgressor to an end,
So helpless, that an infant's careless hand
May pull a giant to his doom.
Marq. Crime!
Sal. Crime.
Marq. Dear heaven, might this be true! I know him cruel —
Ay, guilty — but not within the scope of law.
Sal. Have I no credit?
Marq. Yes; I yield you all —
My faith, my honor. Guide me as you list;
You cannot worst my chance.
Sal. Then hear my tale —
More fitted to draw blood than tears, my lord:
That scheming crawler, Marsio, has hired
A man, who loves Juranio and myself,
To poison us.
Marq. O, horror! Has the wretch
Such depths in his dark soul?
Sal. It so appears.
Marq. I 'll hurl him from my windows! Shall a roof
That hung so long 'twixt heaven and noble men,
Fence off God's justice?
Sal. Softly, sir, I pray!
He must attempt the poisoning, or we lose
Our grasp upon him.

Marq. True. What cause can he
Set up to satisfy him with his crime?
Sal. Against Juranio, 't is jealousy.
Marq. I see. Your kinsman was the cavalier
Who met Costanza in the Park.
Sal. No other:
And plead his suit most bravely, but in vain:
She made her love an offering for your life.
Marq. Poor girl!
Sal. Now, hear my mandates.
Marq. But your plan —
What is your plan?
Sal. It must unfold itself.
I have a shift for Marsio's every turn:
One lost, another wins.
Marq. I am content.
'T is better with you; I have ever marred
Whate'er I touched. Lay your commands upon me.
Sal. Provide a priest, and have such papers drawn,
As the law orders, to unite in wedlock
Costanza and Juranio. At the feast,
See you produce them when I call for them.
Marq. It shall be done. O, signore Salvatore,
See you be well prepared upon your part.
I count my life as nothing; but my daughter,
My only daughter — Look you do not slip:
You might enrage, not foil, his villany;
And draw a double ruin on her head.
Sal. Fear not; even now I hold such evidence
As makes the life of signore Marsio
Not worth a felon's claim. How Pulti tarries!
[*Aside.*]
You will pardon me, if I take leave, my lord?

Marq. Go, signore, go. Ask me to pardon you!
God shield you, sir! You shall have all the prayers
My age may mutter, 'twixt the coming night
And that far darker night, towards which my steps,
By slow degrees, are narrowing to their end.

Sal. Cheer, cheer, my lord! The shadows fly
from us;
Day treads upon the dusky heels of night!
Even now my herald hopes fly far above,
Shaking the morning from their shining wings!
Ho! laugh, laugh, and be merry.

Marq. Ha! ha! ha! [*Laughing.*]
Your hearty courage is infectious, sir!
[*Exeunt severally.*]

SCENE III.

Another Room in the Castle. Enter Costanza *and* Filippia.

Filippia. [*Sings.*]

Love-lorn Lucy
On a bank sat sighing,
Ah, well a day! ah, well a day!
My fickle love has flown away,
And left me here a-dying,

False, false pledges!
Why did I receive them?
Vows are but words, words are but air,
And air can blow both foul and fair:
Why did I believe them?

Ah! light-hearted,
Would thy scorn might slay me!
O! would thy wrongs might end my pain!
Or would that thou mightst come again,
And again betray me!

There 's a light song to cheer you.
Costanza. Woful cheer!
Fil. Why, what 's the matter, cousin? How you droop!
Here 's a strange countenance for a festival!
Take my advice; follow your honest heart;
For those who oftenest trust their knavish heads
Are oftenest led by a fool's bauble. Run,
Run for dear life! Away, girl, Count and all!
I 'll cover your retreat.
Cos. This mockery
Is cruel and useless. How my doom draws on!
It seems to me as if the viewless hours
Have changed themselves to some substantial thing,
And I can hear them roaring by my ears,
Like a vast tide, — alas! alas! how swiftly!
Fil. Did she but know how gayly nimble Time
Is floating on Love's shallop, she would kiss
The slandered gray-beard. I will tell her. No;
'T is Salvatore's secret. [*Aside.*]
Cos. Cousin, cousin,
I cannot marry Marsio! Each step
That brings me nearer to him shows the man
More hideous; and, alas! — I tell you all —
Contrast makes Count Juranio appear
Almost a god to him.
Fil. Why, so he is;

And so is any other honest man.
Marsio 's no man; Marsio 's an outcast imp,
Banished among us for such evil deeds
As set the fiends to staring!
Cos. Misery!
Have you no word of comfort? I implore
Your kindlier feelings, and you meet my grief
With scoffs and jeers. Why do you not sustain
My tottering firmness? Has my lot become
Too low, too mean, for pity? Must I stand
By my own power? So be it, then; I 'll stand,
Though my heart break within me!
Fil. I must tell her.

(*Enter* SALVATORE. FILIPPIA *and* SALVATORE *talk apart.*)

Salvatore. Have you kept counsel?
Fil. By the hardest, though.
Don't glare at me. I have obeyed you, tyrant.
Lord! if you frown so at the maid, the wife
Must feed her love on cudgels!
Sal. Peace, peace, peace!
Your love shall have sound diet. It was well —
Look you, Filippia — it was well I came.
Fil. 'T is always well when Salvatore comes.
Sal. Bah! you mad witch! I love you fearfully.
Fil. And so you show it. I can never tell,
When you come nigh me, whether you intend
To cut my throat or kiss me.
Sal. Instance this. [*Kisses her.*]
Fil. I know not yet.
Sal. Till you are satisfied,
I 'll smother you in kisses. [*Kisses her.*]

Fil. Ruffian, stop!
Look at my ruffle. O! had you rude men
To do our starching! Woo me by main strength!
Sal. Out on your arts! Your wicked witchery
Makes me forget myself — your cousin too.
Fil. She did not note you.
Sal. I must speak with her.
[*Advances to* COSTANZA.]
Lady Costanza, dare you trust your honor
In my poor hands?
Cos. Had I a fear of it,
There I should place it.
Fil. Justly spoken, cousin!
Make him your fate. See what I gain by it, —
A crumpled ruffle, and a bleeding lip.
Sal. Time presses; I must through at once.
[*Aside.*]
Fil. Well, well!
Here 's better than yourself to whisper to.
Sal. Lady Costanza, without argument,
Give me your word to do as I direct,
And I engage to scatter your worst fears,
And crown your brightest hopes with full success.
I hold your future in my happy hands:
My power is ample, and my purpose just.
For — mark this, lady — should I trench upon
Your nicest honor, by the act, I free you
From any compact.
Cos. Signore Salvatore,
You mean this kindly, and I take it so,
But know it baseless.
Sal. Only promise.
Fil. Do!

Cos. 'T is said that drowning beggars sometimes vow
Rich churches to the saint who 'll spare their lives;
So I — passing my word upon your terms —
Promise, if you fulfil your marvellous pledge,
That which defies our voluntary power —
My dearest love.
Fil. Poh! poh! Costanza, "love!"
O! what a doleful effort to be gay!
Pray, use some cooler term — the man is mine —
Say friendship, or affection, or the like:
I dread your rivalry.
Sal. Filippia lays
Our serious feelings, as if they were devils.
Fil. He takes her part! Now I am jealous, sir.
Come, lead her off from this sad theme.
[*Apart to* SALVATORE.]
Sal. Alas!
Here comes the theme itself.

(*Enter* MARSIO *and* JURANIO.)

Marsio. Pray, look you, ladies:
Here is he that once was Count Juranio;
But, now, how fallen, how spent and spiritless!
I tried an hour to work a smile from him,
But lost my labor.
Fil. What 's the trouble, Count?
Sal. Are you a man? [*Apart to* JURANIO.]
Juranio. There is the misery,
That I am man; would I were more or less! [*Aside.*]
Mar. I even took him to your bower, Costanza;
Showed what a lurking-place for love it is;

Pointed your favorite flowers; glanced here and there,
Omitting nothing: but he never smiled.
Then I went through my plans of wedded bliss;
Told him how soon my marriage-day would come;
Invited him to see it. — On my faith,
Methinks I turned a prophet, for his sake —
Did I not, Count? — and in a vision saw
My stretching line of noble progeny.
I named them too — ha! ha! I named them for him! [*Laughing.*]
Called one Juranio. Striving thus to cheer
His melancholy with my happiness:
But yet he never smiled. When he would speak,
'T was only "Marsio, O! were I you!"
And then he 'd blush, and catch his sentence up
With — "I 'd do so and so" — some petty thing,
Beneath my memory. Even now he talked,
So sweetly talked, of "Death, dear, pleasant death!
What a kind thing it is that weary men,
After the jading day of eager life,
Can lie them gently in their earthy beds,
And sleep their cares away!" So well he spoke,
That, for his eloquence, I nearly killed him,
Out of sheer pity.

Sal. What a man is this!
But justice' arm is up. [*Aside.*]

(FILIPPIA, JURANIO, *and* SALVATORE, *talk apart.*)

Mar. (*Apart to* COSTANZA.) They tell me, lady,
You were insulted in the Park, to-day,
By some presuming dunce's love. — Nay, nay;

Come here. They say you used him bravely, too,
As I would wish you.
Cos. Ha! he knows it all:
I see such meaning in his face. I fear — [*Aside.*]
A word, sir, with Juranio.
Mar. With whom?
Cos. With Count Juranio.
Mar. Not a whisper. Lady,
We mostly add men's titles to their names.

(*Enter a Servant.*)

Servant. My lord awaits you, gentlemen.
Mar. On, on!
The feast invites us. Count Juranio,
We 'll drown your gloomy humors in our wine.
Come, gentlemen. To-night is lovers' eve —
Conduct your lady, signore Salvatore;
I too will use the time's sweet privilege:
Think me not rude, Count. By your leave, Costanza.
[*Exit with* COSTANZA.]
Sal. You promise me?
Ju. Ay; use me as you will:
I lack employment for myself.
Sal. Go on.
Fil. Without you, signore?
Sal. Yes. — Make some excuse.
O! where is Pulti? Fate hangs on his steps!
[*Exeunt on one side,* FILIPPIA *and* JURANIO; *on the other,* SALVATORE.]

SCENE IV.

An Ante-Room in the Castle. Enter PULTI.

Pulti. (*Sings.*)

With each grain of Heaven's goodness,
I will mix one of woodness,
And ten solid grains of pure evil;
Do whatever you can,
You must bolt all, my man,
Or starve, quoth to Adam the devil.

(*Enter* SALVATORE.)

Salvatore. Your fiendish ditty is a guide, at least.
Well met! Your news?
Pul. I barely saved my time.
The guests are down, and I am sent to seek you.
Sal. Is the cup drugged?
Pul. I mixed the powders in,
And poured the wine around, ere I came off.
Sal. Two powders?
Pul. Two.
Sal. Victoria! The one
Shall rack him shrewdly, with a piercing colic,
Until the opiate act; when he will fall,
Upon a sudden, in a torpid stupor,
Which will so balance between life and death,
That but a feather's weight might turn the beam,
And land him in eternity.
Pul. It might?

I am no feather, and, by all I love,
I 'll leap into the balance bodily.
Sal. No, Pulti; I 've not closed with Marsio.
To-morrow I must buy the Marquis' debts,
On my own terms; death would upset my bargain.
Pul. Here 's Marsio's poison. [*Gives the vial.*]
Sal. Precious, precious vial!
You hold the happiness of two dear hearts
Pent in your narrow compass!
Pul. Is that all?
Methinks it comes to little, when 't is brought
Down to a liquid form. Had I believed
A lover's prophecies upon this point,
I 'd have been fool enough to build an ark,
Against a second deluge. What a close
To all your rhapsodies! Here 's a scant bath
For a foul fly!
Sal. Enough to drown your wit.
Pul. If that 's the substance of love's happiness,
Pray trust it to my handling. I will bear it,
As friars do rare relics, through the land,
To strengthen bachelors in their religion.
Sal. Prodigious atheist!
Pul. Holy maniac!
Now, which is better, a sound infidel,
Or a cracked devotee? Let Heaven decide.
Sal. Back to your master, knave! his fellowship
Sorts with your feelings.
Pul. 'T is a doleful thing,
That our gay world can yield a healthy man
No company but lunatics or rogues:
The wise are villains, and the honest fools.

Lord! what a raking mid the weeds there is,
To find one modest flower in all the crop!
Sal. I prophecy a cardinal's cap for you,
If you will preach thus in the market-place.
I must be off. O, Pulti, Pulti, Pulti,
If ever man loved man, I dote on you! [*Exeunt.*]

SCENE V.

The Great Hall of the Castle. A feast spread. At which are seated the MARQUIS *and* MARCHIONESS DI TIBURZZI, MARSIO, COSTANZA, FILIPPIA, JURANIO, *and other Guests. Servants in waiting. Enter* PULTI, *and stands behind* MARSIO. *Then enter* SALVATORE, *and seats himself.*

Marquis. We wait you, signore.
Salvatore. Pardon my delay:
My need was urgent.
Marsio. I have kept the wine.
Our cups, o'erbrimming with the sunny juice,
Stand to attend you.
Sal. 'T was a needless pause.
I never taste the vintage. By your leave,
I 'll use the grape, as nature gives it to us,
Thus, in the ripened fruit. For I hold wine
To be a most ingenious fraud of Satan's;
Who is so ready to change Heaven's best gifts
Into some tempting form of sin. 'T is true
A healthy apple cozened mother Eve;
But I have wondered at that barefaced trick
Upon the simple woman. Why did not
The guileful devil change it into cider,

And gull her handsomely? My kinsman, too,
Is of my way of thinking.

Juranio. I! what, I!
Why, Salvatore, I would quaff a sea
Of the rich earthly Lethe, were our night
Stretched to a polar length.

Mar. You hear him, sir:
The Count is wild for wassail. You will not
Refuse my lady's health? 'Sblood! should this dog
Lap water only? Pulti, is it done? [*Apart to* PULTI.]

Pulti. You 'll find it so. — Ho! ho! — [*Laughing.*]

Mar. Hist! be discreet. [*Apart to* PULTI.]

Sal. I will not balk you, to be curious.
A toast, a toast!

Mar. Rise, sirs. Our union! [*They drink.*]

Sal. Simple and pregnant. Cleopatra's pearl
Suffers discredit by your tasteful pledge.
I drank it, with good relish, to the dregs;
Ay, and forgot my enmity to wine,
In seeing with what gust you boused it down.

Mar. You flatter me. Your kinsman holds his peace:
I hope I touched him.

Sal. Him! Why, look you, now;
His cup is dry, — the very moisture gone:
Heavens! what a fiery thirst!

Costanza. Your lover's spirits
Mount to a wondrous height. It makes one sad
To see a man so merry.

Filippia. Wait a while,
And his high spirits shall fly off with you.

Cos. You have a hopeful fancy: it must be
A sorry thing to mark its failures.

Fil. No;
I have fresh hopes to help the lame ones on.
They are like flowers that, dying, run to seed,
And multiply the race. — See, Marsio!

March. What is the matter, signore?

Mar. Nothing, nothing:
A passing pain.

Sal. You drink too eagerly.
A sudden rush of wine into the frame
Shakes it with spasms sometimes.

Mar. Are you a leech?
Physic yourself — 'Sblood!

March. Signore! —

Mar. I am ill. [*They all rise.*]

Sal. Pray will you test my leechcraft?

Mar. I feel faint.
Nay; I am stronger now. Come hither, Pulti.
What does this mean?

Pul. I cannot tell.

Mar. Those men,
Those devilish villains — Pulti, do you see them? —
Look well and merry. Ere this time, the snakes
Should have crawled homeward, with their venom in.
The poison but fulfils what nature skipt:
While I — Augh! Pulti — [*Apart to* PULTI.]

Pul. Let me see. (*Runs to the table.*)
O, Lord!
O! signore Marsio is poisoned! O!
The cups are changed. You drank the —

Mar. Traitor, hold!
Or I will cut you to the belt!

March. Good heaven!
Poisoned?

Marq. Is this your plot? You —

Sal. Wait the issue. [*Apart to the* MARQUIS.]

March. Run, run — a doctor!

Mar. Forty thousand doctors
Were forty thousand short.

Cos. How feel you, signore?

Mar. Out! smooth drab! — O! — O!

Sal. You have sprung the trap,
But caught yourself for game.

Mar. Who did this thing?

Sal. I.

Mar. Hear! he confesses it. Seize on them —
Juranio and that man — my murderers!

March. Ay; seize them, seize them!

[*The Guests draw.*]

Sal. Patience, gentlemen,
I make you no resistance. On my honor,
I will not try to fly.

Mar. A poisoner's honor!
Mercy, what a pang! 'Sdeath! an officer —
Send for an officer! Quick, quick — break up —
I do denounce them both — we 'll have no feast!

Sal. Ay, but we will; a marriage, too.

Mar. How, how?

Sal. We 'll use Juranio, when you are gone.

Mar. Ah, dog! may your tongue rot!

Sal. Before you, signore?

Mar. Silence the miscreant! Are you men, to see —
O, heaven! these pains!

Ju. What means this, Salvatore?

Sal. Peace, my dear boy; the time is mine.

Mar. You think —

You two — your countship and that pliant lady —
You think, I say, when the grave swallows me,
To wed? — Ha! do ye? If the dead can rise —
And I will up! I 'll haunt you till ye pray
To sleep beside me. I will crawl between
Your eager kisses with my wormy lips;
I 'll eat with you; I 'll drink — I 'll drink again —
O, heaven! some water, water! I consume —
Till all my flesh has rotted from me. Gods!
Ha! ha! I 'll make a merry guest! You wretch —
Now I feel easier — you Salvatore,
I 'll fight with you, through all your odious days,
Until I drive you in your grave. O! curse you!
Do I look better? I may yet be well.
O! O! these searching cramps! Where do you go?
Come back, I say! I will not die alone!
I do denounce them — Pulti, Pulti too.
Seize them — seize all! Have pity on me, Heaven!
I will — I will! — The room is full of smoke.
Cut down the poisoners! I am not dead yet!

[*Draws, rushes at* JURANIO, *and falls.*]

O! mercy, heaven! O! curse you — O! [*Faints.*]

Sal. Well done!
He shows his death-bed in perspective.

March. Base,
Base man, to glory in your victim's death!
Sirs, apprehend him. [*The Guests advance.*]

Sal. Gently, gentlemen —
I use my cutlery with the best of you —
Marsio 's not dead. A simple opiate
Caused all this terror.

Fil. 'T is ill news, but true.
Find out some den to keep this monster in.

[*Servants carry off* MARSIO.]

Sal. Wake from your apathy! You stand like marble.
Cos. I never dreamed such horrors.
Ju. What, not dead?
March. O! joy, joy, joy!
Sal. Call in your priest and notary.
Are they in waiting?
Marq. As I promised you.
But I can scarcely see my way through this.

(*Enter a Priest and a Notary.*)

Sal. I am your pilot: trust me.
Marq. As you will.
Sal. Now sign this paper, lady; and you, Count.
'T is hasty, not dishonorable. Keep faith.
Cos. How, sir!
Ju. But, Salvatore, Marsio lives.
Sal. He lives a felon! And I roundly swear,
If you two people are not wed to-night,
I 'll have him hung upon a moving gallows,
And wheel him after you around the world.
I 'll have no trifling.
March. Marsio a felon!
Sal. He sought to poison Count Juranio,
And honored me by joining me with him.
Where are you, Pulti?
Pulti. Here, sir. Room, room, room,
For Marsio's prime minister of drugs!
This vial, and my oath, might go some lengths
To speed his journey to a hotter world.
Advance my relique! [SALVATORE *shows the vial.*]
March. O! the horrid viper!
What an escape poor, dear Costanza made!

Sal. You still hang back?
Cos. My father still is bound.
Sal. He is well cared for. Ere another day,
I pledge myself to buy your father's debts
At my own price. 'Sdeath! do you falter now?
My lord, your promise.
Marq. I command you, daughter:
Obey my friend.
March. Is Count Juranio rich?
[*Apart to the* MARQUIS.]
Marq. Pshaw! madam.
Cos. I obey — perhaps too kindly;
But the mere thought of your security
Sends my heart upward, like a loosened bird,
Dizzy with hope, and strength, and ecstasy;
For I am free again! (*Turns to* SALVATORE.) To you I owe
More than a common show of gratitude;
But, now, forgive me; my o'erflowing thoughts
Would drown the happy prospect of my speech,
By sheer abundance of their offerings.
To you, Juranio —
Ju. Nay, dear Costanza,
Let my heart whisper what your words might be.
Sal. Hide all your roses in your lover's breast.
Go talk it over, go — we 'll never look —
Then come to us, and notary and priest
Shall knit you up.
Ju. Dear kinsman —
Sal. Silence, sir!
This place is nauseous with stale sentiment.
Mind your affairs; I 've business of my own.
Fair lady, have I won?

Fil. Yes, Salvatore. [*Giving her hand.*]
Would it were *worthier!*
Sal. Not for my sake, love:
You cannot add a morsel to content.
Marq. Peace crown you all! I have such friends, at last,
As money could not buy — the gifts of heaven:
I thank it humbly. As for Marsio,
He 'll wake to-morrow, and behold what gulfs
Crime opens 'twixt the richest criminal
And the frank brotherhood of honest men,
However poor, — gulfs that must yawn forever!

THE WIDOW'S MARRIAGE:

A COMEDY.

DRAMATIS PERSONÆ.

Lord Guy Ruffler, ...	*A gallant.*
Sir William Travers, ...	*His friend.*
Harry Goldstraw, ...	*Nephew to Lady Goldstraw.*
Hopeful, Sir John Pollen, Lord Foam, Marks, ...	*Suitors to Lady Goldstraw.*
Darkly,.	*Servant to Ruffler.*
Nick Prior, ...	*Servant to Lady Goldstraw.*
Lady Goldstraw, ...	*An old and wealthy widow.*
Madge, ...	*Her daughter.*
Dolly Flare, ...	*Lady Goldstraw's maid.*

Ladies, Gallants, Tradesmen, Servants, &c.

Scene, London.
Time, Beginning of the reign of George II.

THE WIDOW'S MARRIAGE.

ACT I.

SCENE I. *A Street in London. Enter Sir* WILLIAM TRAVERS *and Lord* GUY RUFFLER.

Travers. GUY, I will not! This dodging petticoats
Round the street-corners — peeping into shops —
Leering, with shameless meaning, under hoods —
Staring hot blushes into modest cheeks —
And fancying a favor if you catch
A wandering glance — is sheer against my manhood.
Tut! man, you slander all your female kin
By this procedure.

Ruffler. (*Looking off.*) Do I? — Pah! look there:
Into the goldsmith's shop! Can they not see
That I am looking at them? Travers, come,
We 'll enter, too: I want a ring — a chain. —
'Sblood! are the women fools?

Trav. There seem to be
Two fools among them.

Ruf. Speak you for yourself?
Stand here a while.

Trav. For what? To be the butt
Of my sharp self-contempt? Ruffler! [*Shaking him.*]
Ruf. (*Still looking off.*) Hey!
Trav. Nay;
I 'm talking to you.
Ruf. As my grandmother.
Trav. You need it. Look you, listen to me, Guy;
Do you hold woman of no higher use —
Ruf. Pish! let me go: I 've business in that shop.
Unhand me, pray. [*Struggles to get away.*]
Trav. No, sir, you shall not go.
I cannot see an insult thrust upon
A modest woman; and the man who can,
Without his nature flaming into wrath,
And his arm lifting with instinctive might,
Deserves to have his sisters, mother, wife,
Tossed in together at a city's sack,
While he looks on in powerless agony.
Ruf. You could not please them better. What a stir,
Among the velvets and the damasked silks,
There was when the invading French were feared!
What rubbing up of jewels, what a dust
Among old finery! How some delicate maid
Would squeak, in her high treble, "Dear mamma,
They say those monsters do not spare the weak:
Let us be caught as ladies!" Then the dame
Would smooth her powder, with a gentle sigh
Of patient resignation. On my life,
I never saw the women in such feather!
You 'd thought the land was dressed for holiday,
Not for invasion. All the time, we men
Stood trembling, like huge jellies, for our throats;

While our brave women — now, you see, I praise
them —
Made nothing of their honors!
Trav. Monstrous stuff!
I would not share your notions of the sex,
To win a tribe of Helens. I can see,
Within the simple innocence and truth
Of uncorrupted woman, a fair spirit,
Ranked, by all-seeing Heaven, not far beneath
Its sinless denizens.
Ruf. (*Laughing.*) Now Heaven forgive
His wicked blasphemy! I 'll draw you woman,
According to her earthly character,
Not as your poets make her. Woman, Will,
Is animated vanity. A toy
Made up each morning, by a forward whim,
That scarcely lasts the day through. The same sigh
Over a broken fan, or a broken heart,
Measures her depth of feeling. A long stare
At the last fashion, on a rival's back,
Shows her ambition. A conspicuous seat
At church, or theatre, where she may be
The conscious centre of a thousand eyes,
Shows her religion, or her taste. The power
To bear hot sentiment, and frigid love,
Her soul's endurance proves. Ask her to give
Her hero's character, and when you have
The color of his eyes, and hair, and cloak,
You 'll praise her nice perception. See her weed
Her eyebrows of gray hairs, or paint her cheeks,
And there 's her industry, and love of art.
Come to her death-bed —
Trav. Nay.

Ruf. Well, end her there:
The thing is soulless, and can go no further.
Yet, for all this, a very pretty doll
For man to dandle.
Trav. If the heavens be just,
You'll pay this one day. Guy, I reverence woman.
Ruf. For what? Here's a discovery, indeed!
For what?
Trav. For many things. And yet there is
One thing I never fully understood, —
Love, love.
Ruf. Why, that's the simplest thing on earth.
Trav. The very simplest! Were you e'er in love?
Ruf. Always.
Trav. With whom?
Ruf. With everything that wears
More than a yard of velvet in its skirts.
You are a world too wise for happiness.
Trav. The man who looks for it beyond himself
Is a mere fool. But, Ruffler, I intend
To marry shortly.
Ruf. Heaven preserve your victim!
What, you'll set traps, ha? Scheme her to your bed?
Play on her weakness? and declare, the while,
How much you reverence her; as travellers say
Some pagans do, who flog unmercifully
Their painted gods, and worship them, by turns.
You talk of taking a poor maid, as though
She were an oyster. — Hist! they leave the shop,
And come this way.
Trav. In decency retire.
Ruf. Not I, by Jove!

Trav. To please me, Guy.
Ruf. Poh! poh!
You are too much humored.
Trav. For a moment, then,
Until I can escape.
Ruf. Well, well; come on.
A woman, more or less, is little gained,
And nothing lost. Sneak, dodge; — I am with you.
[*They walk up the stage.*]

(*Enter* LADY GOLDSTRAW *and* MADGE.)

Lady Goldstraw. La! they are there again. It is too bad:
I cannot walk abroad, to feel the sun,
Without these shadows following. Every day
A pack of courtiers dog me to my door;
Or walk before me, dropping billet-doux;
And one, but Thursday last — I tell you, Madge —
Cast a French plume, that must have cost the knave
A good ten pound, in hope I would return it.
Madge. And did you not?
Lady G. Not I, you silly child!
I set my little foot upon it, thus,
And ground it in the mire; to show my pride,
And brave, contemptuous spirit. Mark those men:
See how the tall one eyes me. Ha! ha! ha!
[*Laughing.*]
A proper fellow, too, and bravely trimmed:
A courtier, doubtless. I do wonder, now,
If 't was that villain twitched my dress and sighed,
As we came through the church-door! — Mercy! Madge,
Don't stare so at them. Fie! you naughty child,
I 'm blushing for you. Marry! when you 've seen

As many men as I, you 'll know a way
To cut your eyes at them, that stirs them more
Than all your rustic glares.

Madge. Come, mother, come.
Yon jackanapes is grinning like death's head,
With much the same expression ; and his friend
Has great ado to keep him back. I fear
The coxcomb will be saucy.

Lady G. Will he, rogue ?—
Let him : I 'll give him better than he sends.
Why, things have reached a pass, when pretty women
Are at the beck of every handsome dog
That strolls the streets ! My husband, the Lord Mayor—

Madge. Tell me the story as we pass along.
Yon bear will slip his keeper, if we stay.

Lady G. So, then,—but how you hurry me away !
[*Exit with* MADGE.]

(*As they go off, enter* DARKLY.)

Ruf. (*Advancing.*) Darkly !

Darkly. Forsooth.

Ruf. "Forsooth !" Geneva-cloak !
You end of texts, and stupid homilies,
You all that 's bad in every Christian sect,
Do you "forsooth" me, sirrah, ha ?

Dark. Amen !

Ruf. A fool ! you sin-begotten tag-rag ! What,
Are you pranked up, now, in your holy mood ?
Come, saint, lay by your amaranthine crown,
And track those women.

Dark. Ah !

Ruf. You sigh! you 'll groan
When you have gotten to the martyrdom,
I am preparing for your sainthood.

Dark. O!

Trav. Guy, if hard knocks can break a road to heaven,
You 're on the way. The man has honest scruples;
Do not outface his conscience.

Ruf. Have you scruples?—
Have you a conscience?—Have you anything
That hints at honesty within your dirt?
I 'll put him to the question. (*Seizes* DARKLY.) Answer me!

Dark. The Lord forbid!

Trav. Indeed!

Ruf. Of course. Go, knave!

Dark. Why should I follow the profane of earth,
The painted instruments of thy desire?

Ruf. Because I order.

Dark. Bear me witness, sir,
Here, in this world, and at the last account,
I sin by man's compulsion.

Trav. Truly!

Dark. Ah! [*Exit.*]

Ruf. A wretch like that would ornament the Shades,
And put the little devils to the blush,
Make Satan pine with envy, and upset
Chaos itself. I never saw his twin.
The club of Hercules could hardly drive
One hand to pen a love-song, while the other
Pilfered his lion-skin, with ohs and ahs
Enough to raise a whirlwind.

(*Enter* HENRY GOLDSTRAW.)

Trav. Who is this?
What, Harry Goldstraw? Happily met again.
We were in Rome together — mind you, sir? —
That day the miracle would hardly work —
You know the virgin that did roll its eyes? —
Because the rain had rusted something, ha!
Much to the Church's scandal.

Goldstraw. Ay; and you
To Fra Anselmo, a most bitter papist,
Did seriously offer to anoint
The clockwork with the chrism, and let the Pope
Go home ungreased. "*Che, che?*" he cried. "Because,
Fra," you replied, "the Pope's eyes roll without it!"

Trav. My friend, Lord Ruffler, Mr. Goldstraw.
(*They bow.*) Boys,
Let's shake up London with a revel. How,
Goldstraw, you flinch?

Gold. I have a reason, sir.
You saw two ladies pass —

Ruf. I told you so:
Here is another hound upon the scent.
Look you, Will Travers, men are all the same;
You are the only Joseph upon earth.
So you were trailing them? O! never mind;
We will not quarrel; we'll divide them justly.
Take the old woman; give me the young thing:
I have a taste for unripe fruit. —

Gold. My lord —

Ruf. Well, you may wince, but so fate orders it.
A fairer piece of Eve I never saw
Than the young baggage. You'd have laughed to see
The little creature stare at me.

Trav. A look
Full of pure modesty, and more designed
For me than you.

Ruf. A most immodest leer.
Hear, the vain puppy, how he claims her glance!

Gold. I pray you, listen —

Ruf. As for your share, — phew!
Think what a bundle of fine clothes you 'll have —
What pots of paint — how many different wigs —
What an array of teeth, all movable,
And warranted to baffle time's decay!
And then her cotton; — why, an Indiaman
Carries no greater cargo! Whalebone too!
A very female Jonah, all encased
In the sea-monster's ribs! And mark —

Gold. My lord,
Know you of whom you speak?

Ruf. Not I, in faith:
Some lady of the suburbs, I suppose,
Who 'd bargain for her girl. You frown? 'Ods blood!
Who is the woman, then?

Gold. My aunt.

Ruf. The devil!

Trav. Shame on you, Guy! You 've given a sorry wound
To the best nature ever lodged in man.
See how a loose tongue, like an archer, blind
With the thick dust of battle, shoots its shafts,
With undiscerning aim, at foe or friend.
Down on your knees!

Ruf. Your pardon. Here 's my hand;
Or, if you like it better, here 's my sword;
Both at your service.

Gold. By your leave, my lord,
I 'll take the hand; it seems an honest one,
Though somewhat hasty.

Trav. Spoken like brave men!
The sword should be a backward arbiter.
If human weakness can forgive a wrong,
Without blood spilled, let it be done; for so —
By just such steps of charity and love —
We climb to heaven.

Ruf. Alas! I scarcely know
How to implore your confidence again.
You seem to bear a grief about with you,
That I, perhaps, might lighten.

Trav. Harry, speak.
A truer mind, and a more slippery tongue,
A better heart, and a more idle head,
Were never bundled up in stranger sort
Than in Guy Ruffler.

Ruf. When I go to service,
My master shall not get my character
From you, my boy.

Gold. Alas! the character
You gave my aunt fills up my former grief.
That you, a stranger, by a casual glance,
Should come so near the thing she really is,
Gives me a sorrowful conclusion. She —
But I 'll not talk. Come to her house with me;
Where, if you be true friends, you may behold
Things more for tears than laughter.

Trav. Ah! I see.

Gold. No, sir, you cannot see, with eyes like mine,
The open folly and the vanity
With which she stains my uncle's troubled grave, —

The faithful guardian of my orphanage,
Whose fragrant memory sheds no balm on her,
Amid the train of fops and fashionists
That flutter round her gold, in buzzing swarms;
Slaves whose mere presence would disgust the sense
Of many a wanton. All these things have sprung,
Not from her heart, which, at the root, is good;
But by the culture of such poisoned sprouts
As grow upon the surface of our nature, —
Self-love and vanity. But come; I 'll preach
More by example, if you feel inclined.

Trav. Nay, Harry, quit these dumps. A woman's whims
Are all too light to bow so strong a soul.

Ruf. I 'll find a way to cure her malady.
I never saw a woman yet of stuff
I could not mould, as wax before a fire.
Some merry plot, half serious and half gay,
I 'll plan. I undertake it, sir; and what
I undertake, I do.

Trav. Go to! Here is [*Patting* RUFFLER.]
My Vanity, my Ego, my great Me:
Match any woman with him, if you can! [*Exeunt.*]

SCENE II.

A Reception-Room in LADY GOLDSTRAW'S *House. Enter* MADGE.

Madge. When will my mother hold her years to be
Beyond man's courtship? O! it sickens me
To see her deck her ruins with bright flowers, —

Through which the ugly seams will peep, withal, —
While I, who, in the course of nature, am as fit
For flowers as Spring is, shut my roses up,
And pine beneath her. Child, forsooth! A child
Of twenty summers, who must know its bounds,
Its nursery, its book, its pretty toy;
Rise with the lark, and lie down with the lamb; —
Must I, indeed? — while she makes daybreak blush
To see her revels, and high noon amazed
To catch her sleeping. If I knew a man,
Of all her tribe, worth loving — Not so fast:
There 's cousin Hal, worth all the bearded race;
But what cares he? Would I were not his cousin!
Ah, well! Hal is so modest too: a fashion
That went out with the tilting-spears and shields.
Poor chivalry! they scorn you; but you died
Rather for lack of heroes, to renew
Your drooping laurels, than your own misdeeds.
If I were Hal — How he torments me!

(*Enter* LADY GOLDSTRAW.)

Lady Goldstraw. Child,
You must be jogging: your embroidery
Needs a few stitches, and your French has gone
The saints know where!
Madge. The saints know little, madam,
Of where the French go. If the French go —
Lady G. Fie!
Your tongue is idler than your hands. Go, go;
Get to your book. I spoil you, silly child,
By my indulgence.
Madge. Nay; I think you spoil
My mother more by your indulgence.

Lady G. Mistress,
Would you be pert?
Madge. Not if I could respect.
Pray hear me, mother.
Lady G. To your room, I say!
I 'll cool your blood upon a water diet, —
Impudent nursling!
Madge. Madam!
Lady G. To your room! [*Exit* MADGE.]
O! what a fume she put me in! I fear
My poor complexion has not stood the shock
Of this emotion. (*Looks at a mirror.*) Yes; a fair escape!
No crack nor line, and not a hair awry.
Prior! (*Enter* NICK PRIOR.) Who waits below?
Nick. Why, Master Hopeful, mam.
Hope 's first to come, and last to go away.
Lady G. No words! Admit him. Now, I wonder why
This whole house treats me with such disrespect?
[*Aside.*]
Go, sir! I 'll get a master for you, sirrah,
To swinge you roundly.
Nick. How the old girl shines!
She must have varnished down her paint to-day.
[*Aside. Exit.*]
Lady G. Ho! here he comes. Lie still, my little heart!
Why wilt thou flutter, tender fool? Ah me!
[*Sinks into a chair.*]

(*Enter* HOPEFUL. RUFFLER, TRAVERS, *and* GOLDSTRAW, *enter behind, observing the scene.*)

Hopeful. Queen of my soul, sweet agony of bliss,

Adored deceiver! daylight is agog
To see thy coming; though bright Phœbus knows
Thy light will shame him! Wherefore, wherefore,
wherefore,
Cruel eye of beauty, didst thou keep thy slave
Sitting upon a hall-stool? Has thy heart
No sympathetic thrill to waste upon
Joints stiffened in thy service, rheumatisms
Beyond red flannel and mustard?

Lady G. Faithless bard,
What, dost thou murmur at thy bondage, then?
I could well-nigh forbid your lips to press
The lilies of this hand.

[*Extends her hand, which he kisses.*]

Hope. Nay, mistress mine,
My grief is closed within my placid heart,
As those fair lilies when they fold to rest
Upon thy snowy bed-quilt. Hear, O, hear!

[*Takes out a paper.*]

This Sonnet to thy glory. Little, lady,
Compared with their sweet source, the verses seem;
As rivers which seem trifles to their springs —
Nay, I am out somehow. (*Aside.*) But give thy ear
To this soft melody of Phœbus's. [*Reads.*]

O! ever-to-be-remembered day and night!
O! never-to-be-forgotten ecstasy!
O! sun-god, with thy sky-born eyes, day-bright,
O'er-look the song-soul of thy votary!
O! teach his love-pen how to soothly write
Of the not-now-forgotten hour, when I
Poured out my love-words to the worthiest wight
That wends, heart-bound, beneath ceruleous sky!

O! dip my ink-dried pen in á sunsét;
  Roll out a white-cloud scroll, without a flaw;
For sand, powder a storm-cloud up; and get
  Venus to set her silvern taper, for
To light thy Poet; and one name he 'll set
  Across the sky, and it shall be — Goldstraw!

Lady G. A sweet, sweet sonnet! much in Petrarch's way.
Yours is a pretty gift of poesy.
Hist! be discreet.
Hope. I hear profane strong steps;
Much like a man with heavy boots might make.
Lo! rivals, madam! Lo! the slaves that tear
My heart out, and destroy my appetite!

(*Enter* LORD FOAM, SIR JOHN POLLEN, *and* MARKS.)

Lady G. Fair welcome, gentlemen! You have missed much —
The poet's latest verse. Read it again.
Hope. At thy command I would do much. But, no,
No common ear shall list to holy verse.
Yet if you will —
Marks. Don't break yourself for us;
Keep something back to live on.
Foam. La! they say
Your verse is stale before the ink gets dry.
Hope. They wrong me foully!
Pollen. (*Aside to* HOPEFUL.) At him! In my day —
In Flanders, yonder — I have seen a throat
Cut for less insults. By the devil's blood!
I smell a coward.

Hope. Cut the miscreant's gorge,
Here, in this presence!

Pol. Ay; and fling his head
Into her lap. When we were leaguers, bully,
Down there at Antwerp, an old Spanish Don
One morning sent his mistress, by the post,
The heads of all her twenty paramours,
Strung on a rope like onions.

Hope. Horrible!
Brought they no tears into her woman's eyes?

Marks. No, sir; she did not peel them.

Pol. Look you, sir,
I am a soldier.

Marks. Then, thank Heaven, I am not.

Foam. La! fairly struck! Good boy, good boy! I kiss
Your worship's hand.

Pol. Small shot and thunder! Turks,
I'll teach your tongues —

[Lady Goldstraw *faints, supported by* Hopeful.]

Hope. Hold, ruffians! Look here,
And see your handiwork.

Pol. 'Ods bayonets!
Twitch her nose, Foam.

Hope. Who twitches dies the death!

Foam. A fan, a fan, la! Merchant, bring a fan!

Marks. "A fan!" No; bring some water.

All. (*Running about.*) Water, water!

Lady G. (*Starting up.*) No; bring no water; I am not afire.

Marks. Nor do you use fast colors for your cheeks,
Or water would not wake you. [*Aside.*]

Pol. Blood and drums!
I beg for quarter.
Lady G. Water me, forsooth!
Do I look withered?
Hope. Spare, my gracious queen, [*Kneels.*]
The wretch who kneels before you, and inclines
His lips unto your shoe-string!
Lady G. For his sake,
I spare you all.
Marks. Had I your guineas safe,
I'd spare your sparing. [*Aside.*]
Foam. La! how kind you are!
Hope. A royal amnesty!
Lady G. But leave me, sirs;
My nerves are shattered.
Hope. Misery, misery!
Pol. 'Swounds!
This thing has fallen like a ten-pound shell
Among a company.
Hope. O! pardon, pardon!
Lady G. I pardon all. Go, I implore!
Foam. Adieu! [*Exit, gayly.*]
Marks. 'Sdeath! must I lose more interest?
[*Aside. Exit.*]
Pol. Soul of me!
Where shall I dine to-day? [*Aside. Exit.*]
Hope. O! agony!
I did not read my sonnet to them. (*Aside.*) Ha!
[*Starting.*]
One look, and then the pall of midnight falls!
[*Exit, wildly.*]
Lady G. One cheek has cracked: I felt it giving
way

When they cried "water." Doll, what, Doll, I say!
Ha! there's the handsome stranger of the street;
And come to court me, doubtless. Lack-a-day!
O! had those brutes cried anything but "water!"
[*Exit.*]

(RUFFLER, TRAVERSE, *and* GOLDSTRAW, *advance.*)

Ruffler. O! such a farce!
Traverse. Such actors too! But, Hal,
Where is your cousin?
Goldstraw. Prisoned by my aunt;
Kept out of sight. Blooming and withering
Show ill in company.
Ruf. Such vanity
I've heard of. —
Trav. Practised.
Ruf. How?
Trav. Why, in yourself;
Is not all womankind in love with you?
Ruf. That's not my fault.
Trav. Guy, you are sharp enough
For others' follies, stone-blind to your own.
Ruf. Bah! hang your sermons! Goldstraw, I've a plan
Working within me, but scarce formed as yet.
Let us to Travers' lodgings; where I'll lie
Till time has brought my struggling thought to light.
Trav. Onward! — But, Hal, if widow, maid, or wife,
Should look upon us, as we pass along,
Pray you remember, all the sweetest looks
Belong by right to Ruffler; all the frowns
To us, by imposition. Forward, then! [*Exeunt.*]

ACT II.

SCENE I. TRAVERS' *Lodgings.* RUFFLER, TRAVERS, *and* GOLDSTRAW, *discovered.*

Travers. YOUR plot comes hardly, Ruffler.
Ruffler. Not at all:
But, as you say, if the old lady's follies
Could reach the end they aim at, she would find
A keen repentance following her success.
She must be married; that 's the starting-point.
Goldstraw. "Married!" Nay, that 's the ending-point, I fear.
For, in a furious outburst of her folly,
Or by the coming of some needy fellow,
Of handsome person and adroit designs,
She may be cozened to clap up a match,
Either with one who dangles in her train,
Or an adventurer who will spend her wealth,
Rob my poor cousin of her heritage,
And break both hearts together.
Trav. A shrewd fear.
For, Guy, suppose yourself a ruined man;
How easy would it be to mend your rents
With Lady Goldstraw's patches!
Ruf. True enough.
Trav. 'T is well all sharpers have not your address,
Or heaven protect rich widows!

Ruf. Hum! Suppose
That I should marry her. [*Laughing.*]
Trav. He takes the bait. [*Aside.*]
'Sdeath! what a life you'd lead her! It would cure
Her amorous fancies till her dying day.
Lord! how she'd shy, and try to throw you off,
And how you'd cling and spur! I understand:
Married in jest, by Darkly, or some knave
With reverend face;—just for a day or so?
'T would work like poison. Ah! you cunning dog,
What nimble wits you have! [*Laughing.*]
Gold. Yes; how they skip,
When Travers pulls the wires! [*Aside.*]
Ruf. Well, there's my plan;
Born by due course of nature, as you see,
Without the aid of doctors.
Trav. *Brava,* wife!
No; pshaw! you gull us. What, you will not dare
To carry out your artful project, man?
I doubt your courage. Hal, what think you, Hal?
Gold. I would be loath to see her ladyship
The victim of a plot.
Trav. Yet, after all,
Could it exceed the antics of to-day—
The lovers, and the sonnet, and the swoon?
And why not touch her feelings, and awake
The torpid heart that smothers in her follies,
And makes her monstrous? Ruffler's scheme is good—
Excellent, exquisite, without a flaw—
And easily practised.
Ruf. Ay, simplicity,
That's your true mark of genius!

Gold. I'll consider.

Ruf. Nay, now, you shall consent. I will not have
The travail of my brain miscarry quite
Through stupid counsel. 'T is the only way;
And if you shrink, I'll offer no more plans.
Live on, and suffer by your obstinacy.

Gold. What think you, Travers?

Trav. Soberly, I think
The plot a sound one: and, besides, if he
Wring the old lady past her sufferance,
We can remit; for then the cure will be,
Beyond a doubt, accomplished.

Gold. I consent.
But deal as a good surgeon; give no pain
Where pain is needless; cut the cancer out,
But spare the patient.

Ruf. Mark me, gentlemen;
I'll have no interference; you must be
But instruments, not artists, in my work.
Prepare yourselves for orders.

Trav. We'll obey. [RUFFLER *struts up the stage.*]

Gold. Travers, I never saw such vanity —
Of all complexions, shapes, and shades — in man.
He takes your thoughts out of your very teeth,
Swallows, and casts them up, as carelessly
As though your brain were his.

Trav. (*Laughing.*) And so it is.
His weakness does not hide his nobler parts
From my respect. We'll hit upon some way
To cure both patients with one medicine.

(*Enter* DARKLY.)

Ruf. (*Seizing him.*) Where have you tarried? By the holy rood,
I feel like basting you!
Darkly. Swear Christian oaths!
Do not afflict me with the filth of Rome —
The bells, the candles, or the holy rood —
The graven images, or painted saints —
The monks, or bulls, or other hornéd beasts —
The —
Trav. Peace! you hypocrite, you sightless mole,
Who burrow in the dirt and lees of things,
Nor see the flowers that root in the decay
Of Roman greatness, to delight our time!
Peace, wretch! that ancient church held up a torch,
To light our fathers through the utter gloom
Of feudal ignorance! Learning lived in her;
Her cloisters saved the wondrous minds that made
Greece beautiful and Rome imperial.
What if she lag behind this rapid age?
Is she not old? and age claims man's respect.
What if the daylight show the torch's smoke?
Did it not serve us in the middle night,
And light us towards the morning? Rome, thou fool!
There 's not a church, from Luther to George Fox,
That on her broad foundations is not built!
Ruf. You hurl a thunderbolt against a gnat.
Peace, father Will!
Trav. You heard the villain prate.
I am no Papist, yet it angers me
To see that noble bulwark of our faith
Touched with irreverent hands.

Ruf. Well, sirrah, well!
Where have you been?
Dark. I tarried round the house
Of the gay gentile, near the offices,
Over against the backside of the court;
And there I saw her handmaids and her men
Bear the repast to its allotted place.
Ruf. (*Mimicking him.*) And, peradventure, thou didst enter in,
To fill thy inward man with broken meats.
Yea, and I marvel that thou didst not burst
Thy hide with stuffing. For, bethink thee, brother,
It falls on fast-day, when it is thy use
To cram thee grossly, just to scorn the church.
Dark. Yea, verily.
Ruf. Out, glutton!
Dark. And it chanced,
A maid of comly mien, and smooth of skin —
Ruf. How did you know the texture of her skin?
Dark. In divers ways.
Ruf. Ugh, losel!
Dark. And I called,
And said unto the maid, in modest tongue —
Ruf. With a most filthy leer.
Dark. Whose habitation,
Or whose dwelling-place, dost thou abide in?
And she answered me, "The Lady Goldstraw's,
Widow to a mayor of mighty London;
A brave and portly dame, stricken in years,
But full of amorous blood." And who the damsel?
I questioned; and she made reply, "Young Madge,
A child of twenty summers." So I rose,
And came my way.

Ruf. Unconscionable liar!
You have been nobbing in stale beer with her,
Eating cold pasties; and, for after cates,
You stole a brace of kisses. Come, put on
Your sanctimonious garb, and follow me.—
Are you prepared? [*To* TRAVERS *and* GOLDSTRAW.]

Trav. Yea, verily!

Gold. In sooth!

Dark. O, O, alas! how the profane ones scoff!

[*Exeunt.*]

SCENE II.

An Ante-Room in LADY GOLDSTRAW'S *house. Enter* TRAVERS *and* MADGE.

Travers. So love died long ago?

Madge. When Venus died,
With her three Graces, and the Golden Age
Came limping downward to these prosy days
Of gain and reason. If we marry now,
'T is this lord's park wedding that lady's field;
Or this man's money-bags and that dame's plate,
Joined at compounded interest; or John's arm
Mated to Polly's thrift. Or give the theme
A wider scope — throw wealth and sense aside —
And then 't is folly caught by beauty's glare;
Or base desire asking the church's seal,
To sin by charter; or sad loneliness
Seeking companionship; or simple malice
Seizing a helpless victim to torment,
While the law nods approval; or — or — or —
For any motive, good or bad, you please,
But not for love. Love has no motives, sir,

No purposes, no aims, no selfish wish;
Love is its own reward.
Trav. Indeed! then love
For nothing sighs — for nothing groans and weeps —
For nothing wrings his hands, and tears his hair;
Or with this nothing being enraged, for nothing
He fires a house, or cuts a rival's throat,
Or leads the Greeks into a ten years' war,
And tumbles blazing Ilium o'er her walls:
And all for nothing!
Madge. Then was love a god;
Men demi-gods, who stalked through history
A head and shoulders taller than the world:
Ah! there were heroes then!
Trav. And heroes now.
Are heroes proven by the knocks they take? —
Is blood the only livery of renown?
I knew a sickly artisan, a man
Whose only tie to life was one pale child,
His dead wife's gift. Yet, for that single tie,
He bore a life that would have blanched the face
Of armèd Hector; bore the hopeless toil,
That could but scrape together one day's food;
Bore the keen tortures of a shattered frame,
The sneèr of pride, the arrogance of wealth;
All the dread curses of man's heritage,
Summed in one word of horror — poverty! —
Ay, bore them with a smile. And all the time,
His ears were full of whispers. In his hand,
The common tools of work turned from their use,
And hinted — death! The river crossed his path,
Sliding beneath the bridge, so lovingly,
And murmuring — death! Upon his very hearth

The tempter sat, amid the flaming coals,
And talked with him of — death! A thousand ways
Lay open, for his misery to escape;
Yet there he stood, and labored for his child,
Till Heaven in pity took the twain together. —
He was a hero!
Madge. Sir, you sadden me.
Trav. Is man, then, so degenerate?
Madge. On my faith,
You prove the thing worth something.
Trav. Would that I
Could prove it in my person!
Madge. Why?
Trav. Fair Madge,
I'd have you love me.
Madge. Horrors! what a man!
How many houses have you? How much land?
How many guineas? Are your cattle fat?
Could you afford a carriage? Sir, you see,
Having no father, I must look to this,
As you'd be loved, in my own person. Come;
Set up your claim. What settlement, Sir William,
Can you make good upon my daughter?
Trav. Sir,
I am a hero of the Golden Age,
Belated in your times. A love like mine
Is its own blessed reward. I nothing seek;
And, therefore, nothing will I give. My love
Is an abstraction, a divine idea,
That settles on your daughter, my good sir,
For want of better habitation.
Madge. Pshaw!
You'll vex me, shortly: I abhor a quiz.

Trav. Why, so do I; and hating thus myself,
I leave myself, and cast my love on you.

Madge. Which love is self-love, by your own confession.

Trav. And being self-love, of the best quality.
Find me, between the poles, such tenderness
As that men lavish on themselves; such sighs
As they can utter o'er their private griefs;
Such tears as their own miseries call forth;
Such perfect and complete oblivion
To all the world, for their own darling selves!
It would shame Hero o'er Leander's corpse,
To hear the anguish that a surgeon's knife
Can waken in his patient.

Madge. Farewell, sir!
I'll hope to meet you in a graver mood.

Trav. I shaped my mood by yours. — But one word more.
Suppose me grave; should I have credit, then?
You shake your head. Pray, when will you believe?

Madge. When I believe in love. [*Exit.*]

Trav. I like thee, Madge:
Would I could love thee, as thou dost deserve;
But love! — O, fie! I'll swear I cannot love.
Yet I must feign it; drop philosophy,
And rave myself into a lunatic.
I like thee, though, beyond a shade of doubt;
And there's a nature underlays thy mirth
That well approves the feeling. 'T is full time
I should set up a nursery, and prolong
The race of Travers; or my father's bones
Will rise against me. He who wills can win.
[*Exit.*]

(*Enter* DOLLY FLARE.)

Dolly. My! what a handsome gentleman! How well
He'd look, if he had Mr. Darkly's way
Of pious conversation! There's a man
The devil fears, I warrant!

(*Enter* DARKLY.)

Darkly. Sister Flare,
How is it with thee, sister?

Dol. Poorly, thank Heaven!

Dark. O! weaker vessel, dost thou feel the need
Of faith, to steady thee?

Dol. I fear I do.

Dark. Um, um! faint soul, thou shalt not ask in vain
The arm of succor, (*Embracing her.*) or the guiding hand. [*Taking her hand.*]
And, peradventure, it might comfort thee
To taste a morsel of refreshing strength:
[*Taking a bottle from her pocket.*]
Albeit, the spirit is strong, the flesh is weak,
And cries for aid. (*Gives the bottle. She drinks.*) Yea, verily! alas!
How much the poor soul needs! But go thy ways;
My strength is waning, even as thine doth wax.
[*Takes the bottle from her.*]
When thou dost falter by the way, look up!—
Even though this carnal vial cleave unto thee,
Defy the tempter, and look up, I say!
[*Throws back his head, and drinks.*]

Dol. (*Taking the bottle.*) I will, indeed. O! sir, you have not left
A drop to try my strength on.

Dark. Marvel not:
Sore was I tempted. Thou of little faith,
O! frail of purpose, canst thou not look up?

[*She looks up, and he kisses her.*]

Dol. (*Starting.*) O! O!

Dark. Does thy strength fail? Look up, I say!

[*She looks up, and he kisses her.*]

Dost thou feel easier? Is the tempter laid?

Dol. I could look up forever.

Dark. Verily,
Thy faith is great, O, blessed sister Flare!
Perchance I may abide beneath this roof;
And if it happen, I will come to thee,
Even to thy chamber, to exhort with thee,
And wrestle with the tempter.

Dol. Dear, good man!
I don't deserve it, sir, indeed I don't:
I feel so dismal-like, when you are nigh,
And I can see your blessed face. O! O!
I fear I am a sinner, sir! [*Weeps.*]

Dark. Look up!

[*She looks up, he kisses her, and exit.*]

(*Enter* RUFFLER *and* GOLDSTRAW.)

Ruffler. Here I am, Harry, in my best array.
But where is Travers?

Goldstraw. Somewhere hereabout:
He strayed off with my cousin. Dolly, girl,
What are you staring at?

Ruf. A pretty maid! —
Hist, hist! I'll wake her. [*Steals up to kiss her.*]

Dol. (*Striking him.*) Out, tempter, out!
Get thee behind me, Satan! [*Exit.*]

Ruf. Blood of mine!
What a she-devil! [*Rubbing his face.*]
Gold. What has come o'er her?
Ruf. Plague on her handling! Now, I tell you, Hal,
That's the first check I e'er received from woman.
She's taken me for you.
Gold. Without a doubt.
You're welcome to the error.
Ruf. Now, suppose
I open on the widow. I intend
To carry the whole matter through by storm.
Who are within?
Gold. Fools: the same silly crowd.
You'd better join them.
Ruf. Mark me put them down,
Clear the whole field, and catch the widow up
Before she can draw breath. —
Gold. Or hear a word
That sounds like reason.
Ruf. Ay, ay! Forward, then!
Sound, trumpets! I am armed to win the day!
[*Exeunt.*]

SCENE III.

A Room in the Same. LADY GOLDSTRAW, LORD FOAM, SIR JOHN POLLEN, HOPEFUL, *and* MARKS, *discovered.*

Hopeful. Star of our lives, make an election now.
Behold thy four slaves suppliant at thy heels;
[*They kneel.*]
And all they beg, imperial dame of hearts,
Is that thou'lt choose, among their number, one,

To make the partner of thy four-post bed.
Would thou couldst honor all, and shame the Turk
By a reversal of his way of life;
Yet since vile law confines thee to but one,
Choose from among us here the worthiest;
And let the remnant of thy slaves depart,
Covering their misery with their handkerchiefs.
As for myself— [*They all start up.*]

All. Hold, Hopeful!

Pollen. Honor, honor!

Marks. We chose you spokesman, and not advocate.
You must not speak, or speak for all alike.

Foam. La! yes; well put!

Lady Goldstraw. How shall I choose aright,
Where no one seems unworthy? Marry, sirs,
A simple woman, immature in years—
Though wise beyond them—here may hesitate,
And hand upon the syllable of judgment.
I like the martial air of bold Sir John—

Pol. 'Sdeath! yes: at Antwerp—

Hope. Peace! an angel blabs.

Lady G. I like the manners of Lord Foam—

Foam. La, now!

Lady G. The thrift of Marks; the wild poetic soul
That throbs in Hopeful—

Hope. Glory to my queen!
She chooses nicely.

Marks. Cease your braying, ass,
Until she chooses.

Pol. (*To* HOPEFUL.) Breathe another word,
And I will scour my rapier in your soul!

Marks. Let us cast lots.

Hope. Back, merchant! Slave, to thee! —
[*To* POLLEN.]
What! dost thou scorn the poet? Flanders' knight,
He of the lyre is master of the blade;
Nor goes out, like a candle, at thy puff!
Lady G. Beseech you, gentlemen! —
Hope. Pray not for him:
His cause doth soil the ruby of thy lip
With present arsenic. On my angry sword
Grim horror sits, and murder is about!
Away! [*The others seize him.*]
Pol. I pray you, hold him; he is mad.
Lady G. O gentlemen — good gentlemen —
Hope. Mad for your bleeding!
Foam. La! be quiet, do!
Marks. Peace, or I'll trounce you!
Hope. Dost thou second him,
Thou thing of measures, and plague-bearing rags?
Receive thy wages! [*Strikes* MARKS. *All draw.*]
Lady G. Murder! murder! murder!
Pol. Murder! I'm slain!
Foam. And I!

(*Enter* RUFFLER *and* GOLDSTRAW.)

Ruffler. Keep the king's peace!
Hope. (*Rushing at* RUFFLER.) Presuming toadstool, die! [GOLDSTRAW *strikes up his sword.*]
Goldstraw. Stand back! you know me.
Hope. But I regard you not.
Ruf. Ha! dogs, you snarl,
You show your teeth, you bite, before a lady!
Lady G. Marry! that they do, sir, and little else.

Ruf. Are these your manners? This the high respect
A man should show before yon paragon
Of beauty, sweetness, and accomplished worth?
Now, as I live, my heart takes fire indeed
At the bare thought, and I would make you dance
To the harsh music of this rapier! —
Lady G. No more — if you do love me.
Ruf. Love you, sweet!
See, one soft word has saved you. Vanish, then!
I banish you her presence, one and all,
Until our wedding-day.
Hope. Man, dost thou think
Thy clamor scares us?
Pol. Poh, poh! soldiers, gull,
Afraid of words! In Flanders, 'sdeath! the French
Said ten words to our one.
Marks. Ha, magpie, ha!
You 'd steal our lady's gold!
Foam. La! yes, indeed.
Marks. We 'll clip you close enough.

(*Enter* TRAVERS *and* DARKLY.)

Ruf. Here come allies.
Draw out your battle; for I have resolved
To drive you out, through yonder door, like thieves.

(RUFFLER *and his friends range themselves on one side; the suitors on the other.*)

Travers. What is this folly?
Marks. It has just come in,
Along with you.
Lady G. Entreat them to desist

O dear! my hair has gotten all awry;
I must look dreadfully. [*Aside.*]
Trav. Nay, gentlemen —
Marks. Pish! draw your sword, and sheath your tongue.
Hope. Ay, slave,
If you be mortal, we will find it out!
Darkly. (*Coming between.*) Or, peradventure, if I might exhort —
Marks. Out, scarecrow! [DARKLY *retreats.*]
Trav. Taste your madness. [*Draws.*]
Pol. Hold, by Mars!
This looks like earnest. (*Aside.*) I proclaim a truce.
Hope. Base-born deserter!
Marks. Coward!
Foam. La! and I
Have no idea of getting my clothes spoiled.
[*Crosses with* POLLEN *to* RUFFLER'S *party.*]
Pol. Why, sirs, we often did it, down in Flanders,
To bury up the dead. A truce! a truce!
A soldier asks it. Or, if you will fight,
Throw down your arms, and beg for quarter.
Marks. Hopeful,
We are out-matched.
Hope. I care not, I! Come on!
The world shall witness how a bard goes off!
[*Advances.*]
Gold. This mummery has gone far enough. (*Coming between.*) Be still,
Mad poetaster; and you, master Marks,
Off to your counter, or I'll call the watch.
Trav. A good idea.
Pol. and Foam. Watch! watch!

Marks. We will submit
To Lady Goldstraw ; but the best of you
Shall not dictate at the sword's point to us.

Hope. Speak, magnet of my heart! thy slaves prepare
To do thy bidding.

Lady G. Now, I really like
That stranger's counsel, for the stranger's sake. [*Aside.*]
Begone! I banish you. Yet, not to kill
Your loving spirits, I'll mix sweet with sour, —
Return again upon my wedding-day.

Marks. Keep up your spirits: I, for one, have hope
To be alive to see your funeral. [*Exit.*]

Lady G. Ungrateful brute!

Foam. La! so do I. [*Exit.*]

Lady G. Mean fop!

Pol. Good-morning to your paint! In faith, I'd take
The same leave of your face, if 't were in sight. [*Exit.*]

Lady G. Ugh! slanderous warrior!

Hope. Madness, madness, madness!
A thousand hissing vipers gnaw your soul,
The nightmare lie beside you, and may dreams —
Grimmer than gorgons, hydras, and the like —
Forever mind you of lost Thomas Hopeful!
This marvellous world to me is black as soot! [*Exit.*]

Lady G. Loving, but vicious!

Trav. (*Laughing.*) 'T was a fearful scene! [*Apart to* GOLDSTRAW.]

Gold. But all a sham. You saw the cut-throats cool
When "watch" was cried.
Trav. Yet Ruffler swaggered bravely.
Gold. Dear aunt, excuse me. This fierce gentleman,
Who saved our lives, is Lord Guy Ruffler; famed
For gallant deeds done in the field of Mars,
And Cupid's, too. [*Introducing them.*]
Lady G. My service to your lordship.
Ruf. Nay, nay; command me, madam.
Gold. Aunt, my friend,
Sir William Travers.
Lady G. (*Apart to* GOLDSTRAW.) Are they both at Court?
Gold. Yes, both in office; and Lord Ruffler, aunt,
Is of great wealth, and greater expectation.
Lady G. He seems to like me.
Gold. Like you! Ah! I fear,
'T is more than liking.
Lady G. Pshaw, you foolish boy!
Well, well, I cannot see, but so it is,
The men will fancy something in me still.
A lonely widow; only I have worn
Better than most, and youth yet lingers here
With some small show of charms.
Gold. I never saw
Years touch one lighter; all the gayety
Of youth is yours, without youth's rudeness, madam.
Lady G. O fie! you flatter.
Gold. (*Apart to* RUFFLER.) I have smoothed your way:
Her heart is open now to all mankind.

Lady G. Lord Ruffler.

[GOLDSTRAW *and* TRAVERS *walk up the stage.*]

Ruf. Madam.

Lady G. You are from the Court.

Ruf. 'T is true, my lady.

Lady G. Are there many there
Of greater beauty than our city belles?

Ruf. You jest.

Lady G. How then?

Ruf. I trust you know the worth
Of the transcendent beauty stored in you;
Your glass must brighten with it every day.
Those eyes, that flash upon me, are not blind,
Or heaven belies its light.

Lady G. O dear! my lord,
You are so sudden! I could scarce expect
To hear such words at once. You frighten me. —
See how my hand is shaking.

Ruf. (*Taking her hand.*) Precious hand,
That trembles at my lips; then, at my lips,
Tremble forever. [*Kisses it.*]

Lady G. O, O, let me go!
'T is cruel to use your strength; and I so weak!

Ruf. I love you madly!

Lady G. Ah! you fib, you do —
You know you do — you naughty, naughty lord!

Ruf. By those bright eyes I swear — and by that brow
Of Parian whiteness — and those curving lips
That match and rival the vermilion dye
Brought from Cathay — and by those cheeks that blush
The Persian rose to paleness — by this hand,

Which now I hold, and never will release,
I swear — and hear me Venus and young Love —
To win a title that shall make it mine!
Lady G. (*Struggling.*) Indeed, my lord, I 'll call for help, I will,
If you presume so. You are crushing me —
A poor weak woman — O, unhand me, O!
Gold. (*Advancing.*) What is the matter?
[*As he advances,* RUFFLER *releases her.*]
Lady G. Nothing, goose, — begone!
[GOLDSTRAW *retreats.*]
I must retire a while, indeed I must.
Stay, if you will — I cannot help it — stay;
But don't expect to see me. Lack-a-day!
The fellow 's squeezed me out of shape, I know.
[*Aside, arranging her dress.*]
Ruf. Shall I not hope?
Lady G. Hope is the guest of all;
I cannot help it if you hope. Adieu!
Sweet ruffian! [*Aside. Exit.*]

(TRAVERS *and* GOLDSTRAW *advance.*)

Ruf. Talk of wooing girls, forsooth!
Hang me, if aught compares with wooing widows.
The hopeful ease, the careless certainty, —
Ah! that 's the thing to whet one's heart upon.
Gold. She took it kindly?
Ruf. "Kindly!" that 's no word.
But I am trammelled with another scrape.
Trav. How 's that?
Ruf. Why, look ye, as we came along,
We met the pretty Madge, and, as I live,
She gave me that same stare.

Gold. She spoke to me.
Ruf. Ay, but she looked at me. And let me tell you —
For I know all about these woman's ways —
A look goes further with them in a day,
And means more too, than fifty thousand words.
Gold. The boundless coxcomb! Madge, too! [*Aside.*]
Trav. (*Laughing.*) Ha, ha! Guy,
Keep your belief; you 'll need it by and by.
Ruf. What do you mean?
Gold. Pish! sirs; let us go in.
I have a cork to draw. — My cousin — 'sdeath! — [*Aside.*]
A jolly bottle of an ancient house,
Ice to the lips, but fire within the blood;
A liquid joy, that, in its native grape,
Basked a whole summer through in old Provence,
And rolled its pulpy fatness in the sun,
And caught the spirit of the Troubadour,
To kindle song amid our colder age!
Ruf. Come, Travers, come, and crack the bottle. Ugh!
This ancient love-making is somewhat dusty:
I 'm dried up to a cinder with my flames.
Where is the wine, Hal? Quick, my throat 's afire!
[*Exeunt.*]

ACT III.

SCENE I. *A Room in* LADY GOLDSTRAW'S *House.* *Enter* MADGE *and* GOLDSTRAW.

Goldstraw. MADGE, can you keep a secret?
Madge. Hal, it seems
You cannot keep the one upon your lips.
Gold. But it concerns you.
Madge. Do I look concerned?
Gold. Am I a fool, that you should answer thus?
Madge. Am I town-crier, that you should fear to tell
This secret which will burst you, if you hold
A moment longer?
Gold. Now, by Midas' ears,
I will not trust you!
Madge. Well, well; I'm content.
Gold. No, you are not.
Madge. Indeed!
Gold. You're mad to hear.
Madge. And you to tell. Ah! cousin Hal, you men
Call woman curious; but it would not be,
If you wise mortals did not, from our births,
Feed us on secrets. First, you tell your sins,
Then slander us for knowing them. Now, I
Have a great secret, that, when yours is out,
I'll give unasked.

Gold. A secret! pray, what is it?
That Lady Picture paints? — Miss Wiggins' hair
Grows on her French maid's head? — Miss Cripple's limp
Accounts for the high price of cork this year? —
That Mistress Flimsy's death was hastened on
By swallowing her set of brilliant teeth,
The day she heard Lord Faithless jilted her
For Lady Lucre? For poor Flimsy's maid
Told Lady Pop's, your cousin's maid, who told
Nick Prior, your mother's footman, who told Maud,
Your chambermaid, who told your seamstress, Blanche,
Who told your Dutch nurse, who unguardedly
Dropped it to Dolly Flare — *et cetera.*
Why, Madge, a secret, such as you would tell,
Has such a pedigree, before you reach
The thing itself, as an old Hebrew king:
I'd go to sleep before you came to it.

Madge. Ho! ho! (*Yawning.*) There is a shameful saying, Hal,
That fools and women talk with many words.
Now, you are not a woman —

Gold. Then, a fool.

Madge. A frank confession.

Gold. Madge. —

Madge. Hal?

Gold. Madge. —

Madge. Hal, again:
What would you?

Gold. Of this secret? —

Madge. What, of yours?

Gold. Well, then, of mine. Lord Guy, Travers, and I,
Have formed a plan to cure your mother's whims. —
Madge. How, all? And she a woman!
Gold. No; the whim
Of second marriage, with the ill it brings
To your repose.
Madge. O, take no thought for me:
My secret will release you.
Gold. 'Sdeath! you wasp,
What is it?
Madge. Finish yours.
Gold. Thus far I will.
Make no real opposition to our plot;
Flatter Lord Ruffler, treat Sir William well;
And be instructed, as we go along,
Either by them or me. Will you consent?
Madge. Is there no malice in it, no true grief,
Intended towards my mother? For, remember,
Were all her fancies multiplied by ten,
She is my mother still; nor do her ways —
Strange though they be, and open to rebuke —
Sever the bond between us.
Gold. Madge, I swear,
A fortnight hence she 'll thank us for her cure,
And vow the bitter medicine was sweet
Wherewith we drugged her. Have you faith in me?
Madge. Some little, Hal. But work your own designs;
Bring me as seldom in them as you can;
I will not thwart you.
Gold. And your secret, now?
Madge. Am I of age to marry?

Gold. You? poh! poh!
A very child.
Madge. And so my mother thinks.
Gold. Why, then I 'll swear — for she ne'er thought aright —
You 're old enought to be Methuselah's wife,
On his last birth-day! How old are you, Madge?
Madge. Twenty.
Gold. A fib!
Madge. Too true! [*Sighs.*]
Gold. 'Sdeath, and you sigh!
What 's twenty?
Madge. 'T is twice ten; but double that.
I have lived twenty years a lonely maid;
I might live twenty more; or die between,
Like a good purpose that neglects its time,
And dies for want of action. Tell me, Hal,
How do you like Sir William Travers?
Gold. Well:
A noble fellow; all that 's good in man
Finds lodging with him.
Madge. Lodges there, and sleeps?
Gold. No, no; enacts a royal part, and fills
Its fair abode with splendor.
Madge. Say you so?
Gold. Of course; who could say less?
Madge. I 'm glad of it.
Gold. And why?
Madge. He has proposed to me. —
Gold. He! he!
The man 's a fool — a stark, rank, raving fool!

Madge. Thank you, sweet sir! You're pleased to flatter me.
A fool to wed me!
Gold. Yes, a very fool:
There is a spice of folly in us all.
You are not suited for each other. — No;
Neither in rank, tastes, fortune, friends, nor aught
That makes a marriage proper. What, good goose,
Would you wed him?
Madge. I thought of it.
Gold. O, pah!
He is too wise for you — and knows it well;
He is most absolute and settled down
In his opinion of his intellect.
Why, Madge, he holds such mortals as ourselves
As little better than born naturals; —
Things to be driven, here and there, at will,
Like shuttlecocks.
Madge. Then he's too good for me? —
More flattery!
Gold. Zounds! no; he's not too good —
Who is? — but then — but then — damn it! —
Madge. You swore!
Gold. Now, Madge, I tell you — you are not quite mad —
If you intend to wed, choose some mere man,
A fellow like myself, perhaps; and love him —
Love him with your whole heart — because he needs it.
Don't take an intellect, a thought-machine,
To look up to, and worship. Zounds! I'm mad;
And you're both fools! [*Walks about passionately.*]
Madge. Dear Harry, so I would;

I like your counsel, you are very wise;
But no mere man, like you, affords the chance.
I 'd love a man, like you, with all my heart,
If one, like you, like you would counsel me;
And teach, like you, this poor heart to confess
How it could love a man, like you, indeed.
Ah, me! [*Weeps.*]

Gold. What is the matter, Madge — sweet Madge?
[*Takes her hand.*]
Look up; you shall not wed this Travers, dear:
No one shall force you, dearest, dearest Madge; —
[*Embraces her.*]
By heaven, they shall not! my adored one, my —
[*Sinks on his knee.*]
By all the saints, I do believe I love her!

Madge. Ha! ha! ha! [*Laughing.*]

Gold. Out, you witch! [*Starts up.*]

Madge. You really love me?

Gold. Yes; the thing is out; I 'll put the best face
That I can upon it.

Madge. No; you half hate me.

Gold. And if I do —

Madge. No oaths. You love me too
Nearly enough to take compassion on me,
And marry me yourself?

Gold. Indeed, I do.

Madge. Yet you were rather late to find it out.

Gold. True, true: but 'twas a thing forever mine;
So much a part of me, I never thought
Upon it, as we do on outward things:
As one may have a leg, an arm, an eye,
And use it daily, without daily saying,

This is my leg, or arm, or eye; and this
Is its true function, and just so it works.

Madge. Too plain to see, too present to fear loss,
Till loss was threatened: I can understand.
But, Hal —

Gold. Dear Madge.

Madge. You spoke?

Gold. No; you.

Madge. Well, then —

Gold. Why, true —

[*Embraces, and is about to kiss her, as* DARKLY *enters.*]

Darkly. (*Groaning.*) O! O! —

Gold. 'Ods blood! Ha! Darkly, ha! [*Laughing.*]
My cousin, sir — I say my cousin, sir —
My aunt's true daughter — by some accident,
Got something in her eye.

Dark. I do perceive
The maid hath something in her eye, forsooth,
Even at this distance. And perchance her eyes —
Being thy cousin's — do lie round about,
Even in the girdle that confines her garb.

Gold. (*Jerking away his hand.*) Ha! ha! my hand? —
O, yes — I put it there —
Only to steady her.

Dark. Ah, me! I've heard
The sufferer this wise must be steadiéd.
Hast thou removed the mote? O, neighbor Goldstraw,
First cast the beam out of thine own! A beam
Tempting to damsels, called by the profane
Men of Charles Stuart, the love-light — woe is me!

Gold. You sanctimonious sharper, blab one word,
And I will flay you!

Dark. Ah! the wrath of love!
Some mouths are closed with promises, and some
Are sealed with gold, and other some —

[GOLDSTRAW *puts a purse into his hand.*]

Gold. Ha! shut?
What have you seen?

Dark. Naught.

Gold. Liar! did you not
See Harry Goldstraw kiss his cousin's cheek?

Dark. Nay, verily.

Gold. False slave, what know you, then?

Dark. Naught that concerns them.

Gold. Well said! Madge, I play
Lord Ruffler's part, his master. Mark me now;
I 'll put him to the most extreme ordeal.
Patch-text, you canter, you — you hobbling knave,
There 's something in you, and I 'll rip it out!
Speak, or I 'll murder you!

Dark. And shall I speak
The things that are of false Beelzebub?
Coin cunning lies, to please thee? O, alas!

Gold. Talk, you psalm-singing villain — talk, I say —
Or you and life shall not get off together!

[*Beats him.*]

Dark. O! O! my death draws on. Deliverance
Is opening to the martyr! O! O! O!

Gold. I am quite blown. My faith is strengthened, brother,
By thy endurance. For each day you keep
My secret, I will give you half a pound;
If you betray me, a whole pounding waits,
To which this was but shadow.

Dark. Verily
Man cannot serve two masters. If I take
Thy golden lucre, I am bound to thee,
Even at thy chariot-wheel.

Gold. Enough, begone!

Dark. Master and damsel, peace be with you both! [*Exit.*]

Madge. Will he betray us?

Gold. While the money lasts,
No fear. A soul more sordid never skulked in man.

Madge. Hark, some one comes. Your friends.

Gold. Fly, love! But, Madge,
Think of the plot. And, Madge —

Madge. Quick, hurry, then.

Gold. Remember me.

Madge. I feared you meant to kiss me.

Gold. Well feared!
[*Attempts to kiss her, she slips past him.*]

Madge. Well gone! [*Exit.*]

(*Enter* RUFFLER *and* TRAVERS.)

Ruffler. See little Madge there, see!
She 's always dogging me.

Travers. Poor dog!

Ruf. 'Sdeath! Hal,
Your aunt is all one glow. It puzzles me
To keep her in the bounds of prudence. I
Should be your uncle, without aid of priest,
If I allowed her ardor to have way.
The waiting-maid, who boxed my ears for yours,
Is gentler grown to-day, I warrant you.
I must say nothing; but you 'll see, you 'll see. —
Lord! what a pliant thing a woman is!

Gold. Poor Doll! You have not wronged her?
Ruf. "Wronged her!" phew!
I pleased her well enough. Say nothing, Hal:
You 'll cross my suit else. Here my widow comes.
Stand by, and see me woo her.
Gold. (*Apart to* TRAVERS.) O! that man!
He has more antics than a tutored ape.
[*Exit with* TRAVERS.]

(*Enter* LADY GOLDSTRAW.)

Ruf. My life!
Lady Goldstraw. Heigh ho!
Ruf. Star of my destiny,
Where have you hidden, while my moments ran
To dross and blackness? I have heavy news;
Doleful to you, perchance, and to poor me
Darker than cloudy midnight.
Lady G. Marry, now!
Cheer up, my lord! hold up your lordly head!
Let me, my lord, like a bright star, essay
To struggle through your lordship's gloomy dumps.
Ruf. She stole that speech from Hopeful. (*Aside.*)
Woe is me!
Ruin, destruction, horror, blood, and death,
Stare in my face, and beckon me away!
Yet you, you, author of my joy and grief,
Lull me to rest with dulcet melody!
Lady G. The Lord 'a mercy! noble gentleman,
What irks your lordship?
Ruf. My father, lady,
The proud and cruel Earl of fifty towns,
Some villages, and miles of fruitful land,
Hearing his heir in thy sweet thraldom lived,

Sends here a messenger of trusty faith,—
John Rook, his butler, — with this dread command:
"Either give up your courtship of the fair
And much-respected Lady Goldstraw, son,
Or wed her instantly, upon the pain
Of my displeasure." Now, I knowing well
Thy cruelty — for all beauties must be cruel —
Droop in my spirits, and prepare to die.

Lady G. Poor soul! and will you die outright, indeed?
I am no crueller than the rest, my lord.

Ruf. You find me choosing out my means of death.
Whether to throw me from some rocky height
Into a den of wolves; or watch my chance
For sharks and porpoises, to boldly plunge
Into their hungry maws; or by some drug;
Or by the ignominious cord; or,
Snatching at once the nearest means of death,
With this fell rapier — [*Offers to stab himself.*]

Lady G. O! O! help, help, help!
Think of the carpet — I will marry you —
My best new Turkey-carpet!

Ruf. Angel, speak!
Has Turkey's loom embroidered life for me?
And wilt thou wed me?

Lady G. Spare my modesty.

Ruf. But when?

Lady G. O, la!

Ruf. Now, lady; or the stars
Shall say — we rose upon his bloody corpse!
[*He coughs.*]

(*Enter* DARKLY.)

Here is my chaplain, — a grim, worthy man,
Of dismal piety, and awful hopes.
Darkly. O! O!
Ruf. To him let us confide ourselves.
Then I in triumph, with the morrow's sun,
Will bear thee to my father's gorgeous halls;
Saying, "Great Earl, behold my beauteous bride!"
Lady G. How prettily you talk, my lord! So you
One day will be an earl, and I —
Ruf. A countess!
To show how small a thing a title is,
Laid on thy natural majesty.

(*Enter* TRAVERS, GOLDSTRAW, *and* MADGE.)

Behold,
My plighted bride! (*Presenting* LADY GOLDSTRAW.)
Madge. What, mother —
Lady G. Silence, child!
Goldstraw. You will not, aunt —
Lady G. Will not! and why?
Madge. O, shame!
Lady G. Hush, or I'll wring your ears!
(*Apart to* MADGE.)
Gold. Pray hear me, madam.
Lady G. Send welcome words, or none.
Travers. And you, my lord,
Heir to an earldom, run your noble blood
Into a puddle!
Ruf. Puddle her again,
And at the word you die!
Gold. It shall not be:
O, aunt! —

Madge. O, mother!

[*They lay hold on* LADY GOLDSTRAW.]

Trav. Base, degenerate lord,
By Jove, you shall not! [*Seizes* RUFFLER.]

Ruf. And by Mars, I will!

Dark. O! the blasphemers! [*Groans.*]

Ruf. (*Breaking from* TRAVERS.) What, am I betrayed—
Made over like a pawn—my love enslaved!
Come forth, my faithful steel, and show the world
How freedom brightens in thy awful glare! [*Draws.*]
Scum of the earth, release my love and me,
Or I will pave a highway with your hearts,
Though you were giants leagued with amazons!
Off, Travers!—Follow, Darkly!—Stand aside!
My sword shall be my groomsman, and grim death
My only guest and witness; dying groans
Shall be my marriage-bells, and thou my bride!

[*Seizes* LADY GOLDSTRAW, *and exit with her, followed by* DARKLY.]

ACT IV.

SCENE I. *A Boudoir in* LADY GOLDSTRAW'S *House. Enter* LADY GOLDSTRAW.

Lady Goldstraw. I don't half like it: money, money, money —
Nothing but money; and the ink scarce dry
Upon our marriage-contract. How is this?
But Lady Ruffler — I am Lady Ruffler —
Heir to an earldom, a peer's wife, in sooth.
"How does your ladyship?" a duchess cries:
"Ah! poorly, thank your grace," I say; and then
Her loose-tongued highness has familiar jokes
About the ills of a new-wedded pair:
Says, "Ruffler should be pleased;" and pinches me —
Yes, faith, I feel her grace's fingers pinch —
The gay, bold, wicked duchess! Ah! dear me!
That covers much. And then my husband's love —
The brave, young, handsome fellow! Poor, poor soul,
He loves me dearly; and that covers more.
What are a thousand pounds or so?

(*Enter* NICK.)

Nick. Your grace,
Your most imperious ladyship —
Lady G. Fie! Nick,
You over-rank me, fie! Call me plain Lady —
Plain Lady Ruffler.

Nick. Well, plain Lady Ruffler —

Lady G. Presuming knave! such words to rank like mine!
Have you no proper reverence, impudent!
For aristocracy, and birth, and titled names?
Have we not been the pillars of this land?
What would you do without us?

Nick. I don't know.
We do all your work now, and I suppose,
Mayhap, we'd do our own then. What would you,
Your royal highness, do without us, hey?
Who'd dig for you, who'd wait, who'd till your land? —
Who'd fight your battles, die in flocks for you,
And give you all the praise, and gold, and rank,
And stars and garters, and that sort of thing,
While we starve on forgotten? Please your grace,
I heard an old mechanic say all that,
Over a pot of porter.

Lady G. How now, Nick?
What, will you murmur?

Nick. No; you see I don't.
When we begin to murmur, then look out
For thrones, and crowns, and things! Your gouty lords
Will feel the people's broad, rough, hob-nailed shoes
Upon their toes.

Lady G. Dear, dear! Nick Prior, I vow,
If you frequent that odious porter-house,
I'll turn you out of doors.

Nick. Why, true enough,
A man might learn in better places, mam;
But we will learn it somewhere.

Lady G. What brought you here?
Nick. A flock of woodcocks. O, your ladyship,
There is a crowd of fellows at the door,
With bills as long as Lent, to see my lord. —
There is more aristocracy for you!
They make a noise too, and the people stop.
Lady G. Admit them, then. (*Exit* NICK.) I sent that Nick to school
For no good purpose. So, more bills to pay,
More money to be sunk! Has my lord nothing?

(*Enter three Tradesmen.*)

All the Tradesmen. Please your ladyship —
Lady G. Well, well!
First Tradesman. Hush, I 'll speak.
Please, mam, the others sent us up, to see
If we can get some money on our bills.
Here they are, mam. (*Throws down a huge bundle of bills.*) Pay all alike, or none:
That 's our agreement.
Lady G. Give me time to look.
First T. For certain, madam; but we hope you 'll take
A shorter time to look than we have had:
For, please you, madam —
Lady G. You have said enough.
[*Exeunt Tradesmen.*]
"For furnishing Miss Polly Trifle's house, [*Reading.*]
Five hundred pounds! Ditto for furnishing
Miss Flaunt's apartments, seven hundred pounds!"
Dear me! and all within six months — the monster!
[*Takes up another bill.*]
"One brocade tissue silk, for Miss" —

(*Enter* Ruffler, *beating in a Servant.*)

Ruffler. Hey! slave,
You 'll open doors, you will, and flood my house
With such another deluge of old bills,
To vex my lady, hey!
Servant. Indeed, my lord —
Ruf. Indeed your lord! and being such, I 'll trounce you! [*Beats him. Servant cries.*]
Silence your bellowing, calf! Do you not see
Your clamor grieves my lady? Stupid dolt!
She cannot bear to hear a human cry.
Ser. Then spare your blows.
Ruf. 'T is not my blows disturb her,
But your most hideous yells. (*Beats him.*) Peace, slave!
Lady G. My lord —
O, dear! — my lord!
Ruf. What say you, sweet?
Lady G. Forbear;
'T was not his fault; Nick Prior let them in.
Ruf. Hah! call Nick Prior. (*To Servant.*) I 'll make him twice a man:
I 'll double all his bones, by breaking them.
Lady G. Pray, pray, forgive him! I adopted Nick,
Sent him to school, and made a fool of him:
Besides, I ordered him to bring them up.
My lord, 't would break my heart.
Ruf. Enough, my love.
Go, sirrah! you are innocent, it seems.
Receive those blows but as a specimen
Of what I can do, when my hand is in,

Not a genuine flogging. (*Exit Servant.*) Well, my witch,
It seems you called these trading devils up;
I pray you, lay them.
Lady G. What's the gross amount?
Ruf. Some thousands — ten — or twelve — or so.
Lady G. Lord, Lord!
I cannot pay it; it would ruin me:
Let them take half.
Ruf. And half dishonor me!
Is this affection? Is this woman's love?
Or have I married with a huckster?
Lady G. La!
Well, call them in. But, O! my lord, the way,
The naughty way, in which you made these bills!
Ruf. Naughty! my charities.
Lady G. Five hundred pounds,
To stock a lady's house, for charity!
Ruf. 'Sdeath! yes: she'd nothing to her back, poor thing,
When first I met her.
Lady G. Like enough. My lord,
I'll pay this once; — but no more charities.
Ruf. Ho, there!

(*Reënter Tradesmen.*)

Lady G. (*Writing.*) Here is an order on my banker. —
My money in the funds must melt for this. [*Aside.*]
Make it go far. [*Gives a paper.*]
Second Tradesman. (*To Ruffler.*) I'll send the velvet gowns.
Lady G. What did you say?

Second T. My lord bespoke some gowns.

Lady G. For whom?

Second T. A lady.

Lady G. Doubtless! When?

Second T. To-day.

Lady G. More charities!

Ruf. Ay, faith! she's hardly clothed;
There's scarce a rag between her and the wind.

Lady G. And so you get her velvet gowns, 'ods love! —
And on my wedding-day!

Ruf. Tailor, look here.
Make me a pair of breeches.

Second T. Yes, my lord. [*Goes to measure him.*]

Ruf. Ass, take that! (*Cuffs him.*) They are not for me.

Second T. For whom?

Ruf. My lady, to be sure: and here's the price.
[*Throws a purse at him.*]
She shall have breeches, if I have no gowns.
'Ods blood! she needs them. Can one ride the horse
She's mounted on to-day, with decency,
In woman's gear?

Lady G. O heaven! — O patience, heaven!
[*Aside.*]

Ruf. One moment, gentle lady. Look you, tailor:
[*To Second Tradesman.*]
I want a taffeta body-cloth and hood,
Picked here and there with gold embroidery,
For Jennet, my gray mare. Upholsterer,
[*To Third Tradesman.*]
Provide me with a bed of eider down,

Roomy and thick, and of the choicest feather,
For Juno, my sick spaniel. Ay, and, tailor,
Make me six court-suits. See the stuff be rich.
Goldsmith, you 'll match some jewels to the clothes;
[*To First Tradesman.*]
A casket for each suit. And — nay, you may go:
I have a thousand wants; but these are chief.
Ah! goldsmith, I forgot the rapiers;
A rapier for each suit; and in the hilt
Of each Toledo see you place a gem,
For which a gentleman may not be shamed.
And, tailor —

Lady G. Nay, my lord, I 'll have a robe —

Ruf. A robe, the devil! Will you ruin me?
How shall I have my horse-clothes and my bed,
My jewels and my rapiers, and such things,
If I indulge your monstrous luxury?
Shame, shame! be modest.

Lady G. Pray, whose money buys
Your trumpery, good sir?

Ruf. Ours, to be sure.

Lady G. "Ours!" my fine lord: are you beside yourself?
Am I to go worse covered than your horse?
Get me a taffeta body-cloth and hood,
To match your Jennet's; stand me in her stall;
Or let me lie beside your ailing dog.
'Ods mercy! if I must be ruined thus,
I claim a share, above your jade or cur,
In the destruction of my own estate!

Ruf. La! now, my dear, sweet, gentle, loving wife,
Did I not know you far too well, I 'd say

That you are really in a passion, chuck!
[*Pats her cheek*]

Lady G. Keep off your hands!
Ruf. Why, then, hang out a sign,
Like those we see upon the new-made doors,
"Beware the paint!"
Lady G. Savage! insult your wife
Before the faces of these vulgar knaves!
Ruf. Insult you, love! because I would preserve
The painful labor of your dressing-maid?
Am I a tasteless Vandal or a Hun,
To mar so delicate a work of art?
'Ods death! you wrong me grievously, sweet wife.
Lady G. Why are you waiting, tradesmen? You
are paid. [*Exeunt First and Third Tradesmen.*]
And you, sir goose? [*To Second Tradesman.*]
Second T. To take your measure, madam.
Lady G. Ay, for the robe.
Ruf. No; for the breeches, wife.
Lady G. Out of my house, insulting cur!
Ruf. What, love,
Has he insulted you? Outrageous patch,
Here in her husband's presence! By the gods,
I'll make your bones ache for your sinful tongue!
Will you not stir? So then, take that, and that!
[*Exit, beating him out.*]
Lady G. O! what a temper, what a tongue, what
arms,
And what incessant use he makes of them!
Ha, marry! and the breeches, my fair lord;
I'll make you wish you never offered them.
I'll close your wasteful courses too, sweet sir;
Even if I put my whole estate in trust.—

(*Enter* GOLDSTRAW *and* MADGE, *sorrowfully.*)

Well, what 's the matter?
Madge. My new father, mother!
Goldstraw. And my new uncle, aunt!
Lady G. But how is this?
Are these sad eyes the welcome that you give?
Gold. Ah! aunt, your bride-bells should have tolled a knell;
Your friends, in crape, should have walked, two by two,
Behind the hearse that drew you to the church;
The priest, in black, have read the burial-rites;
And when 't was over, better far for you
If you had leaped into your grave alive!
Lady G. To spoil your fancies, I was wed at home.
Poh, poh! you prate.
Gold. Dear madam, have you heard?—
Lady G. Of what?
Gold. Of Ruffler?
Lady G. Give his title, sir.
Gold. Ay, when he gets it.
Lady G. When he gets it!
Gold. Yes,
Along with his estate.
Lady G. You called him rich.
But that is nothing,—I 've enough for both.
Gold. If he could cheat you, how might I escape?
Lady G. Where are his father's lands?
Gold. In chancery:
And his petition for the earldom, too,
Is laid upon the table of the Lords,
Session by session, with a general laugh.
Lady G. A swindler, eh?

Gold. Worse, madam, worse, I fear:
A noted rake, a ruined gamester, aunt —
A common drunkard, a notorious cheat —
A murderous bully, thrice tried for his life,
But thrice he dodged the gallows.

Lady G. Mercy! mercy!
I can't believe it.

Gold. Heaven avert the time,
When you may be compelled!

Lady G. (*Taking his arm.*) Your arm, I pray.
Harry — O dear! — you see I'm calm enough.
I do not tremble, do I? Has my cheek
Lost its accustomed color? Look, boy, look!
I bear me as a lady. — Saints above,
I shall go raving mad! [*Exit with* GOLDSTRAW.]

Madge. I cannot laugh;
Yet I suppose I should. This may be wit;
Yet, to my poor dull brain, it seems like cruelty.
Hal has my word to keep the secret too:
Would I had pledged it to that Travers! —

(*Enter* TRAVERS.)

Travers. (*Aside.*) Ha!
My name upon her lips! Fair Madge, you're caught,
Caught in the very act.

Madge. Of what, sir?

Trav. Tut!
I heard my name.

Madge. I grant: so may a rogue,
When he is called in court.

Trav. How, angry, Madge?

Madge. O! no, sir; pleased, pleased with your pretty tricks —

Pleased with your gambols — with the holiday
You three stout gentlemen have given yourselves
Over a poor old lady!

Trav. Say the word,
And I will end it.

Madge. No; 't is well perhaps,
Just punishment perhaps, if men have right
To take heaven's functions, and rebuff our sins;
Or seize the church's office, and patch up
Our moral rents — mere patchwork, though, for all.
Harry persuaded me; he may be right. —
I would I were a hundred leagues away!
I 'll hide myself; for since our house became
A moral hospital, sin seems so rank —
In doctors, nurses, patients, and spectators —
That I could wish a plague were on us all,
To spot our skins, and let our hearts alone.

Trav. 'T is but a comedy.

Madge. So you design;
But Heaven knows how 't will end. Man's comedies
Do often end in sobs, and tears, and blood.
[*He takes her hand.*]
Let go my hand, sir! Till your play be o'er,
The best among this feigning company
Shall not receive it. [*Exit.*]

Trav. She is worth a crown!
Would I could really love her! But this love —
Pshaw! 't is a mere infirmity, a toy
Of painted candy, that tastes well enough
Until we swallow it; but, then, there is
No rest until we cast it up again.
Yet for all that, sweet Madge, I 'll marry you.
Ah me! I wish I really were in love! [*Exit.*]

SCENE II.

An Ante-Room in the Same. Servants cross the stage, carrying dishes, wine, &c. Enter DARKLY *and* DOLLY FLARE.

Darkly. Lo! where the servants of iniquity
Bear carnal meats in to the revellers!
Dolly. But, Mr. Darkly, hear me. I believe
You meant no harm to a poor orphan girl,
Yet, O! you've done one, sir.
Dark. Avoid thee, woman!
Why dost thou still pursue me with thy tongue,
And break upon my meditations thus?
I tell thee, as a servant of the truth,
I know not what thou mean'st.
Dol. Then listen, sir.
You know the time you sought me, to exhort
And drive the tempter from me? —
Dark. Truly, maid:
And it befell that, waxing strong in faith,
I was caught up in spirit, and abode
Above an hour entrancéd.
Dol. And I, too,
I was caught up in spirit.
Dark. Happy soul!
And when I woke, I found thee standing by,
Weeping and wailing at what thou didst call
Thy "loss of honor;" and it so befell,
The night being dark, thy honor being but small,
We could not find it. Although I arose,
And lit a taper, and did search the room,
Even from the centre to the ends thereof.

Dol. It is not possible you do not know
My meaning, Mr. Darkly!
Dark. As a lamb,
So am I innocent of thy intent.
Unless, perchance, thy so-called honor be
A bead, a trinket, or such vanity,
As maids delight in.
Dol. Were you quite entranced?
Do you remember nothing?
Dark. I was rapt
Above this sublunary sphere; the world
Fell from me like a garment; yea, the flesh
Was melted in the spirit, as a vessel
Cast in amid the burning.
Dol. Then I'll speak
Right up and down. —
Dark. Speak, but beware the wrath!
If thou dost stain my hearing with such talk
As enters in the organs of the vile,
Lo! I will curse thee with a cleaving curse!
I'll plunge thee quick into the fiery pit,
Where roaring devils broil, and hiss, and stew
On brimstone embers of eternal woe! —
Where groaning Satan stamps his cloven foot,
Lashes his barbéd tail, and howls their sins
Into the splitting ears —
Dol. (*Stopping her ears.*) O stop, sir, stop!
Indeed, I'll hold my tongue — indeed, I will.
Dark. Thou hast been biding with unholy men.
That man of stripes, that pagan, who afflicts
The humble servant, hath deluded thee —
Yea, even Ruffler, whom men hail a lord.
Therefore, I say to thee, depart with him;

Dwell in his tent; and make thy habitation
Among his handmaids. For, of verity,
That which man breaketh, let him also mend.
Go, I have laid commandment on thee, go!
And if he scorn thee, hie unto his wife,
And lay thy sorrows down before her feet:
So when she gives thee gold and silver coin,
Make thou return to me; and I will counsel
What pious use thy money may go to.

Dol. Is that your best advice?

Dark. Yea, verily.

(*Enter a Servant, with a dish.*)

Young serving-man, tarry a little while.
What dost thou bear? (*Opens the dish.*) Strong meats.
Ah me! ah me!
A beggar waiteth close beside the porch;
His need is greater than thy lord's. Go, thou,
And stand behind thy master, where he sits;
But make no mention of this silly dish.
[*Takes the dish.*]
And if he asks thee, answer, "By the way
I slipped and stumbled." For I say to thee,
Much evil must be done, that good may come
[*Trips up the Servant.*]
Damsel, I will endure thy company. [*Exit with* DOLLY.]

Servant. (*Rising.*) Well, that must be a very pious man! [*Exit.*]

SCENE III.

A Banqueting-Room in the Same. A table spread for a feast, at which are seated RUFFLER, TRAVERS, GOLDSTRAW, POLLEN, FOAM, HOPEFUL, MARKS, LADY GOLDSTRAW, MADGE, *and other Ladies and Gentlemen. Servants in waiting.*

Travers. (*Apart to* RUFFLER.) Go to it boldly, Ruffler. All these fellows
Have been instructed in their parts, and all
Have sworn to aid you; some inspired by fun,
And some by malice or revenge.

Ruffler. But, Will,
You did not trust them with my plot?

Trav. O no;
Their natural wickedness was spur enough.
They volunteered a thousand graceless things
More than I asked. Begin.

Ruf. Sirrah, the woodcock!

First Servant. Please you, my lord, I stumbled.

Ruf. Stumbled, ha! —
Take that! [*Throws a bottle at him.*]

Lady Goldstraw. My lord is merry. [*To the company.*]

First S. O, my head!

Ruf. Poor soul, he 's hurt! I 'll heal you, Come, kneel down. [*Servant kneels.*]
Travers, that sauce. Let me anoint his wound.
[*Pours sauce over servant.*]

First S. O Lord! I 'm scalded!

Ruf. Scalded! Quick, some wine —
'Ods blood! some wine! He 'll die upon my hands.
[*Gives a bottle of wine.*]
Drink all, my boy; down with it, every drop;
Or I 'll not answer for you. [*Servant drinks.*]

Lady G. Joyous heart!
The very life of company. O dear!
The man is surely mad. (*Aside.*) Ha, ha! my lord,
[*Laughing.*]
You have a humor of your own.

Ruf. How, wife,
Do I enact the good Samaritan,
To have you call it humor? Now, 'ods life!
I feel a virtuous anger at your scorn.

Madge. I cannot bear this; it will break my heart!
[*Aside. Exit.*]

Lady G. I meant no scorn.

Ruf. 'Sdeath! do you answer me?

Lady G. I 'm dumb, my lord.

Ruf. This Burgundy is sour:
Who brought it in?

Second and Third Servants. We did, my lord.

Ruf. Then drink it.
[LADY GOLDSTRAW *shakes her head at them.*]
What, you refuse when I command? [*Starts up.*]

Servants. No, no!
We 'll drink it. [*They drink.*]

Ruf. All!

Lady R. You 'll make them drunk, my lord.

Ruf. The better, love; they will not see your state.

Lady G. My state!

Ruf. Ay, madam, your unseemly state.
It grieves me to call notice to a sight
Which all here have observed, too plainly, madam.
Pray, ladies, lead her to her room, and use
Your dearest care about her. [*The Ladies rise.*]

Lady G. (*Starting up.*) Marry! queans,

Touch me, and I 'll be even with your eyes!
You base, ungrateful ruffian, thus to lie —
Ay, never wince — to lie, to lie, to lie —
Over and over in your teeth — to lie
About a lady! The Lord Mayor, my husband —
Ruf. Hang the Lord Mayor, your husband! Never cast
His old dry bones into my face again!
The devil has him.
Lady G. And his widow too,
I fear. O gentlemen, if you be such,
How can your manhood brook, unmoved,
This villain's insults?
Goldstraw. He 's my uncle, aunt.
Trav. Your husband, madam.
Pollen. Captain of your squad.
Foam. La! yes.
Marks. And guardian of your property.
Hopeful. (*Drunk.*) Ex-queen of my affection —
Lady G. Silence, cowards!
I will not learn my duty from your lips,
Pale-hearted cravens! —
Servants. (*Drunk. Sing.*)

The devil 's a gentleman, I contend —
Tra, ra, la, la! the bottle stands —
His horn 's his beginning, his tail 's his end,
And his —

Lady G. Dare ye, dare ye, knaves,
Sing filthy rhymes before your mistress' face?
Out of the house — out, every one of you!
Ruf. Budge, and I 'll skin you!
Hope. (*Drunk.*) Scorn not poesy — hic!

Ruf. Well said, my poet! Come, a song, a song!
We'll tame her temper with our harmony.

(*Sings, passing the bottle.*)

Drag it round the table's bound,
By the glassy muzzle.
He who goes in ragged clothes
Has a mouth to guzzle.

All. [*Chorus.*]

For Rhenish wine is fit for swine,
So is wine of Landes;
But the bowl to reach the soul
Is immortal brandy!

Ruf. [*Sings.*]

Drink it down without a frown;
When we cannot tap it,
When the cup we can't get up,
We'll duck our heads and lap it.

All. [*Chorus.*]

For Rhenish wine is fit for swine,
So is wine of Landes;
But the bowl to reach the soul
Is immortal brandy!

Ruf. How like you that?
Lady G. Come, ladies, if there's left
One grain of self-respect among you all,
And leave these drunkards. Husband, ribald, brute!
Tear up my rooms, break all my furniture,
Murder my servants, set the house afire —
Do all the devilish pranks your drunken brain
Can stumble over; but, in Heaven's good name,

Drink yourself dead! Never come out of this —
This beastly cloud of shame and infamy —
To torture me with your gross, odious life!
Die, gorged with your own baseness — die, and rot!
And I will bury you, and kiss your body,
Which, living, I abhor! [*Exit with Ladies.*]

Ruf. Indeed! Ho, ho! [*Laughing.*]

All. [*Laughing, sing.*]

For Rhenish wine is fit for swine,
So is wine of Landes;
But the bowl to reach the soul
Is immortal brandy!

[*The curtain falls, amid roars of drunken laughter.*]

ACT V.

SCENE I. *A Room in* LADY GOLDSTRAW'S *house. Enter* LADY GOLDSTRAW, *sadly.*

Lady Goldstraw. O sorrow, sorrow! Was there e'er a fool
Before my time — an old, blind, doting fool?
Off, painted face — off, curls — off, all that 's false!
[*Rubbing her face, and tearing off her false hair.*]
Henceforth I 'll make my age my guardian:
He may respect a thing that 's reverend,
Even in me, who merit no respect.
Ah! silly vanity of womankind,
What an example may you see in me!
Who fought with nature, struggling to put off
The gentle touches of her slow decay,
Until she turned upon me, in her wrath,
And gave me all my wishes. A young lord
Who tears my peaceful mansion inside out;
Squanders my well-stored wealth on revellers,
Dogs, horses, wantons; and rewards my grief
With scorn, and mockery, and tempestuous rage
That aims too plainly at my hapless life;
But, missing that, torments me with cruel wounds,
Bleeding from all but mortal parts. Ah me!
Would I were in my grave! But, gentle Madge,
Left to the care of this wild dissolute,
What were thy portion? There I am pulled back,
And bound to life again. My child, my child!

This heart awakens from a long, long trance ;
And throws itself upon thee with a love
That will not be cast off except in death ! [*Weeps.*]

(*Enter* RUFFLER, TRAVERS, *and* GOLDSTRAW.)

Ruffler. What, in the water, drowning in your tears !
How 's this, old girl ? Why, what an ancient look
You have to-day ! Where has your color gone,
Your curls and gewgaws ? Now, for all the world,
You seem like some old ruin that has stood
A thousand years, then tumbled all at once.

Lady G. Scoff ! I deserve it.

Travers. (*Apart to* RUFFLER *and* GOLDSTRAW.) Ha ! the physic works.

Ruf. Travers, what 's that ? (*Pointing to the false hair upon the floor.*) Has the wool come to life
Within the carpet ? — Does it grow in curls ?
[*Turning it over with his sword.*]

Lady G. That is my hair. —

Ruf. No ! by the Lord, 't is mine :
It grows upon my carpet.

Lady G. Jesting still !
The bloom you saw upon my withered cheeks
Was paint, the curls around my sunken brow
Were false, and there they lie, never to rise.
When I have dressed my age in proper guise,
You 'll see more changes yet : A poor, old woman !
I shall be sixty-three the fourth of March.

Goldstraw. Her age, by Jove !
[*Apart to* RUFFLER *and* TRAVERS.]

Ruf. A woman tell her age !
Here 's a good symptom, Travers. Now tell me
I cannot manage women ! [*Apart to him.*]

Trav. So I do:
You are malignant to a lady's maid,
But harmless to her mistress.

Ruf. Envy, envy!
There's Madge.—But, pshaw! I'll not waste words on you.

(*Enter* DOLLY FLARE, *weeping.*)

Dolly. O, mistress, mistress!—

Lady G. Well, what is it, child?

Dol. O, mam, your husband!—

Lady G. There he stands, my girl:
He'll answer you.

Dol. He cannot; he's afraid
To look his victim in the face.

Lady G. What, what?
Do I hear rightly? How is this, my lord?

Ruf. 'Sdeath! mind your private ways, mend your own sins,
And leave me to myself! What right have you
To interfere with me?

Lady G. The right I claim
Is delegated from a higher power
Than earth affords—the right of every one
Who lifts a voice to aid the sufferer.

Ruf. Fine talk, fine talk!

Lady G. You turn aside, my lord.

Ruf. To laugh.

Lady G. You dare not look her in the eyes!

Ruf. Here, Doll, come here, and let me stare at you. [*Takes her by the shoulders.*]
By heaven! I think she'll blush into a blaze,
If I look longer. Dare not look at her!

'Ods blood! I dare do more, before you, too;

[*Kisses* DOLLY.]

And yet I never wronged her.

Dol. Don't believe him!

Ruf. Presuming hussy, do you say to me —
To me, remember, who can fathom you —
That I betrayed you?

Dol. Yes, I do, indeed.

Ruf. Lord love the women, they are worse than men!

Trav. Why, Guy, you have confessed it!

Gold. Yes, to us;
Ay, boasted of it.

Ruf. Have you no regard
For a man's feelings? 'Sblood! there stands my wife.
You treacherous villains, do you counterplot?
Carry the war to Africa?

[*Apart to* TRAVERS *and* GOLDSTRAW.]

Lady G. A shame
Upon your falsehood!

Ruf. (*To* DOLLY.) Baggage, leave the house!
You plot against me, you connive with rogues.

Lady G. Come with me, Dolly; I cannot do much,
But what I can I will. This last is worst:
I feared and hated the bold debauchee,
But now I brave you, and despise you, sir!

[*Exit with* DOLLY.]

Ruf. You rascals!

Trav. Why?

Gold. We only spoke the truth.

Ruf. Well, well; but out of time. There's Madge, too, Madge —
Another female trouble in my path.

Trav. As how?
Ruf. The old complaint — love, love.
Trav. (*Laughing.*) Ha! ha!
I'll take her off your hands.
Ruf. Take her, indeed!
What, you cold, bloodless lizard, take my Madge —
You who can rail at love a June-day through!
You icy reptile, if you had my blossom —
My delicate young bud, my fragrant Madge —
What would you do with her? Press her to death
Between the pages of some monstrous book,
As girls do flowers? Parch her with learning? Or,
With a vile course of your experiments,
To reach the mysteries of the human heart,
Pull her poor nature all to pieces, ha,
As country-maids do, leaf by leaf,
The flower they try their simple fortunes on?
What are you laughing at?
Trav. At you.
Gold. (*Laughing.*) Ha! ha!
Ruf. And you?
Gold. At both of you.
Ruf. A merry set.
But here comes Madge. Observe her, how she haunts me:
Yet I can't help it. Do you blame me, sirs?
If girls will fall in love, all I can do
Is to endure with my best modesty.
Trav. Of course, of course! [*Laughing.*]
Gold. (*Aside.*) Which is the greater fool,
Mere vanity or conscious excellence?
Here are two coxcombs, by two different ways,
Both meeting at one point, and both astray.

Ruf. Withdraw, withdraw! I wish to treat myself
To a small dish of feminine affection.

Gold. Heaven speed you, king of hearts!

Trav. We take our leave
Of your imperial highness; yet our leave leaves you
In most amusing company — with yourself.

[*Exit with* GOLDSTRAW, *laughing.*]

(*Enter* MADGE.)

Madge. Father.

Ruf. My child. Nay, fear me not, approach.
What would you, daughter?

Madge. A strange suit, good sir:
Divorce my mother.

Ruf. If you'll take her place.

Madge. How can I answer till your hand be free?

Ruf. I bear my wife, your mother, no more love
Than a physician bears some desperate case
Given to his hands, who sees but the disease,
Not the poor wretch who suffers; upon that
I spend my skill.

Madge. But now the patient mends.
You've brought her to plain clothes, and simple talk,
Clean cheeks, true hair, and modest carriage.
I pray you, give her to my nursing hands,
And let me do my part.

Ruf. She may relapse.

(*Enter, behind,* LADY GOLDSTRAW.)

Madge. I will go bail for that.

Ruf. Offer your bail.

Madge. My lips.

Ruf. I take the bail. [*Offers to kiss her.*]
Madge. Nay, father, father,
You push paternal privilege too far.
Ruf. Unnatural child, my heart weeps blood for you!
Give me the bail, and in another hour
She shall be free: if not—
Madge. Well, if a kiss—
A formal, legal kiss—can set her free;
Here, take it. [*Offers her cheek.*]
Ruf. Now, don't flinch.
[*As he goes to kiss her*, LADY GOLDSTRAW *comes between, and he kisses her.*]
Ugh! Heaven be praised,
I took you for the devil!
Lady Goldstraw. Your close friend,
And therefore kissed me. Madge, my love, come, come.
Madge. But, madam—
Ruf. Ay, keep faith; the bail 's unpaid.
Madge. Can I not kiss my father—only once?
Lady G. Not if that kiss unclosed the doors of heaven,
And all the world could troop in after you.
O, villain, villain! [*Apart to* RUFFLER.]
Ruf. Will you not agree?
Lady G. "Agree!" you bold, base monster, who would stain
The only pure thing that is left to me!—
"Agree!"—I could say that—but, no, not now;
Not in the hearing of my child, whose ears
Would be polluted by the faintest hint
Of your most virtuous thought. Begone, begone!

Out of the world! you sully human sin
By fouler projects than belong to earth.
Away! you are prepared in quality
For the most darksome corner of the pit.
Away! the gates will gape to let you through.
[*Exit with* MADGE.]

Ruf. What an infernal blast she blew at me!
I feel quite singed by her sulphureous breath;
And all because my daughter wants a kiss.

(*Enter* TRAVERS, *sorrowfully.*)

Why, Will, what saddens you?

Travers. The saddest news;
Matter to make your inky locks turn gray.
Ah! Ruffler, when you planned this merry jest,
I little thought, my friend, that you would be
Its chiefest victim.

Ruf. Do not rack me, Will:
Speak out.

Trav. Well, Darkly—Heaven preserve you, Guy!—

Ruf. Will Travers, by the blessed sun above,
I'll tear you into tatters, limb by limb,
If you torment me!

Trav. Then, dear Guy, poor Guy,
Darkly has told to me, in confidence,
That he has taken orders as a priest,
And you are married, absolutely, Guy,
To Lady Goldstraw.

Ruf. Married to that woman!—
That parchment skin-full of old rattling bones—
That relic of past ages—that old hag,

Who rides a broomstick, if there be a witch—
That—Hell! O, hell! You joke with me.
Trav. Alas!
If I were only jesting!
Ruf. Blast your wits!
Here 's your rare plot!
Trav. Yours.
Ruf. No; yours, I say!
You cut the whole thing out from first to last.
I would be whipped if such a bungling job
Called me its father. O, my luckless fate!
And you, you botcher, hope you to escape?
By heaven, I 'll make you eat her, paint and all!
Trav. Had I the stomach!—
Ruf. 'Sblood! it pleases you:
I see you laughing.—Laugh again, fair sir,
And you shall laugh your last!
Trav. Poh! poh! you 're hot.
Ruf. Go to the devil, and be cooked, I pray,
In all the dishes that the French cook veal—
You most egregious calf!
Trav. Fair words, my friend!
Ruf. Foul deeds, my foe!
Trav. Well, then.
Ruf. And nothing more?
Draw, goose! I 'll fray your feathers—draw, thin-blood—
I 'll bleed you sweetly!
[*Draws and passes at* TRAVERS. TRAVERS *disarms him.*]
Trav. Have you reached your wits?
Ruf. Pshaw! fencing-master, trickster! 't were a reach,
To get my wits through you.—O, horrible!

Trav. Nay, Guy, be patient.
Ruf. Zounds! you talk to me!
There 's Lady Alice, in the country yonder —
Stuck down among the weeds and cabbages —
I almost love her, and she dotes on me.
If I were loose, I 'd run down to her place,
And marry her, by Satan! — just to get
A guardian for myself. O! fool, fool, fool!
Trav. Prithee, be calm!
Ruf. Prithee, be — There, again,
I came nigh swearing! See what you have done:
Ruined my hopes for life, perilled my soul,
And — O! if I were in some open plain,
Some empty place, where I might curse my fill
In peace and quiet! Where has Darkly gone?
Trav. Fled from your wrath.
Ruf. And were he shod with wings,
Plumed with the speed of restless Mercury,
Armed with Jove's thunder, Pallas' Gorgon shield,
Mars' spear, the horrid club of Hercules —
Trav. The Parcæ's chattels, Vulcan's forge and limp,
Cybele's towers, the Titan's mountain load. —
Go on! If he were freighted with these pagan wares,
I swear you 'd find him: but with empty hands,
And lithe legs stirring with a new-born terror —
Like a shrewd thief who sees the officer,
Himself unseen —
Ruf. Lord! what a tedious tongue!
Out on your "peradventures" and "becauses,"
And "ifs" and "buts"! You talk a deed to death,
Murder a purpose with philosophy,

And sigh and moralize above its corpse,
As if it died by nature.

Trav. Do forbear!
Your words are simply noises. I can make
A better meaning from the cluck, cluck, cluck,
Of a half-empty bottle of stale wine.

Ruf. O, yes; I've caught your plague: a single fool
Often infects a kingdom.

Trav. Hark you, Guy:
I say you're married — married to a wife —

Ruf. And you respect her; or I'll make you, sir!
A husband's title is the only one
To warrant kicks, and cuffs, and hair-pullings,
And other matrimonial tendernesses.
'Sdeath! I intend to make the most of her:
I'll paint her up again, and frizz her curls,
And make her beautiful as a Spring sun,
That shines into the Winter ere you think,
Melting the crusted snow to violets,
And mottled crocuses, and golden grass. —
By Jove! you'll envy me.

Trav. (*Laughing.*) Ha! ha! more words.

Ruf. Zounds! true. I cannot talk my grief away.
Where is this holy devil, Darkly, hidden?
I'll make him swear, before his mother's face,
That he's no son of hers. Poor Alice too!

Trav. The country-girl?

Ruf. Yes: it will kill her.

Trav. Ah!
What a kind heart you have!

Ruf. And you, you churl,—
You trimming politician, scheming Machiavell,—

Who'd trample heaven and earth beneath your feet,
To gain an end! — Now, Will, I coolly tell you,
That if your crafty brain do not contrive
Some way for my escape, I'll murder you
In cold, black blood! — Take care!

Trav. Take poison!

Ruf. Pah! [*Exit.*]

Trav. His physic works too. Just one nauseous drop,
Of the same drug he feeds his patient on,
Has soured the doctor's nature to the core;
And brought his heart up, in a dreadful state,
All spotted through and through with Lady Alice!
How stubborn is this criminal, the heart,
That will not speak except upon the rack
Of strong affliction. Now for the last stroke.

(*Enter* LADY GOLDSTRAW.)

Lady Goldstraw. Sir William, pity me.

Trav. I would do more.
Say how my feelings may be put to proof.

Lady G. Remove my husband for a single day;
But give me time to say a prayer or two,
And make provision for my helpless child,
And I will slide into my timely grave
So quietly that, when you ask for me,
My friends shall give no answer.

Trav. Say no more.
Ruffler is dearer than my life to me;
But weighed with you, how light a thing he seems!
You who not only bear a store of charms
That might make Juno pine upon her throne,

And Venus drop the round Hesperian prize,
Before your fuller beauties —
Lady G. O! sir, O! —
Trav. Nay, hear me, lady. This alone outweighs
A world of Rufflers; but you wear a crown —
Unconsciously, and like a true-born queen —
That makes his life scarce worth the pleasant pain
Of taking it.
Lady G. How dreadfully you talk!
Trav. Your wit strikes deeply — you have guessed my secret —
I see it in your eyes. Heaven's meaning glows
Through their deep azure, and their fringéd lids
Are heavy with the tears of ecstasy. [*Takes her hand.*]
If I interpret these celestial signs,
With half the cunning of astrologers,
You love me. — Nay, the word is on your lips.
As well might thunder burst upon the world,
From the warm splendor of a sunny sky,
As dread denial from that rosy mouth!
Lady G. O me! O me! A fragile woman, sir,
In plain, cheap clothes.
Trav. What covers you is dear,
And gains a sanctity from every touch
That makes it radiant.
Lady G. Can this be, indeed?
Trav. It is, I say! Ah! promise me one smile,
One look of cheer, one glance, and Ruffler — Nay,
I'll not profane your senses with his name.
I know a way to free you. I require
No wages for my service. The mere act
That brings content to you repays itself.
Lady G. Can it be done with safety?

Trav. Ay; but who
Sums up the venture for a prize like this?
Adieu! time calls for action. Sweet, adieu!
A clear relapse, by Jove! [*Aside. Exit.*]
Lady G. Sir William, stay!
I call that love, real love. But how can he
Shuffle by Ruffler; as if husbands grew,
Like o'er-ripe fruit to us, and only needed
A little shaking to fall off? I fear
The law binds tighter than Sir William thinks.
Yet wits like his are full of happy schemes.
[*Looks into a mirror.*]
Dear me! I have disfigured this poor shape
By my absurd ideas. These homely robes
I wore as penance for my marriage-rites,
These cheeks were washed with penitential tears,
These locks were shorn with penitential hands:
Art shall repair my folly. Love me now!
How will he love me when I come to him
In all my former glory! Ha! ha! ha! [*Laughing.*]
Another heart! Who has the impudence
To call me old or faded? Madge, you child,
Get to your books again: leave the field clear
For my triumphant progress! Open doors!
Let my state-chambers brighten up again!
Call in the barbers, milliners, and knaves,
That deck our person for the envious world!
'Ods love! we'll queen it, while our crown is on!
[*Exit, proudly.*]

SCENE II.

(*A Drawing-Room in the Same. Enter* RUFFLER, TRAVERS, GOLDSTRAW, *and* MADGE.)

Ruffler. I 'm sick of it.
Madge. And I.
Travers. I tell you both,
Your wife, sir, and your mother, gentle lady,
Has not withstood the test.
Madge. Nor ever will.
'T is in her nature, sir; to weed it out,
Were to pull up her being by the roots.
I grant that 't is a hurtful growth; yet it
Has twined itself through many better things,
Which are apparent to a daughter's eyes,
Though lost on you. Let us endure the ill
For the good's sake. I love her; that implies
I love her as she is, not as you 'd make her;
Nor can I now foretell if any change,
Even for the better, might not change my love.
What think you, Hal?
Goldstraw. That you 're the best of daughters,
But not, in that respect, the best of friends.
Sir William's purpose seeks your mother's good,
And only indirectly aims at you.
Madge. Well, well!
Ruf. Pray you, consider me, good sirs.
Am I a thing to push about at will?
In faith, you 'll find me somewhat bulky when
You come to move me.
Trav. But I promised you—

Did I not, Guy? — the body of Saint Darkly,
Alive or dead. And more —
Ruf. That is enough:
Let me but hack his carcass into reliques,
And I will do the world some service yet.
I 'm ready for my part.
Trav. So are the rest. [*Leads* MADGE *apart.*]
I 'll claim your pledge anon.
Madge. My pledge!
Trav. The hand,
The hand, fair lady, when the play is o'er.
Madge. How many poets have been tricked of that!
[*Aside.*]
Gold. Your whispers are too loud for secrecy,
Though quite too low for satisfaction, Madge.
If you 'd be private with Sir William Travers,
Withdraw; I 'll hold the door, to let you pass.
Madge. Why, Hal! — [*Taking him apart.*]
Gold. Why, Madge!
Madge. What, jealous of my words!
Gold. If they were worthless —
Madge. There! that pretty thing
Will do unspoken. I foresee a time,
A very dreary time, for little Madge.
Gold. Or very merry, if she 'll stand a while
Out of this artificial, hot-bed world,
To let that spice of coquetry dry up:
A very pretty flower, to deck a maid;
A thorny stalk within a marriage-bed.
Trav. Come, Ruffler.
Ruf. Ay, ay, Will; 't is come, good dog —
And go, good dog — and — O! you heartless wretch,

Had you my weight of misery at your heart!
Poor Lady Alice! [*Exit with* TRAVERS.]

Gold. Narrowly escaped.
Here comes your mother, in full tire again,
Blooming with paint, and odorous as the East
With borrowed perfumes. All her curls have grown,
Within an hour, beneath Sir William's breath;
And what she lacks in youth, she gains in art—
A sorry patchwork!

Madge. A sad spectacle!

Gold. Her shroud would more become her.

Madge. Hal!

Gold. Forgive me.
Your father's grave rose in my memory,
And seemed to claim a partner.

(*Enter* LADY GOLDSTRAW.)

Lady Goldstraw. You here, child!
Get to your studies; make yourself more fit
For male companionship, before you thrust
Your greenness forward.

Madge. Madam!—

Gold. Madge!—Aunt, aunt,
Pray keep your honey-moon without eclipse.

Lady G. My honey-moon! You saw—why should I blush?— [*Aside.*]
You saw Sir William Travers pass this way?

Gold. An hour ago, with your good husband, aunt;—
In high words too.

Lady G. I like not that. (*Aside.*) High words?—
Such as—

Gold. "Base fool!" And "By your leave, you lie!"
And "If you dare be brave, slave!"—
Lady G. That will do.
O dear! my heart misgives me. Did he mean
To kill my husband? Risk his precious life
Against a drunken brawler! (*Aside.*) Harry, run:
They 'll come to mischief.
Gold. Never fear.
Lady G. Run, run!
Procure an officer.—You stony fool,
Why stand you gaping, when their blood may flow
Even while you stare at me?

(*Enter* HOPEFUL, FOAM, POLLEN, *and* MARKS.)

Who let you in?
Hopeful. Fallen idol, he who oped the wooden doors
Of our lost Paradise was Nick, thy man.
Marks. We would congratulate you.
Foam. La! yes, madam;
We kiss your hand.
Pollen. I bow my colors down.
Lady G. You stand there still?
[*Apart to* GOLDSTRAW.]
Gold. In wonder.
Lady G. At these fools?
What brought you here?—what keeps you here?—And why,
In Heaven's sweet name, do you not quit my sight?
I 'm on the rack, yet dare not groan! [*Aside.*]
Marks. Your speech,
Hopeful, your speech!
Hope. Renowned enchantress, list!
We who upon your fateful wedding-day

Showered our blessings on your orange-wreath,
Seeing that wreath has changed to stinging thistles,
Thought it might not be an ungracious act,
To come and gratulate your ladyship
Upon your husband's death. Since that alone —

Lady G. Has he run mad, at last?

Hope. Mad!

Marks. Sober truth:
We saw the body.

Hope. With more fatal stabs
Than Cæsar gathered in the Capitol.

Pol. Why, once in Flanders —

Lady G. Silence! I shall die
Before I understand you. Master Marks —

Marks. Your husband 's dead: there 's the blunt truth for you.

Lady G. O, Heaven! — I — Harry — How did he die?

Pol. Why, like a soldier!

Lady G. Mercy!

Marks. Stabbed to death.

Lady G. By whom? — Quick!

Marks. No one knows.

Lady G. Thank Heaven! [*Aside.*]

(*Enter* TRAVERS, *his hands bloody.*)

You here! —
What 's this — this stain upon your hands? Speak! speak!
You did not kill him?

Trav. He is yours no more.
Ask me no questions.

[*Takes her hand. She shrinks away.*]

Lady G. Murderer!

All. How?
Trav. Look there!

(*Enter* RUFFLER, *as a ghost, pointing to a wound on his breast.*)

Is it a phantom of my feverish brain?
Or —
Lady G. Terrible!
Trav. You see it, too!
All. See what?
Trav. Thou gory horror, wherefore art thou here?
I say, I slew thee, in fair, open fight!
Monsters like thee should track the murderer,
Not the true man!
Gold. Poor gentleman! the loss
Of his old friend has quite bewildered him.
Lady G. Kind Heaven, destroy my sight! Let me not look
Upon this thing, and live!
Gold. Aunt, are you crazed?
Here's nothing but a chair — a table here.
Ay, that's the portrait of your former husband:
He looks upon you sorrowfully, I grant;
But so he must have looked throughout his life.

[*Holds* MADGE *back.*]

[RUFFLER *advances towards* LADY GOLDSTRAW.]

Lady G. Keep it away! — Stand off! — I had no hand —
Mine are not bloody — in this butchery!
Look at my hand — O, horror! blood here, too!
Ha! ha! we three wear one foul livery!
Ha! ha! how like you scarlet, gentlemen,
For a lord's lady?

[*Bursts into a laugh, and faints, supported by* GOLDSTRAW.]

Madge. (*Rushing forward.*) Mother! —

Trav. Give her air.
Ruffler, go wash your ghostly colors off.

[*Exit* RUFFLER.]

Fear nothing, lady: 't is the crisis, now;
That past, all will be well.

Madge. Ah! my poor mother! —
Inhuman men! — Hal Goldstraw, you as well —
You could consent to this!

Trav. Hist! she awakes.

Gold. Dear aunt!

Trav. How feel you, madam?

Lady G. Has it gone?

Gold. What has been here?

Lady G. My — my —

Trav. You pause.

Lady G. You here!
Dare you to question me?

Trav. Why not, my lady?

Lady G. Where is my husband?

Gold. Madam, you should know
How long the good Lord Mayor has been entombed.

Lady G. Sirs, would you mock me? Am I not a bride?
Was I not married yesterday?

Gold. Dear aunt,
Your thoughts are wandering. You have been a widow
Some fifteen years or more.

Lady G. Did I not wed
A loose, low ruffian, by the name of Ruffler?
Was he not killed? And am I not — O, heaven!

[*Covers her face.*]

Trav. He will feel flattered at the character

You have bestowed upon him. Ruffler lives,
And is within your house. A sober man,
I can assure you; and no more your husband
Than your fair daughter, there.

Lady G. Strange! Madge, come here.
You have been weeping. Dry your pretty eyes.
It has been all a dream — but such a dream!
I have been ill and feverish. — All a dream!

Trav. O, yes; there was a German who believed
Dream-life the true one, and our actual state
A mere illusion: in that faith he died.

Lady G. I 've heard of such things. It was wonderful!
I have had other waking fancies, too;
But they are over now. Those gentlemen,
Companions of my folly, if they stay,
Must not suggest my weakness: it has past.

Hopeful. Queen of my heart! —

Lady G. (*Laughing.*) That is sufficient, sir.
I abdicate in favor of my child.
The crown of hearts will hardly slide across
My many wrinkles: here 's a smoother brow,
More worth the dignity of general love,
And thus I bless it.

All. Long live Madge, our queen!

(*Enter* RUFFLER, *dragging in* DARKLY, *and followed by* DOLLY FLARE.)

Ruffler. Howl, villain, howl! Your agony delights me;
And you, she-devil, add your cries to his;
A merrier concert never struck my ear.
Now, here, upon your knees, before us all,
Confess your lies. Say, are you under orders?

Darkly. Under your orders, as the hireling lies
Beneath the master's.

Ruf. But you lie without them,
Much to my sorrow. Am I married? — Speak!

Dark. No, no!

Ruf. You never saw me wed?

Dark. No, no!

Ruf. You were not present? You were in the moon,
The sun, in heaven, in —

Dark. No! O! let me say
One great concluding no, and end this choking.

Ruf. Now, for your penance, I consign you over
To Dolly Flare, forever.

Dark. But my faith
Forbids vain penance. I am under vows
Never to mate with woman.

Ruf. Under vows,
You deadly papist! and not wed a woman!
I'll join you to an ape, then.

Dark. Must I take
Thy Jezebel, thy minion, thy cast ware?
Nay, throw her from the window to the dogs!

Ruf. That might improve her fate.

Dark. (*To* Dolly, *who approaches him.*) Avaunt, thou witch!
Child of iniquity, thy touch defiles me!

Dolly. Not more than yours has me.

Dark. Speak, and I'll curse thee.

Dol. Curse away, then: I care not for your curse.
My lord, forgive me: I have lied of you,
For that man's sake.

Ruf. Ho! ho! the fox is up!

Darkly, sweet saint, lift up your sacred head.
Here, take her hand. (*Joins their hands.*) I join you two in one,
And throw you, thus, across the nuptial line,
As boys do cats. — There, scratch yourselves to death!

Dark. O! O! the heathen rages! Wife of mine,
Let us remove our habitation hence.
I am inclined to cleave to thee — [*Stealing off.*]

Ruf. Hold, there!
You shall not stir until I see you wed.
Hey! Reynard, would you dodge?

Dark. O! O! [*Retires with* DOLLY.]

Ruf. And you,
My quondam wife, are you inclined to try
A serious union with a young gallant?
Here 's Travers, heart-free.

Trav. Whew!

Lady G. Excuse me, sir,
Your friend has been explaining all to me.
The process of your jest was somewhat harsh,
Yet I confess 't was healthful; and, though built
Upon a fiction, that may move my mirth,
I see no reason why the same events,
If true, might not have drained my silly eyes
Of their last tear.

Ruf. Travers is scorned, then?

Lady G. No;
Not scorned, but not accepted.

Trav. Cheer up, Guy;
There 's something left me. Lady, by your leave,
The play is over, shall I gain the hand?
[*Offers to take* MADGE'S *hand.*]

Gold. (*Interposing.*) Sir, by your leave, I urge a prior claim. [*Takes her hand.*]

Ruf. Ho! ho! Will Travers, we are gulled, I think; [*Laughing.*]
Apollo 's tumbled from his pedestal!
Nay, hark you, now, superior intellect,
You look less like Minerva than her owl!
O! this is too good! Some one hug me tight,
Or I shall split with laughter! Travers gulled
By two mere mortals!

Trav. 'Sdeath! you monstrous dunce!

Ruf. (*Apart to* TRAVERS.) I am beginning to reform my faith:
I thought Madge Goldstraw loved me. Seriously,
I fear all women do not love us, Will.

Trav. You should respect them — if you know yourself —
For that one fact.

Ruf. But Lady Alice!

Trav. Poh!
Guy, Guy, the truth will out: I really love,
With all my heart, I really love sweet Madge.
I scoffed at love, once —

Ruf. Bravo! baby Cupid,
This is thy vengeance! Travers, are you paid?

Trav. Beyond my sin: The gods do naught by halves.
Where goes the hand? [*To* MADGE.]

Madge. Where the heart went before.

Gold. A gentle herald! Do not envy me
The dearest blessing that has crossed my path.
You have a happiness within yourself,
A soul made fruitful by a teeming mind;

Mine is all here, within this little hand.
Your sanction, madam.
Lady G. Take it. 'T is a match
Your uncle planned, and smiles upon, I know:
The sod lies lighter on his grave for this.
Trav. Come, Guy, I want some country air. I 'll plant
Myself among your weeds and cabbages,
Poultry, and pigs, and Lady Alices.
Ruf. 'Sdeath! mend your phrases.
Lady G. Gentlemen, no jars.
You, who have made my marriage-day so bright
With heart-felt blessings, must not bring the night
Ere I enjoy the sunshine. I would see
The bowl pass round among this company.
Will goodness not become me — make me fair? —
Ruf. There 's the old sin, in a new shape — beware!
Lady G. True; I 'll be cautious. You have had a day
Of harmless merriment; thank Heaven, I pray,
For the enjoyment; and preserve your wine
Safe from the bitter taint of tearful brine,
Till you can pledge me in my altered carriage: —
What shall the toast be, sirs?
All. The Widow's Marriage!

POEMS.

THE

PODESTA'S DAUGHTER;

A DRAMATIC SKETCH.

SCENE. *Before and within the Gate of an Italian Church-Yard. Enter, as if from the wars,* DUKE ODO, VINCENZO, *and a train of Men-at-arms.*

DUKE ODO. (*Dismounting.*)

HARK you, Vincenzo ; here will I dismount.
Lead on Falcone to the castle. See
He lack no provender nor barley-straw
To ease his battered sides. Poor war-worn horse !
When last we galloped past this church-yard gate,
He was a colt, gamesome and hot of blood,
Bearing against the bit until my arm
Ached with his humors. Mark the old jade now —
He knows we talk about him — a mere boy
Might ride him bare-backed. Give my people note
Of my approach, and tell them, for yourself,
I will not look too strictly at my house :

An absent lord trains careless servitors.
I wish no bonfires lighted on the hills,
No peaceful cannon roused to mimic wrath.
Say, I have seen cities burn, and shouting ranks
Of solid steel-clad footmen melt away
Before a hundred pieces. Say, I come
For rest, not jollity; and all I seek
Is a calm welcome in their lighted eyes,
And quiet murmurs that appear to come
More from the heart than lips. Remember this.
Yon old gray man who wanders through the tombs,
Like Time among his spoils, is the first face,
Of all the many strange ones we have passed,
That I can call by name: I 'll question him.
See Marco's bed be soft. Let him be laid
In the south turret, close beside my room:
His wound aches cruelly. I must not forget
The cry of love with which he dashed between
My broken corslet and the Frenchman's spear.
There, lead Falcone gently. Loose his girth;
Unhook his curb. He ever fretted thus
To part from me.

VINCENZO.

Lord! signor, here 's a task!
First, lead this furious devil to his crib,
Throttle the cannon, blow the bonfires out,
Tell o'er another Iliad of your fights —
A hundred battles to Achilles' one;
Keep down such yells of joy as might outbrave
The lungs of thunder; make a bed for Marco —
A soft bed, bless me! — the outrageous bear
Would growl, like Cerberus, if he were laid

Upon the cloudy couch of amorous Venus.
Then — Well, you say it, and —

DUKE ODO.

You will obey ;
Bettering my plans with your inventive brain :
Only there must be hinderances enough
To heighten your good service. Fare you well !

(VINCENZO *and the train ride on towards the castle.* DUKE ODO *enters the church-yard, and approaches the* PODESTA.)

Good-even, signor !

PODESTA.

Welcome ! An old man
May fitly bid you welcome here ; for I,
Standing upon this grave-yard, sometimes feel
Like an unseized inheritor who treads
Hereditary acres, long kept back.
I am next heir to this domain of death :
Ere many days, I 'll come with funeral pomp
To claim my full possession. Welcome, then !
No breach of hospitality shall prove
My right unworthy. I was thinking thus —
Framing such salutation for a guest —
While you stood in the gateway.

DUKE ODO.

Merry sadness !

PODESTA.

Ay, signor, 't is as well as weeping mirth.
Laughter and tears ! their issue is the same ;

One treads upon the other's flying heels,
Heaven takes up each into its steady breast,
Life rolls along beyond the power of both,
And either is soon over.

DUKE ODO.

True as sad.
I pray you, Podesta —

PODESTA.

How! You know my office?

DUKE ODO.

One at the gate informed me.

PODESTA.

Who were they —
Those horsemen that went clattering up the street?
Yon wall concealed them.

DUKE ODO.

Servants of the castle.

PODESTA.

What a rude stir the lazy varlets made!
'T is now all play with them. The duke 's abroad,
Battering down castles, while malicious time
Is busy with his own. He 'll find neglect
Makes as sad breaches as his cannon-balls.
The whole world rots together, men and things;
That 's comforting to mortals.

DUKE ODO.

How the graves
Have thickened here!

PODESTA.

Ay, truly; and should man
Consent to leave these landmarks of the dead
Stand a few centuries, he would make his home
Within the peopled cities of decay;
And the bewildered swain, furrowing the fields,
Would drive his plough zig-zag between the stones
In sowing-time.

DUKE ODO.

This consecrated ground,
Within my memory, was an open field.
Here I have seen the golden heads of grain
Shaken together in an autumn gust;
Where yon ambitious marble lifts its pile
Of sculptured trophies, I have seen the peasant,
With hearty, laughing labor, strike his spade
To found the May-pole. Glancing eyes and feet,
Timed to the lute and rattling castanet,
Figures of rustic grace and rustic strength,
Gaudy with flaring ribbons, I have seen
Whirled in a transient frenzy round and round
That festal tree. Where is the ripened grain?
Yonder the spade was struck, with heavier heart,
For other purposes; and other sounds
Than May-day dance and music have been heard
Around the crusted sculptures of that tomb.

Alas! the very flowers which twined the pole
Have turned to marble; colorless and sad
They stiffen round yon column, and appear
Such flowers as winter, in a jealous mood,
Might breed upon the bosom of his snows,
In mockery of spring. Where are the forms
Of maiden beauty and of manly power
That crushed the tender grass beneath their feet?
Sleep they in their own footsteps? Does the grass
Grow over them secure? The votive wreath,
Hanging upon the headstone of this grave,
Perchance conceals a name which one time passed
From lip to lip like cheering news; the eyes
Of young and old grew bright with heart-born ease,
To hear her foot-fall on the cottage-floor;
And some, no doubt, burned with a warmer fire
That smouldered shyly, and went out unseen —
An inner torture. Let me raise the garland.
"Giulia," and nothing more. Whose grave is this?

PODESTA.

My daughter's.— Heaven protect your life! how pale,
How very pale you turn!

DUKE ODO.

What, I? — Indeed? —
Well, well, I am a soldier, and my wounds
Will twinge sometimes. Besides, I felt a shock
Recoil upon me, at my sudden burst
Into your sacred grief. Pray pardon me.—
Whose tomb is that? — yonder great, haughty work,
That seems to rise, like purse-puffed insolence,

Among the humbler grave-stones, crying, "See,
Even in death I keep my wonted state!"

PODESTA.

Signor, you wrong the dead. The clay beneath
Asked only to be tombed in open ground,
Where the deep sky might stretch above his head,
The bright flowers grow, and the south breezes bring
A noise of running waters, and a gush
Of drowsy murmurs, rustling through the trees,
Forever round him. 'T was his fancy. He
Shuddered with horror when the thought would come
Of his ancestral crypts, where daylight turned
Into an oozy dampness, worse than night.
"How shall I lie with patience all the years
Earth has in store for her, beneath a place
At which my dullest instincts cower with fear?
Lay me beneath the sun," he ever said.
Age has its toys, like childhood; this was his.
So, when he died, through superstitious dread —
But more through love — with smothered discontent,
They laid him there, and piled that pompous mass —
Which wrongs the spirit of his last request —
High over him. That tomb is old Duke Odo's.

DUKE ODO.

Heaven rest his soul!

PODESTA.

Amen! My Giulia loved him —
Though she had little reason — to the last.

DUKE ODO.

How long has she been dead?

PODESTA.

Why — let me see
Since young Count Odo buckled on his arms —
He is the duke now, but I still forget —
Is nigh a score of years: my daughter died
A twelvemonth from the day he journeyed hence.
O, weary time! And Ugo, too, is dead;
Daughter and son are lying side by side:
The fruit has fallen, but the old trunk stands,
Forlorn and barren, rooted yet in life.
'T is a long story; would you hear it all?
Past griefs are garrulous, and slighted age
Is pleased to listen to its own thin voice.
Sit there on Giulia's grave — the sod is fresh —
I 'll find a seat on Ugo's.

DUKE ODO.

Nay, nay, signor;
A maiden's grave is of choice sanctity:
I 'll stand and listen.

PODESTA.

Please yourself; I 'll sit.
This tale could not be told to every ear; —
Though, after all, 't is a mere history
Of how a maiden lived, how loved, how died:
A simple matter, such as gossips vex

Our sleepy ears with round a winter's fire.
Yet, for all this, a sympathetic heart,
Like that you seem to own, is only fit
To hold the pure distilment of such tears
As early sorrow sheds. Shall I go on?
Or do I blunder in my thought of you?

DUKE ODO.

Of me! O, heaven! (*Aside.*) No, no.

PODESTA.

Well, let me think.
On her twelfth birthday my child, Giulia —
I now may say it, she is dead so long —
Was fairer than the rose she loved so much,
White as the lily were her virgin thoughts,
Her pride as humble as the violet;
Her fancies trained as easily as the vine
That loves a strong support to grow around,
And grows not upward, if not upward held:
So all her pliant nature leaned upon
Me and her brother, Ugo. Sweeter far
Than rose or lily, violet or vine,
Though they could gather all their charms in one,
Was the united being of my child,
Just as she stepped beyond her childish ways,
And lightly trod the paths of womanhood.
Only there was this one defect in her —
If a half beauty may be called defect —
She was too rare, too airy, too refined,
Too much of essence, and too little flesh,
For the rude struggles of rough-handed earth.

Even her very life seemed bound to her
By frailer tenures than belong to us.
There was no compact between heaven and earth
Regarding her. She had no term to live,
No time to die. Within her life and *death*
Seemed ever striving for the mastery;
And she on either smiled with equal cheer.
She was a product of her native air,
Born from the breath of flowers, the dews of night,
The balm of morning, the melodious strains
That haunt our twilight, waning with the moon.
Each unsubstantial thing took form in her;
Even her country's sun had shot its fire
Through all her nature, and burnt deeply down
Into her soul: — Here was the curse of all!
Count Odo — mark the contrast — so we called,
Through ancient courtesy, the old duke's son —
Came from the Roman breed of Italy.
A hundred Cæsars poured their royal blood
Through his full veins. He was both flint and fire;
Haughty and headlong, shy, imperious,
Tender, disdainful, tearful, full of frowns;
Cold as the ice on Ætna's wintry brow,
And hotter than its flame. All these by turns.
A mystery to his tutors and to me —
Yet some have said his father fathomed him —
A mystery to my daughter, but a charm
Deeper than magic. Him my daughter loved.

DUKE ODO.

Loved! Are you sane?

PODESTA.

The thing seems strange enough,
That love should draw my tender flutterer
Around this jetting flame ; but so it was.
She loved so truly, and she flew so near —
But I forestall the end.

DUKE ODO.

O, misery ! [*Aside.*]

PODESTA.

My functions drew me to the castle oft,
Thither sometimes my daughter went with me ;
And I have noticed how young Odo's eyes
Would light her up the stairway, lead her on
From room to room, through hall and corridor,
Showing her wonders, which were stale to him,
With a new strangeness. For familiar things,
Beneath her eyes, grew glorified to him;
And woke a strain of boyish eloquence,
Dressed with high thoughts and fluent images,
That sometimes made him wonder at himself,
Who had been blind so long to every charm
Which her admiring fancy gave his home.
Often I caught them standing rapt before
Some barbarous portrait, grim with early art —
A Gorgon, to a nicely-balanced eye,
That scarcely hinted at humanity ;
Yet they would crown it with the port of Jove,
Make every wrinkle an heroic scar,
And light that garbage of forgotten times

With such a legendary halo, as would add
Another lustre to the Golden Book.
At first the children pleased me; many a laugh,
That reddened them, I owed their young romance
But the time sped, and Giulia ripened too,
Yet would not deem herself the less a child;
And when I clad me for the castle, she
Would deck herself in her most childish gear,
And lay her hand in mine, and tranquilly
Look for the kindness in my eyes. She called
Odo her playfellow — "The little boy
Who showed the pictures, and the blazoned books,
The glittering armor and the oaken screen,
Grotesque with wry-faced purgatorial shapes
Twisted through all its leaves and knotted vines;
And the grand, solemn window, rich with forms
Of showy saints in holiday array
Of green, gold, red, orange, and violet,
With the pale Christ, who towered above them all,
Dropping a ruby splendor from his side."
She told how "Odo — silly child! — would try
To catch the window's glare upon her neck,
Or her round arms;" and how "the flatterer vowed
The gleam upon her temple seemed to pale
Beside the native color of her cheek."
Prattle like this enticed me to her wish,
Though cooler reason shook his threatening hand,
And counselled flat denial. Till at length
Ugo, my son, stung by the village taunts
Which the duke's menials had set going round,
Grew sad and moody with an inward shame,
That soon ran over in a wrathful stream
Of most unfilial censure. "Look you, sir," —

Beating his sword-hilt with his furious hand,
Till blade and scabbard rang like clashing brands —
"This never shall be said! By Mary's tears,
I'll cleave the next bold slanderer to the beard!
And you, sir — you who are the cause of it —
Look that your house be stainless. Breed no trulls
For your liege lord; or, if you needs must pimp,
Look further from your home!" Here was a strait!
The partial justice of his hot rebuke
Pardoned its disrespect, and sealed my lips
Against reproaches: so I stammered out,
"Ugo, you rave." "Rave! only look to it,
Or I may rave in action!" Down the hall,
Black as a thunder-cloud, he swept along,
Darkening the way before him. I awoke.
The shameful fear stood imminent; even now
Might be an age too late. But, though delayed,
Duty must be no reckoner of time;
An act good once is good forever. So,
When Giulia sought me for the usual walk,
I put her tears and her aside together;
Not sternly, kindly, but inflexibly.
Then all at once that rapid sorcerer,
The human heart, lit a new light within her.
Still as life may be, flushed from brow to breast
With modest scarlet, by my side she paused,
Tracing the mazes of bewildered thoughts.
I turned and left her; yet whene'er I stopped,
And cast a backward glance, fixed as before,
Her eyes inverted on her inner self,
And all her senses idle, Giulia stood,
Seeming her own excelling counterfeit.
Some strange thing stirred within her, that was plain;

So I, with just the sapience of our race,
Set my poor wits to reasoning down my fears.
Half up the hill, Count Odo, like a stag
Lured by the mimicked bleating of his doe,
Burst from the bushes, and before me stood
With such a wonder as the antlered king
Must feel before the hunter. Not a word
Nor sign of greeting did he make to me:
One flash of his dark eyes along the path —
A look which crossed my person as if I
Were rock, or tree, or mere transparent air —
And then his haughty nature towered aloft,
Magnificent as sunrise, calm as fate.
Back through the thicket, deigning not to part
The netted branches with his hand, he strode,
Wrapped in the grandeur of his boundless pride.
But other shapes his refluent passion took
Ere his heart settled; for the servants said
The house became a bedlam. In his wrath
He slashed the pictures which poor Giulia loved,
Tore up the missals, hacked the carvéd screen;
And with his impious hand, sheer through the glass
Of the great window — through the very Christ —
Hurled a great oaken settle, overweight
For two stout yeomen. Said the old duke naught?
Yes, merely this: — "Let all the pictures hang,
Spread out the books, cover the screen no more,
Let heaven have entrance through the broken panes:
These wrecks shall be Count Odo's monuments —
The guide-posts pointing him to better things."
And he was wise. Ugo seemed pleased a while;
For Giulia was dumb about the castle.
I went and came, but never saw my child

Standing upon our threshold for my hand,
As in days past; and when Count Odo's name
Came up at table, not a word from her,
Who once would leap, like lightning, at that sound,
And bear it off triumphant from our lips,
Ringing his praises till her listeners tired.
Only, at times, I caught a shy, quick glance
Of bashful cunning glittering in her eyes,
As covertly, under her downcast brows,
She shot them round her. Her familiar cares,
The usual duties of our small abode,
Were duly ordered. Her accustomed walks,
At morn and evening, through the forest path,
Whereon she sowed her little charities
Among the woodmen, and reaped golden stores
Of grateful smiles, were taken as of old.
Sometimes, indeed, I marked a peevish haste
When aught delayed her, and a curt rebuff
When I or Ugo proffered company;
And sometimes from these walks she would return
With something heavy at her heart, a grief
That often rose to her convulséd lips,
And then dropped backward to her heart again.
I counted this a shadow, cast on her
By the distressful sights of poverty
Within the forest; and I talked at large,
In the smooth, flowing phrases of the rich —
When their world-wide philanthropy unlocks
The liberal mouth, and seals the pocket up:
In good round sentences I held discourse
On the huge evils of our social state,
And theorized, and drew fine instances,
Until the starving beggar at my door

Was clean forgotten. I cajoled the poor,
I flattered them, I called them God's own care;
Asked how the ravens fed. The smitten rock,
The quails and manna, were rare figures: thus
I shifted all the burden on the Lord,
And felt the lighter. I have changed since then.
My daughter listened; but, at times, I feared
Her mind was far away, and all my words
Buzzed in her ears, like a crone's spinning-wheel,
That only chimes in with her vagrant thoughts,
Unheard until the slighted threads divide,
And startle her with silence. Giulia, thus,
Would rise with something like a guilty pang,
And busy her about the household work,
Leaving my words unquestioned. So things went,
Till generous autumn shook his jolly torch
Around the land, and seared the rusty grass,
And scorched the trees, and shook their fruitage down,
And piled the dripping wains with purple grapes,
And turned the year into a jubilee.
Then Ugo in all sadness came to me,
Flushed with the chase, yet redder dyed with shame,
And in the pauses of his sighs told this:
A wounded boar, flying before his spear,
Forsook the closer covert of the wood,
And, mad with terror, harrowed through the glades,
Trailing his life behind him. Towards the town,
Followed by Ugo and his baying hounds,
The forest ruffian sped; but when the dogs
Laid their hot muzzles to his straining flank,
Into the open road he plunged amain,
And scoured the peaceful pathway. Naught availed;
His shadow kept not closer than the pack.

His strength gave way, and Ugo's crusted spear
Again was busy in his bristling side;
When, swerving from a blow, with sudden dart
He cleared the road, drove through a copse of oaks,
And Ugo heard a woman scream. O joy!
O sorrow! turning what we take as joy
Into thy own sad likeness, how is man
Balanced between ye! And what heart may say
"This thing is pleasure," till its fleeting sense
Be past and gone forever? Ugo stood,
As if Medusa stared him in the face,
Breast-high amid the coppice; and beheld
Beneath a patriarchal oak Count Odo stand,
With one strong hand upholding Giulia,
While in the other flashed his wary brand,
Cutting and thrusting at the desperate boar.

DUKE ODO.

I passed that spot, threading the forest path,
An isle of greensward in a sea of leaves;
"Here," cried I, gazing on a stricken oak
Whose mouldering remnants told of greatness gone, —
"Here the avenging hand of God has struck,
In lightning and in thunder reaching down!
Yon ghastly culprit, lopped of every limb,
His bark curled upward in a hundred scrolls,
His fruitless acorns filled with barren dust,
Points to a crime as clearly advertised
As if a herald blew it to the wind."
My thought was just; two hearts were here betrayed
While heaven was near them. But did Ugo leave
These hapless children to the raging beast?

PODESTA.

Help was not needed. Ugo's hunter eye
Saw in that hand a weapon overmatch
For a bayed boar, without the hounds that hung
Still tugging at the monster's brindled haunch:
So, undiscovered, from the wood he turned,
And bore the heavy secret home to me.
Why rage did not o'ercome him in that hour,
Why he, in wonted fury, did not slay
The two together, is heaven's mystery.
Shame — loathful, cruel, degrading, abject shame —
That quite unmanned him, this alone was his;
No thought of vengeance. "She may yet be pure,"
Said Ugo; and the misery of a thought
That dared suppose her other bowed his head,
Crimson with meaning, to his outstretched palm.
"If she is not, Count Odo lives one hour;"
And he glanced sideways at the horologe.
Soon Giulia came; our fears might breathe a while.
She heard with patience, and replied with tears,
Heightening her fault, and taking Odo's blame.
"The guilt is mine," she said; "I met him still:
I staid not to be wooed, I went for it.
I knew it to be wicked, but I bore
The crime for its strange sweetness. Woe is me!
That sin has bounties, while poor virtue starves."
I reasoned with her, setting love aside,
That young Count Odo never could be hers;
I showed the gulf between our wide estates;
I said a dukedom could not wed a plot
Of narrow acres; and I raised a fear
Of dismal vengeance, from the old duke's hand,

Upon my head. Count Odo, even he,
Treated with justice merely, must endure
Some direful grief. At this she blanched and shook.
I balanced chances with the nicest art:
"What if the duke consent, would Odo too —
That hot, proud boy, who from his regal height
Looks, like an eagle, down upon the world —
Would he — ha! ha! — lead such a bride as you —
A new Giralda — to the altar-stone?
Why, child, the pathway between home and church
Would show more perils than the Cretan maze."
Then I advised her. "Daughter, be content
With heaven's appointment; humbly walk the ground,
Nor fly your fancies where you cannot follow;
He is as far above you as the stars."
This she believed; naught was too high for him,
Nothing too low for her, compared with him.
But when I named the danger of such loves,
How reason can be melted in the glow
Of tempted passion; when I almost spoke
In broad, blunt terms, as Ugo spoke to me —
So hard it was to make my meaning clear —
All the proud innocence of woman's soul
Bounded aloft in dreadful majesty;
And such indignant eloquence outburst,
At the gross taunt, that I, by helpless signs,
Was glad to beg her mercy. Well, the end
Of this long tossing to and fro of words
Was that my daughter, bowing to my will
With that obedience she had ever shown,
Promised to shun Count Odo from that hour.
She kept her faith; though Odo came by day

With missions from the castle that outsummed
His several hairs, and were of less respect;
Though, in the evening, I have seen his form
Skirting the roadside where my daughter took
Her silent walk with Ugo; though the night,
From nocturns unto cock-crow, could not rest
For the unceasing tinkle of his lute,
And such faint scraps of doleful melody
As he might venture with his trembling voice.
Now a new fear began. His father's eyes
Could not have missed Count Odo's altered ways;
And soon dread proof was given of what a man,
Good in all else, would forfeit to uphold
The perilled lustre of his heritage.
Ugo and Giulia, in a lonesome place,
By a masked ruffian were assailed; and though
Both mask and sweeping cloak gave Ugo odds
Against the villain, there was stirring work,
And wounds on both sides. Had not Giulia's voice,
Shrieking in terror at the bloody sight,
Prevailed more surely than brave Ugo's sword,
Heaven knows what purpose might have been
achieved.
The vintage came, with it the festival;
And, strange to say, Duke Odo left his books,
To throw a chilling stiffness on the dance
With his unusual presence. How my heart
Shrank into nothing, when the aged duke,
Tottering along the greensward, slowly came
Before my daughter, and, with gallant words,
Lightly among the dancers led my child.
"Ugo," I whispered, "in the name of heaven,
Stand near your sister — hear the duke's discourse —

Perhaps he 'll traffic in his son's behalf.
That girl is doomed past saving!" Ugo said,
"Let him but trade with me; I 'll name a price
To stagger his whole dukedom!" By and by,
With smiles and nods and gentle courtesies,
The duke returned to me. I almost snatched
My startled daughter from his outstretched hand;
And as the rustics cheered him to his horse,
Through the confusion, on the wings of fear,
I fled with Giulia; nor till bolt and bar
Rang in their sockets, and I saw the spear
And rusted sword I bore a while in Spain,
Felt I the safer. Ugo came behind:
He had heard nothing but the common talk
'Twixt high and humble; — questions from the duke,
And meek replies from Giulia. Once, indeed,
He wheeled his ponderous learning slowly round
To bear upon her knowledge; and seemed pleased
To find she knew this planet is a sphere,
Gold not a salt, and spirit not a substance;
That nature's movements are through various laws,
Diverse, and yet harmonious. But when she,
Radiant with faith, proclaimed the central light,
Without which reason were a helpless drudge,
From which, and to which, all creation flows,
And called it God, — ah! there her soul had flown
A league beyond his books; and from that thought
The fool and the philosopher might start
On equal ground. The duke was still a while.
Then they talked o'er the poets: — Petrarch's love,
And Laura's coyness, Tasso's holy war,
And the stupendous Florentine. Just here
The duke's smiles grew most fatherly, and here

The dance was ended. "Saw you not," said Ugo,
"Count Odo join his father near the wood?"
"In good faith, no!" That question had upset
My growing confidence. "Some plot is here —
Some plot to be outplotted." "Have her wed —
Ay, wed her to a clod, a slave, a beast —
To anything that can be made a groom;
But keep her honest!" Ugo shouted forth.
"A wise thought! Call your sister." Giulia came.
A little hope was fluttering in her heart,
And warming one small spot on either cheek;
That died away and never woke again,
At my first sentence. "Marry!" — she was firm —
"Not all that cowards fear — not all the pangs
This groaning earth has borne since man left Eden —
Not all the cheating baits of fruitful sense —
Ambition's crown, toil's gain, fame's tainted breath—
Not all the spirit dreams of future bliss —
No, nor the dictate of the holy church —
The Pope's commandment, barbed with every ill
That may be thundered from Saint Peter's chair —
Should fright, bribe, master, or so far corrupt
The heart which God assigned her to keep pure!"
She spoke this with her virgin eyes aflame,
Blazing like Mars when he has clomb the sky,
And looks down hotly from his sovereign height.
I talked to her until the daylight wore,
And evening lent its pathos to my words,
Of what a daughter owes a parent's love —
And I had been both parents joined in one;
Of the great blessing which her mother laid
Upon her infant's forehead, as she stood
Upon the verge of Paradise, and saw,

Forward and backward, heaven and earth at once.
Would she be false to that? Move saintly eyes;
And wet the golden floor of heaven with tears?
I showed the duke's omnipotent command;
The long and sweeping arm of potentates;
The feeble shield of justice, when the voice
Of poor, oppressed humanity is drowned
In the loud roar of an impending doom.
I made my gray hairs plead to her. I talked
Of Ugo's blighted prospect, and the fate
Which hung above us, sure to fall at last;
Talked till my passion worked me into tears,
And she gave way — not slowly, all at once,
With desperate haste. "Do with me what you will;
But, O! in pity, get me to my grave
As soon as may be. Life is wearying me;
I would have rest from that which is within,"
Said Giulia; and her shaking hand she laid,
With a low, plaintive sob, upon her heart.
I offered comfort. "You shall not be wed" —
"No, by the saints!" roared Ugo, bursting through
A flood of running tears. "Only, my child,
We'll meet their arts with arts. We'll gossip round
That thou hast been betrothed. Some village beau —
Florio, thy cousin, will be proud of it —
Shall be a frequent suitor at my house;
And he shall be thy company to mass —
He'll spread thy cushion with a tender care,
I warrant me!" and then I tried to laugh.
"Why, here's a plot to found a play upon! —
Thou didst like Florio." "I shall hate him now,"
Giulia replied; and her eyes glared at me

With steely lustre, a blank outer light.
"Give me but time. Just lead the duke astray
Until I put my goods in proper trim,
And we will fly the country, and his wrath,
If nothing better offer." Giulia raised
The hollow spectre of a long-lost smile,
And went her way.

DUKE ODO.

There was a murder done!

PODESTA.

It may be, signor; but my acts were squared,
Both to my daughter's interest and the duke's,
As well as my poor judgment would allow.

DUKE ODO.

Forgive my comment, and resume the tale.

PODESTA.

The rumored marriage reached Count Odo's ears.
'T was said, at first, he doubted; but his pride,
Now he was older, and held firmer rein
Above his passions, did not vent itself
In chilling looks and following agonies:
The pictures, books, screen, window, well had taught
Their storied lesson. Marble calmness now,
A mien that never altered with the times,
Was his high state. But when the rumor grew
A settled matter, and the people talked
Of Florio and Giulia in one breath,
Coupling their names as if they could not part,

Count Odo kindled. In a forest-path
He came on Florio. Face to face they stood.
Florio in terror, and the scornful eyes
Of Odo ranging him from head to foot.
He spoke at last: "Florio,"—his voice was soft
As the south wind—"Florio, the world has said
You are betrothed to Giulia; is it true?"
Then the habitual lie was stammered forth.
A while Count Odo's hand upon his sword
Hung, like a mountain pard upon the spring,
And the long veins went twisting through his neck,
Swollen with torture; but some power within
Wrested the clenched hand sharply from the sword,
And his face calmed, and a most lordly smile
Lit up his features, as he cried aloud,
In strong, firm accents, as a martyr might—
"God bless you, Florio!" and burst in tears.
'T was the old fight twixt heaven and hell renewed,
And, as of old, the battle-field was pitched
Within the heart of man. Count Odo left
Ere Florio could catch his scattered thoughts.
On the next day a blare of trumpets woke
The drowsy village, in scarce time to see
The rearward horsemen of a warlike band
Vanish within the forest. Some one said,
"That is Count Odo riding to the wars."
The wars have gone against us: since that day
Thousands of hostile spears have ever lain
Between Count Odo and his distant home.
Sometimes for years in cities he was pent,
Sometimes in adverse battles he engaged,
Sometimes he skirmished through a long retreat,
Hanging between the enemy's flushed van

And the down-hearted soldiers of our rear;
But never has a rumor of his name —
For the foe barred direct intelligence —
Reached us uncoupled from the words of praise.
His father died —

DUKE ODO.

And knew not the deceit?

PODESTA.

How could he know? He died before my child,
Pining, 'twas whispered, for his absent son.
Within a month poor Giulia followed him.
I can recall the time as yesterday.
A low fog lay upon the sodden land,
And on my spirits; from the sluggish clouds,
That trailed their ragged skirts along the hills,
Thick, moody showers were falling now and then;
And when they ceased, the poplars, drop by drop,
Kept their sad chime awake upon the roof.
Since Odo left us, Giulia had walked
Her birth-place like a stranger. All the world,
Its sights of beauty clustering round her feet,
And all the mystery that hung above
In the deep blue of heaven, seemed alien now;
Their power and their significance were gone.
The sun burnt out before her like a torch
Before a blind girl, and within her sight
The brightest moon was blurred by dim eclipse.
She seemed forever lost in solemn thoughts:
Yet when we questioned what she mused upon,
"Nothing," she said, and I believed it true;
For strongest grief is thoughtless, and retains

Only a stupid sense of pain, no form,
Or else we should go mad. Ugo, the while,
Softened his nature to a woman's ways,
And through the house he went, with silent speed,
Forestalling Giulia in her wonted cares;
Or in the garden-walk some flower she loved,
In happier times, he planted full of bloom,
And smiled to see her bending o'er the bush,
Even with her vacant eyes: but I have marked,
When thus her memory stirred, the flower was wet
With other drops than morning's. As the year
Rounded to winter, Giulia's cheek assumed
A kindred color with the falling leaf,
And her eyes brightened, and her thin white hands
Grew thinner yet, her footstep lost its spring,
And life seemed beating a slow-paced retreat
From all its outposts. Just before the day —
The irksome, dismal day — of which I spoke,
She looked as if her frame had suddenly
Crumbled away beneath her, though its life
Still haunted round her heart. She knew her state,
And called us to her. "Father, first to you,
I have no blame, nothing but thanks to give,
And dying blessings. Ugo, so to you,
Who bore the wayward tricks of my disease
With so much kindness, such unfaltering love!" —
God bless her, she was patient as a saint! —
"I do not ask the motives of your acts;
For, since you chose them, they must be the best,
I have one word to leave behind me — hark!
I loved Count Odo, and I die for it.
This ring, which slides about my finger so,
He gave me once — pray bury it with me.

But I beseech you — ay, you promise me
Before I ask it; that is very kind —
If Odo should return, to make him know
That I by deed, or word, or sign, or thought,
Was never false to him. And tell him, too,
Into the grave, with this one pledge of love,
I go rejoicing; and he 'll see it shine
Upon my finger thus in Paradise.
Odo, dear Odo — father — brother — God,
Have mercy on me!" And she closed her eyes,
Shutting the world forever from her sight. —
Soldier, you weep!

DUKE ODO.

Weep! am I stone, old man?
O shallow reason! O deep heart of youth!
What fearful issue has your conflict wrought!
O father, blinder than the burrowing mole,
To trust the mere deductions of your brain
Before the holy instincts of that love
Which, like a second revelation, God
Has founded on our nature! O, false pride!
Dark, sensual demon, that would rather writhe
An age of agony than ope thy lips —
Curse to thyself, and curse to thy possessor —
O, hadst thou slept one moment, what a flood
Of golden sunshine happy love had poured
Upon the desert darkness of two hearts!
Old man, old man, it is a fearful thing
To know what narrow mists, what threads of will,
Divide a life of full, contented bliss
From years of starved and utter misery;
How near our guideless feet may be to one,

Yet choose the other! Had a bare distrust
Of your presuming wisdom crossed your mind—
Had Odo come to you with candid heart,
And interchanged frank questions and replies—
She who is mouldering here might still have bloomed
To fragrant ripeness, and we fools, who stand
Watering the relics of our own misdeeds,
Might not be mourners. Woe to us, blind men,
We knit the meshes that ensnare ourselves!
Now hear your story closed by other lips.
Who was the masked assassin of your child?—
Count Odo, mad with the romantic wish
To rescue Giulia: he it was who fought
With stubborn Ugo, burning with a flame
As high as that which lighted chivalry.
Why came Duke Odo to the festival?—
To prove your daughter worthy of his son;
And found her so, beyond his topmost hope,
And would have crowned her with a diadem,
Holding the trinket honored!

PODESTA.

Gracious heaven!
And who are you?

DUKE ODO.

Count Odo. Do not stir:
From this grave hence, our paths lie far apart.
[*Exit.*]

THE IVORY CARVER.

PROLOGUE.

THREE spirits, more than angels, met
By an Arabian well-side, set
Far in the wilderness, a place
Hallowed by legendary grace.
Here the hair-girded Baptist, John,
Had thrown his wearied being down,
And dreamed the grand prophetic lore
Of what the future held in store;
And here our patient Christ had knelt,
After the baffled devil felt
The terrors of his stern reproof,
And, gazing through the rifted roof
Of palm, had childlike sobbed and prayed
His soul to calmness; here allayed
The mortal thirst which raged within,
Then turned, and all our world of sin
Uplifted on his shoulders vast,
And forth to toil, shame, death, he passed.

A holy place the spirits chose
For blest communion; but the woes
Which follow sin had left a trace
Of gloom on each angelic face:—
Man's sin, the only grief which mars
The joy of heaven, and sadly jars
With its eternal harmony.
One, chief among the spirits three,
Grander than either, more sedate,
Wore yet a look of hope elate
With higher knowledge, larger trust
In the long future; and the rust
Of week-day toil with earthly things
Stained and yet glorified his wings.
"O, woe!" exclaimed the spirits twain,
"Time comes, time goes, and still the train
Of human sin keeps pace with it.
The seasons change, the shadows flit
Across the world, tides ebb and flow,
But human guilt and human woe
Are ever stirring in the blood,
Are ever fixed at their full flood.
Alas! alas! alas! even we,
Poised in our calm eternity,
Can only see new changes bring
New forms of sin. The offering
To death and hell is overstored,
Heaven 's poor; and yet the patient Lord
Bears with mankind for mankind's sake.
Shall never vengeful thunders wake
Among earth's crashing hills, and bare
The horrid lightning in his lair?

Shall never the tornado sweep,
The earthquake yawn, the rebel deep
Scour the rich valleys, till the world —
Back into early chaos hurled,
With all her pomps and grandeurs rent —
Though barren, may be innocent?"
"Never! The sign is set on high,
'Twixt sunny earth and weeping sky:
One tittle of the spoken Word
All hell can change not," said the third.
"Patience, dear brothers: ye who ask
Quick, sweeping changes, set a task
Beyond earth's power. She slowly draws,
By due procession of her laws,
Good out of evil. In the ground,
Dark and ill-featured, seeds abound,
Trees grow and blossom, and the flower
Buds into fruit; yet, hour by hour,
No change we mark, until the fruit
Drops down full-ripened. Let us suit
Our hopes to man. The child of clay
Through his own nature wins his way;
Moving by slow and homely means
Towards the blind future, he but gleans
Behind your wide intelligence,
Leaping the stumbling bars of sense.
Full armed with bounden wealth of thought
Ye stand, and wonder at man's naught;
Scorn his poor ways and sluggish rate,
Rather than gratulate the state,
Uncramped by narrow time and space,
In which ye move. Ye face to face

See all things as they are, he sees
By dim reflection; for the lees
Of earth have settled in his soul,
And made a turbid current roll
Between his mind and essence. Yet
Even earthly natures may beget
Grand ends, and common things be wrought
To holiest uses. I in thought
Have seen the capability
Which lies within yon ivory: —
This rough, black husk, charred by long age,
Unmarked by man since, in his rage,
A warring mammoth shed it. Lo!
Whiter than heaven-sifted snow,
Enclosed within its ugly mask
Lies a world's wonder; and the task
Of slow development shall be
Man's labor and man's glory. See!"
His foot-tip touched it; the rude bone
Glowed through translucent, widely shone
A morning lustre on the palm
Which arched above it. All the calm
Of the blue air was stirred again
With ecstasy, as the low strain
Of heavenly language rose once more.
"Genius of man, immortal power,
Of birth celestial, 't is thy hour!
The doors of heaven wide open swing
One moment. Hasten, ere thy wing
Be locked within the lucid wall,
And darkness for dull ages fall
On earth and man, our common care!"
While yet his accents filled the air

Which rippled on the heavenly shore,
A fourth intelligence, who bore
The semblance of a flickering flame,
Steep downward from the zenith came,
Dazzling the path behind him. Still,
Waiting the greater angel's will,
He rested quivering. "Spirit, bear
This ivory to the soul that dare
Work out, through joy, and care, and pain,
The thought which lies within the grain,
Hid like a dim and clouded sun.—
Speed thee!" He spoke, and it was done.

THE IVORY CARVER.

Silently sat the artist alone,
Carving a Christ from the ivory bone.
Little by little, with toil and pain,
He won his way through the sightless grain,
That held and yet hid the thing he sought,
Till the work stood up, a growing thought.
And all around him, unseen yet felt,
A mystic presence forever dwelt,
A formless spirit of subtle flame,
The light of whose being went and came
As the artist paused from work, or bent
His whole heart to it with firm intent.
Serenely the spirit towered on high,
Fixing the blaze of his majesty
Now north, now south, now east, now west:
Wherever the moody shadows pressed
Their cloudy blackness, and slyly sought
To creep o'er the work the artist wrought,
A steady wrath in the spirit's gaze
Withered the skirts of the treacherous haze,
And gloomily backward, fold on fold,
The surging billows of darkness rolled.

"Husband, why sit you ever alone,
Carving your Christ from the ivory bone?

O carve, I pray you, some fairy ships,
Or rings for the weaning infant's lips,
Or toys for yon princely boy who stands
Knee-deep in the bloom of his father's lands,
And waits for his idle thoughts to come;
Or carve the sword-hilt, or merry drum,
Or the flaring edge of a curious can,
Fit for the lips of a bearded man;
With vines and grapes in a cunning wreath,
Where the peering satyrs wink beneath,
And catch around quaintly-knotted stems
At flying nymphs by their garment hems.
And carve you another inner rim;
Let girls hang over the goblet's brim,
And dangle in wine their white foot-tips;
While crouched on their palms, with pouting lips,
Long-bearded Pan and his panting troop
In the golden waves their faces stoop.
O carve you something of solid worth —
Leave heaven to heaven, come, earth, to earth.
Carve that thy hearth-stone may glimmer bright,
And thy children laugh in dancing light."

Steadily answered the carver's lips,
As he brushed from his brow the ivory chips; —
While the presence grew with the rising sound,
Spurning in grandeur the hollow ground,
As if the breath on the carver's tongue
Were fumes from some precious censer swung,
That lifted the spirit's wingéd soul
To the heights where crystal planets roll
Their choral anthems, and heaven's wide arch
Is thrilled with the music of their march;

And the faithless shades fled backward, dim
From the wondrous light that lived in him.—
Thus spake the carver,—his words were few,
Simple and meek, but he felt them true,—
"I labor by day, I labor by night;
The Master ordered, the work is right:
Pray that He strengthen my feeble good;
For much must be conquered, much withstood."
The artist labored, the labor sped,
But a corpse lay in his bridal bed.

Wearily worked the artist alone,
As his tears ran down the ivory bone;
And the presence lost its wonted glow,
For its trembling heart was beating low,
And the stealthy shadows came crawling in,
With the silent tread of a flattered sin;
Till the spirit fled to the Christ's own face,
Like a hunted man to a place of grace;
On the crown, the death-wrung eye, the tear,
On the placid triumph, faint yet clear,
That trembled around the mouth; and last
On the fatal wound, its brightness passed,
Shrinking low down in the horrid scar,
And flickering there like a waning star.
Slowly he labored with drooping head,
For the artist's heart from his work had fled.
He moaned, he muttered his lost one's name,
He looked on the Christ with a look of shame;
He called, he listened, no voice replied;
He prayed her to come again, and chide
The hateful work which his hand began;
He promised ships, rings, toys, drinking-can.

With level stare, through the thickening shade,
Hither and thither his eye-balls strayed;
But ne'er turned upward where, just above,
A single star with a look of love —
Divine, supernal, transcending sense —
Shone on him a splendor so intense
That it half replaced the spirit's light,
And thwarted the leaguering bands of night.
Albeit he did not see the star,
Sense is not a perfect pass nor bar
To the mystic steps of love; his heart
Felt a dumb stir through its chillest part,
Felt a warm glow through its currents run,
And knew, as the blind man knows the sun,
That the night was past, and day was come.
Bravely he bent o'er the ivory bone;
But dull and dusk as a time-stained stone,
From some mouldering sculptured aisle redeemed,
The face of the slighted figure seemed;
Till with heart and soul the artist cast
His mind on the visionary past,
When the face put on a purer hue,
While again the wondrous presence grew;
And the star's and the spirit's leaguéd light
Baffled the cunning of plotting night.

"Father, why sit you ever alone,
Carving this Christ from the ivory bone?
Unlovely the figure, and passing grim
With cramping tortures in every limb.
A ghastly sight is the open wound,
The wicked nails, and the sharp thorns bound

O'er his heavy brow's crowned agony: —
Fearful is Christ on the cursed tree!"
"And see you nothing," the artist said,
"But pain and death in this sacred head? —
No triumph in the firm lip see you?
No gracious promise which struggles through
The half-closed lids; or no patient vow
Sealed on the breadth of this mighty brow?
Is my purpose idle, my labor vain?"
They answered, "We see but death and pain."
A little word had frozen his blood;
All silent the woful artist stood,
Turning the figure, now here, now there,
With the stolid wonder of despair.
Blankly his eye-balls he swept around,
As one who wakes from a dream profound,
And doubts the actual world he sees,
Yet knows his visions but fantasies.
"Nothing?" the artist murmured again.
"Nothing," they answered, "but death and pain.
O, father, come to the sunny heath,
Where the violets nod in their own sweet breath,
Where the roses, prodigal as fair,
Squander their wealth on the thankless air,
And all the glory of heaven and earth
Meets in the hour of the lily's birth;
Where the wheeling sky-larks upward throng,
Chasing to heaven their morning song,
Till its music fades from the listening ear,
And only God's placid angels hear,
As they hush their matin hymn, and all
Serenely bend o'er the crystal wall.

Hasten, dear father; there 's nothing there
So dread as yon figure's dying stare;
For sun and dew have a cunning way
Of making the dullest thing look gay:
There 's a wonder there in the coarsest stone,
Which you cannot solve, yet still must own.
Or, if it suit not your present mood,
Come with us then to the darksome wood;
Where cataracts talk to hoary trees
Of the world in by-gone centuries,
Ere the dew on Eden's hills had dried,
Or its valleys lost their flowery pride;
When earth beneath them, and heaven above,
Were lulled in the nursing arms of love,
And all God's creatures together grew —
A peace in the very air they drew —
Until sin burst nature's golden zone,
And nature dwindled, and sin has grown.
Come, father, there 's more of joy and good
In our merry heath and solemn wood,
Than the cold, dead hands of art can reach,
Or its man-made canons darkly teach."
"Children, dear children, it may not be:
This work the Master hath set for me.
All are not framed of the self-same clay;
And some must labor, or none could play."
The bright flowers blossomed, the sky-larks sang,
Deep in the forest the cataracts' clang
Went up, unheard, in the silent sun;
The childish ears, which their charms had won,
And the tongues they woke, were there no more —
They lay with the clay that breathed of yore.

Up sprang the artist, and glared around,
Dashing the Christ to the shuddering ground,
With a cry whose piercing agony
Made hell reëcho with welcome glee,
And all the trembling angels pale
At the terrors of that human wail.
"Was it for this I was singled out
From the cringing, slavish, coward rout
That blacken foul earth? Was it for this
I bore the low sneer, the open hiss,
The cross, the passion, the cheerless toil—
Which nothing fosters, and all things foil—
Only that Thou shouldst be glorified
In the Saviour who sitteth by Thy side?
And is this Thy servant's rich reward?
Are these the blessings which Thou hast stored
For the faithful few?—From sons of men
Choose me for Thy chiefest rebel, then!
Thrice cursed be the murderous, cheating thought
That led me blindly! The hand that wrought
This ivory fraud, thrice cursèd be;
For it slew the hearts that lived for me!
Thrice cursed be the sight of heaven and earth!
Thrice cursed be the womb that gave me birth!
Thrice cursed be the blood on Calvary poured!
Cursed, cursed be Thy hollow name"—The word,
That might have uttered unpardoned sin,
Died on his shuddering lips; and within,
Like a dead weight, on his palsied tongue
The impious thought of his fury hung.
Around, above, with one rapid stoop,
The waiting shadows of evil swoop;

And in and out, through the vast turmoil
Of cloudy currents, that twist and coil
In endless motion, unnumbered forms —
Countless as sands in the desert storms —
Were drifted in masses indistinct;
No limb to a neighboring shape seemed linked.
Now a woful head came staring through,
Then withered hands, where the head withdrew;
Now a brow with wrathful furrows knit,
Then the trailing hair of a girl would flit,
Like a meteor, from the dusky throng
That whirled with the cloudy tide along.
One, more audacious than all the rest,
Who wore his crimes, as a haughty crest
Nodding its plumes o'er a conqueror proud,
Stepped boldly forth from the writhing cloud,
Stepped boldly forth on the solid land,
And clutched the Christ with his sinful hand.
Instant the shadows were rent in twain,
Dashed here and there o'er the frighted plain,
And the star burst blazing from above;
Stern vengeance mixed with its holy love,
As full on the brow of the child of hell,
With the crash of a flaming battle-shell,
The beams of the angry planet fell.
Right boldly the startled demon gazed,
And backward, with dauntless front upraised —
Upon whose terrific waste still gloomed
Hate unsubdued and wrath unconsumed —
He faced the star-beams, and slowly strode
Into the depths of his drear abode.

Motionless sat the artist alone,
Fixing his eyes on the ivory bone,
Yet seeing nothing. The vengeful star,
As the routed shadows fled afar,
Softened its lustre, and gently glanced
On his torpid breast. As one entranced
Stirs with dumb life, in the solid gloom
Of some unhealthy, damp-dripping tomb;
Feels his coffin-lid with groping hands,
Or clutches the grave-clothes' tightened bands,
And then with a murmur turns him o'er,
Drowsily dozing to death once more:
So seemed the artist. The star-beams brought
A dim sensation, a vague half-thought,
That glimmered a while around his brain,
Then faded, and all was dark again.
But still the warm, loving splendor shone;
And close to the side of the greater one,
Two stars, in their new-born freshness, came
Down from the throne of mercy, a flame
With all its brightness. A silvery trail
Died out behind them in sparkles pale,
As they wheeled within the lustrous sphere
Of the elder star, and shot their clear
Commingled rays o'er the abject clay,
That prone, unmoving, and silent, lay,
With a dull, cold load of stupid pain
Pressed on his heart and his senseless brain.
As the springtide sun, that sets aglow
The tufted meadows with melting snow,
And turns by degrees the icy hills
To balmy vapors and fruitful rills,

So shone the stars on the torpid man;
Until, as the first hard tear-drop ran,
A thought through his gloomy bosom stole.
At once, with a shock of pain, the whole
Broad human nature arose amazed,
With all its guilt on its brow upraised.
Ah, me! 't was a mournful sight, to see
The three stars shining, so peacefully,
On the raging breast of him who poured
His puny wrath at our gracious Lord.
A while, with stubborn and wilful might,
The artist strove to drive from his sight
The kindly look of the starry trine;
Yet, turn as he might, some power divine
Would soften his will, he knew not why,
And draw to the light his troubled eye.
Long, long he looked; till his heavy grief
Of heart gushed forth, and a full relief
Of balmy tear-drops fell, round on round,
Like the blood which marks yet heals a wound.
He staggered, he bowed his stubborn knee,
He fixed his eyes on the shining three;
And the tears so magnified his gaze,
That the face of heaven seemed all ablaze
With light and mercy. He knew the stars
That looked through his earthly dungeon-bars.—
"I see," he shouted, "ye live, ye live!
Death is a phantom! O God, forgive!"

Steadily worked the artist alone,
Carving the Christ from the ivory bone.
Again the bright presence shone around
With a light more dazzling, more profound.

Through day, through night, through fair, through
foul,
The artist wrought with a single soul;
And when hand would tire, or eye grow dim,
He looked at the stars that looked at him,
Until power and vision both were given,
And he carved the Christ by light from heaven.
Under each cruel thorn-point he hid
A world of grief, and each drooping lid
Was closed round its mortal tears of pain;
But the nostrils curved in proud disdain
Of death and his feeble tyranny,
And the mouth was calm with victory.
High over all, the majestic brow
Looked down on the storm which raged below,
Big with the power and the god-like will
That said to the sinking heart—"Be still!"
And it was still. For who once had looked
On that mighty brow, saw not the crooked
And veinèd fingers that clutched the nails,
Nor the fitful spasm that comes and fails
In the dropping legs, nor the wide wound;
O, no! the thorn-wreath seemed twisted round
A victor's head, like a diadem,
And each thorn-point bore a royal gem.

Silently sat the artist alone;
For the Christ was carved from the ivory bone.
The presence bowed with a holy awe,
And paled in the light of the thing it saw:
But the three stars sang a single word,
Faint and subdued, like a widowed bird

That sings to her own sad heart alone,
And feels that no creature hears her moan.
The artist echoed their timid psalm,
Bowing to earth, with palm clasped in palm;
And, "Pardon, pardon, pardon," he prayed,
As the Christ upon his heart he laid.
"Pardon, O, pardon!" the three stars sang:
"Pardon, O, pardon!" All heaven rang
With dulcet sounds, as the angel throng
Joined in the depths of the choral song,
With harp, and viol, and timbrel sweet.
"Pardon, O, pardon!" the saints repeat,
With shrouded faces and solemn close,
As hearts remembering their human woes.
And martyrs, who bore their fiery scars
Like trophies gathered in long-past wars,
Cried "Pardon, pardon!" And heaven's wide hills,
And fruitful valleys, and golden rills,
And long, long levels of sunny sky,
Were vibrant with living sympathy;
And folded and gathered into one
The waves of the multitudinous tone,
Until, like a wingéd thing that glows
With the first joy of its wings, arose
In pride of triumph the mighty sound,
And circled the mercy-seat around;
Till the glory grew, the sign was given,
And another joy was born in heaven.

EPILOGUE.

Three priests from Saint Peter's church have come,
To carry an ivory Saviour home.
Long years of unceasing strategies —
New bribes, new threats, and new treacheries —
It cost our holy father; until
The prior who held it at his will —
"Cursed be his name!" say the brotherhood
Of the house wherein the treasure stood —
Lost all their wealth on a single cast,
And the Pope secured the prize at last.
How it was managed, heaven only knows;
But by one thing's fall another grows:
And though the prior was cursed, mayhap,
In a year or two a cardinal's cap
Covered more sins than that little slip,
And bore more curses, from every lip,
With as proud a grace to its lord's behoof
As if the cloth were of Milan proof.
Howbeit, I give the slander o'er.
The three priests stand by the convent door,
And the monks, with groans of wrath, essay
To bring the Christ to the light of day.
Three times they had nearly dropped their load: —
All chance, perhaps; but the shoulders broad
Of stout Father John came just in need,
Though his oaths were a little late indeed.

"Is this a matter," said burly John —
His breath and his temper almost gone —
"To bruise one's shoulder about? 'Ods blood!
Bring the true image; or, by the rood!
You shall feel the vengeance of the Pope!"
"Why, brothers, you did not think, I hope,"
Said Father Francis — his open eyes
Bewildered with sorrowful surprise —
"To cheat an old connoisseur like me,
With such a bold dash of villany.
Full fifty better Christs I have seen
Rotting away in the Madeleine.
Here 's cause for penance! here 's much to tell! —
Is this your ivory miracle?"
"Hush!" whispered young Anselm's saintly lips.
"But see the modelling about the hips,"
Broke in sour Francis. "And only see,"
Blustered John, boldly, "the holy tree! —
Of English oak! while the chips we own
Are made from cedar of Lebanon.
Either the Church or the artist lies: —
Who doubts it?" Within his reddening eyes
There burnt a general *Auto-de-fe,*
For whomever might his words gainsay.
Anselm waved slowly his small, white hand,
And speech was hushed, as the little band
Of priests and friars drew softly round,
Like men who tread upon holy ground;
For Anselm was half a saint at Rome.
The general country for leagues would come
To hear his preaching. His sermon o'er,
The alms-box groaned with its golden store;

And alone each thoughtful soul would go,
With his happy features all aglow;
As if bounteous heaven's transfiguring grace
Were sown broadcast o'er each shining face,
And each were revolving in his head
The words which a parting angel said:
So that young Anselm came nigh to be
A saint ere he put off mortality.
Why he was not a bishop, at least,
Or something more than a common priest,
Is a shrewd question we 'll not press home —
They don't make bishops of saints at Rome.
Sometimes a bishop becomes a saint;
But that is after the fleshy taint
Has well worn off in the grave's decay:
And anything can be made from clay;
Saints, poets, heroes, — the thing 's all one —
A scratching of pens, and the work is done.

Slowly round Anselm the listeners drew,
Fixing their eyes on his eyes of blue.
He mused, but spoke not. His spirit now
Was lost in the wonder of the brow;
Or chained to the grand victorious scorn
About the nostril; or downward borne
In the weight of agony and grief
That loaded the tear-drops; or relief,
Perchance, he sought in the steady smile
Round the parted lips: But all the while
No word he spoke, though his constant eye
Blazed with the splendor of prophecy;
As full on the ivory Christ he bent
A look that o'ergathered all it sent —

A fruitful commerce of thoughts sublime,
That burst earth's limits, and mocked at time.
So long he looked, and such meaning grew
Twixt the ivory and the eyes of blue,
That the priests who saw do stoutly tell
How the figure moved. "A miracle!"
Shouted Father John, with hanging jaw; —
"'Ods blood! and the first I ever saw."
"A miracle!" One clamorous cry
Went up through the low, damp evening sky,
From a score of gaping cowls, that hid
More fear than grace beneath every lid;
And the caverned hills, around the plain,
Swelled with it, then cast it back again —
A hollow echo, a jeering shout,
Which silenced the lips that gave it out.
Then gently turned Anselm towards the priest,
His great soul filled with a solemn feast
Of thoughtful love; in the blest repose
Which follows the spirit's higher throes,
Aloud to the silent throng he spoke,
Kindling as thought upon thought awoke.

"O ye, who in midnight caverns dwell,
While the ever-during miracle
Of changing seasons goes through its round
A stone-cast beyond your narrow bound; —
Even though you will not or cannot see
The marvel born in the growing tree,
The opening flower, or the gracious sun
That gives equal alms to every one:
Shall ye be the first to raise a cry
Of 'miracle!' if some passer by

Venture within your hideous cell,
Where the gleam of twilight never fell,
With a flaring torch of smoky pine? —
Shall ye call the light a thing divine,
Because a mere sudden, curious chance
Has worked on your own dull ignorance,
And given you vision, and taught you lore
That lay from the first at your very door?
Must signs and wonders forever be
Guides on the road to eternity?
Unhood yourselves, and look round you, then,
On earth, air, ocean, your fellow-men.
Know that the miracle does not lie
In the roar of jarring prodigy;
But lapped in the everlasting law,
Whose faithful issue last spring ye saw,
When chill earth warmed in the vernal ray,
The snow was melted, the ice gave way,
When the grass rose trembling from the clod,
And pointed its narrow leaf to God.
Who, when this ivory was first revealed,
Saw any marvel, plain or concealed,
In the glorious sculpture? Nay, ye turned
Your senseless shoulders, and boldly spurned
The heavenly thing; till your failing sight —
Caught by a trick of the shifting light —
Fancied some movement, or here, or there —
A crooking finger, a waving hair —
When sudden awe on your weakness fell,
And all cried as one — 'A miracle!'
O shallow sceptics! O seekers blind!
The marvel is not the one ye find;

It lies not in moving limb or head,
Though the frame had writhed, the thorn-wounds bled,
The sweet mouth spoken, tears dimmed the eyes —
No, not in these the true mystery lies;
But in the grand irradiate whole,
Warm with its fresh and immortal soul,
Sealed with the seal of eternal youth —
God's presence revealed in simple truth!
I tell you, here standing, this shall preach
When Pope, priests, church, and the creed ye teach,
Have passed, like the heathen dreams, away,
And flowers take root in your haughty clay.
When a stranger, on the Appian road,
May ask where Saint Peter's ruins stood;
And a simple hind, who tills the soil
O'er Rome's foundations, may pause from toil,
And say he knows not. Even then shall stand
In the musing stranger's distant land,
Sculptured from bases to pediments
With all that studious art invents,
A temple of marble veined with gold,
Built only this precious Christ to hold.
Air-spanning arches and columns broad,
All stooping beneath their splendid load —
Wide-vaulted chambers whose frescoes rare
People the solemn religious air
With heavenly synods — and heavenly notes,
Blown out from the organ's golden throats,
Shall rise like a general voice, to tell
Man's joy in yon ivory miracle.
And daily within that holy fane
Shall come a sin-stricken pilgrim train,

From every country beneath the sun,
To gaze on this image; and each one
Shall loosen his burden of despair,
And stride again to the blessed air
With new power to do, new strength to bear.
For here, in this sacred face, is met
All that mortal ever suffered yet:
All human weakness, all shame, all fear,
Hang in the woe of yon trembling tear;
And all the will, the valor, the power,
That grapple and hold the adverse hour,
Are throned like kings on yon fearless brow;
And the vassal flesh shall cower and bow,
As nature bows unto nature's laws!" —

Here Anselm's speech made a sudden pause.
Lost in the grand passion at his heart,
With flashing eyes, and lips wide apart —
As one whose full subject overbore,
In torrents, the power to utter more —
He stood all trembling. Like heavy clouds
Moved by one wind, the friars in crowds
Gloomily under their portal swam,
In half-voice chanting a vesper psalm;
And the priests were standing there alone
With night, the Christ, and four stars that shone —
Brighter and brighter as daylight fled —
Strangely together, just overhead.

THE SONG OF THE EARTH.

PRELUDE.

CHORUS OF PLANETS.

Hark to our voices, O mother of nations!
Why art thou dim when thy sisters are radiant?
Why veil'st thy face in a mantle of vapor,
Gliding obscure through the depths of the night?
Wake from thy lethargy! Hear'st thou our music,
Harmonious, that reaches the confines of space?
Join in our chorus, join in our jubilee,
Make the day pine with thy far-piercing melody—
Pine that his kingdom of blue sky and sunshine
Never reëchoes such marvellous tones.
No, thou art silent, O mystical sister,
Silent and proud that thou bear'st on thy bosom
The wonderful freight of the God-lighted soul.—
We hear thee, we hear thee, beneath thy thick
mantle,
The war of the winds through thy leaf-laden forests,
And round aisles of thy pillared and hill-piercing
Caverns sonorous; hear the dread avalanche
Torn from its quivering mountainous summit,

Ribbèd with massy rocks, crested with pine-trees,
Thundering enormous upon thy fair valleys;
Hear the dull roar of thy mist-spouting cataracts;
Hear the faint plash of thy salt seething billows,
Lifting their heads multitudinous, or shoreward
Climbing the cliffs that o'erhang them with trembling,
And tossing their spray in exultant defiance
Over the weed-bearded guardians of ocean.
Sister, we listen; thy strains are enlinking,
Melodiously blending to ravishing harmony;
Clouds are departing, we see thee, we yearn to thee,
Noblest of planets, creation's full glory!
Bending we hearken, thou mother of nations,
Hark to the sky-rending voice of humanity!

SONG OF THE EARTH.

O vex me not, ye ever-burning planets;
Nor sister call me, ye who me afflict.
I am unlike ye; ye may revelling sing,
Careless and joyful, roaming sunlit ether,
Urged with but one emotion, chaunting still
Through lapsing time the purpose of your birth,
Each with a several passion; but to me
Are mixed emotions, vast extremes of feeling—
Now verdant in the fruitful smile of heaven,
Now waste and blackened in the scowl of hell.
Ye know me not, nor can ye sympathize
With one like me, for wisdom is not yours.
Ye sing for joy; but wisdom slowly comes
From the close whispers of o'erburdened pain.
I am alone in all the universe!
To me is pain; I can distinguish sin;
But ye with constant though unweeting glance
Rain good or ill, and smile alike at both,
Nor understand the mystery of your natures.
To me is wisdom—wisdom bought with woe,
Ages on ages passed, when first I strayed,
With haughty scorn and self-reliant pride,
From purity and God. For once like you
God spoke me face to face, me soulless led
From joy to joy; yet He was mystical—
Too obvious for thought—I knew Him not.

But now, through sin, I understand like Him
The heart of things, the steep descents of guilt,
And the high pinnacles of heaven-lit virtue.
Bend down, ye stars, bend from your silver thrones,
Ye joyful wanderers of ether bright;
For I, soul-bearer of the universe,
Would teach your ignorance with the lips of song!

O Mercury, hot planet, burying deep
Thy forehead in the sunlight, list to me!
I groan beneath thy influence. Thou dost urge
The myriad hands of labor, and with toil
Dost mar my features; day by day dost work
Thy steady changes on my ancient face,
Till all the host of heaven blank wonder look,
Nor know the fresh, primeval moulded form
That rose from chaos, like the Aphrodite,
Smiling through dews upon the first morn's sun.
The leaf-crowned mountain's brows thou hurlest down
Into the dusty valley, and dost still
The free wild singing of the cleaving streams
To murmurs dying lazily within
The knotted roots of pool-engendered lilies,
That sluggish nod above the slimy dams.
All day the axe I hear rending through trunks,
Moss-grown and reverend, of clustered oaks;
All day the circling scythe sweeps off
The ruddy bloom of vain-aspiring fields,
Clipping to stubbles grim the vernal flowers.
Thou portionest my meadows, and dost make
Each fruitful slope a spot for sweaty toil.
Thou tearest up my bosom; far within
My golden veins the grimèd miner's pick

Startles the babbling echoes. Ancient rocks,
My hardy bones, are rent with nitrous fire,
To rear the marts, to bridge the leaping streams,
Or to usurp the ocean's olden right,
That selfish trade may dry-shod walk to power.
The very ocean, grim, implacable,
Thou loadest with the white-winged fleets of commerce,
Crossing, like wheeling birds, each other's tracks;
Until the burdened giant, restless grown,
Bounds from his sleep, and in the stooping clouds
Nods his white head, while splintered navies melt
To scattered fragments in his sullen froth.
Malignant star, I feel thy wicked power;
My children's busy thoughts are full of thee:
Thou 'st chilled the loving spirit in their hearts,
And on their lips hast placed the selfish finger —
They dare not know each other. All that is,
All that God blessed my teeming bosom with,
Is priced, and bartered; ay, the very worth
Of man himself is weighed with senseless gold —
Therefore I hate thee, bright-browed wanderer!

Daughter of the sober twilight,
Lustrous planet, ever hanging
In the mottled mists that welcome
Coming morning, or at evening
Peeping through the ruddy banners
Of the clouds that wave a parting,
From their high aërial summits,
To the blazing god of day —
'T is for thee I raise my pæan,
Steady-beaming VENUS, kindler,
In the stubborn hearts of mortals,

Of the sole surviving passion
That enlinks a lost existence
With the dull and ruthless present.
Far adown the brightening future,
Prophetess, I see thee glancing —
See thee still amid the twilight
Of the ages rolling onward,
Promising to heart-sick mortals
Triumph of thy gracious kingdom;
When the hand of power shall weaken,
And the wronger right the wrongéd,
And the pure, primeval Eden
Shall again o'erspread with blossoms
Sunny hill and shady valley.
'T is to thee my piny mountains
Wave aloft their rustling branches;
'T is to thee my opening flowrets
Send on high their luscious odors;
'T is to thee my leaping fountains
Prattle through their misty breathings,
And the bass of solemn ocean
Chimes accordant in the chorus.
Every fireside is thy altar
Streaming up its holy incense;
Every mated pair of mortals,
Happily linked, are priest and priestess,
Pouring to thee full libations
From their over-brimming spirits.
Clash the loud-resounding cymbals,
Light the rosy torch of Hymen,
Bands of white-robed youths and maidens
Whirl aloft the votive myrtle!
Raise the choral hymn to VENUS —

Young-eyed VENUS, ever youthful,
Ever on true hearts bestowing
Pleasures new that never pall!
Brightest link 'tween man and heaven,
Soul of virtue, life of goodness,
Cheering light in pain and sorrow,
Pole-star to the struggling voyager
Wrecked on life's relentless billows,
Fair reward of trampled sainthood,
Beaming from the throne Eternal
Lonely hope to sinful mankind—
Still among the mists of morning,
Still among the clouds of evening,
While the years drive ever onward,
Hang thy crescent lamp of promise,
VENUS, blazing star of Love!

O MARS, wide heaven is shuddering at the stride
Of thy mailed foot, most terrible of planets!
I see thee struggling with thy brazen front
To look a glory from amid the crust
Of guilty blood that dims thy haughty face;
The curse of crime is on thee. Look, behold!

See where thy frenzied votaries march
Hark to the brazen blare of the bugle,
Hark to the rattling clatter of the drums,
The measured tread of the steel-clad footmen!
Hark to the laboring horses' breath,
Painfully tugging the harnessed cannon;
The shrill, sharp clink of the warrior's swords,
As their chargers bound when the trumpets sound
Their alarums through the echoing mountains!

See the flashing of pennons and scarfs,
Shaming the gorgeous blazon of evening,
Rising and falling 'mid snowy plumes
That dance like foam on the crested billows!
Bright is the glitter of burnished steel,
Stirring the clamor of martial music,
The clank of arms has a witchery
That wakes the blood in a youthful bosom.
And who could tell from this pleasant show,
That flaunts in the sun like a May-day festal,
For what horrid rites are the silken flags,
For what horrid use are the gleaming sabres,
What change shall mar, when the battles join
This marshalled pageant of shallow glory?
For then the gilded flags shall be rent,
The sabres rust with the blood of foemen,
And the courteous knight shall howl like a wolf,
When he scents the gory steam of battle.

The orphan's curse is on thee, and the tears
Of widowed matrons plead a fearful cause;
Each thing my bosom bears, which thou hast touched,
Is loud against thee. Flowers and trampled grass,
And the long line of waste and barren fields,
Erewhile o'erflowing with a sea of sweets,
Look up all helpless to the pitying heavens,
Showing thy bloody footprints in their wounds,
And shrieking through their gaunt and leafless trees,
That stand with imprecating arms outspread,
They fiercely curse thee with their desolation.
Each cheerless hearth-stone in the home of man,
Where ruin grins, and rubs his bony palms,
Demands its lost possessor. Thou hast hurled

Man's placid reason from its rightful throne,
And in its place reared savage force, to clip
Debate and doubt with murder. Therefore, MARS,
I sicken in thy angry glance, and loathe
The dull red glitter of thy bloody spear.

I know thy look, majestic JUPITER;
I see thee moving through the stars of heaven
Girt with thy train of ministering satellites.
Proud planet, I confess thy influence:
My heart grows big with gazing in thy face;
Unwonted power pervades my eager frame;
My bulk aspiring towers above itself,
And restless pants to rush on acts sublime,
At which the wondering stars might stand agaze,
And the whole universe from end to end,
Conscious of me, should tremble to its core.
Spirit heroical, imperious passion,
That sharply sets the pliant face of youth,
That blinds the shrinking eyes of pallid fear,
And plants the lion's heart in modest breasts —
I know that thou hast led, with regal port,
The potent spirits of humanity
Before the van of niggard time, and borne,
With strides gigantic, man's advancing race
From power to power; till, like a host of gods,
They mock my elements, and drag the secrets
Of my mysterious forces up to light,
Giving them bounds determinate and strait,
And of their natures, multiform and huge,
Talking to children in familiar way.
The hero's sword, the poet's golden string,
The tome-illumining taper of the sage,

Flash by thy influence ; from thee alone,
Ambitious planet, comes the marvellous power
That in a cherub's glowing form can veil
A heart as cold as Iceland, and exalt
To deity the demon selfishness.
O planet, mingle with thy chilling rays,
That stream inspiring to the hero's soul,
One beam of love for vast humanity,
And thou art godlike. Must it ever be,
That brightest flowers of action and idea
Spring from the same dark soil of selfish lust?
Must man receive the calculated gifts
Of shrewd ambition's self-exalting hand,
And blindly glorify an act at which
The host of heaven grow red with thoughtful shame?
Shall knowledge hasten with her sunny face,
And weeping virtue lag upon the path?
Shall man exultant boast advance of power,
Nor see arise, at every onward stride,
New forms of sin to shadow every truth?
Roll on, roll on, in self-supported pride,
Prodigious influence of the hero's soul ;
I feel thy strength, and tremble in thy glare!

O, many-ringéd SATURN, turn away
The chilling terrors of thy baleful glance!
Thy gloomy look is piercing to my heart—
I wither in thy power! My springs dry up,
And shrink in horror to their rocky beds ;
The brooks, that whispered to the lily-bells
All day the glory of their mountain homes,
And kissed the dimples of the wanton rose,
At the deed blushing to their pebbly strands,

Cease their sweet merriment, and glide afraid
Beneath the shelter of the twisted sedge.
The opening bud shrinks back upon its shell,
As if the north had puffed his frozen breath
Full in its face. The billowing grain, and grass
Rippling with windy furrows, stand becalmed ;
Nor through their roots, nor in their tiny veins,
Bestirs the fruitful sap. The very trees,
Broad, hardy sons of crags and sterile plains,
That roared defiance to the winter's shout,
And battled sternly through his cutting sleet,
Droop in their myriad leaves ; while nightly birds,
That piped their shrilling treble to the moon,
Hang silent from the boughs, and peer around,
Awed by mysterious sympathy. From thee,
From thee, dull planet, comes this lethargy
That numbs in 'mid career meek nature's power,
And stills the prattle of her plumèd train.
O icy Saturn, proud in ignorance,
Father of sloth, dark deadening influence,
That dims the eye to all that 's beautiful,
And twists the haughty lip with killing scorn
For love and holiness — from thee alone
Springs the cold, crushing power that presses down
The infinite in man. — From thee, dull star,
The cautious fear that checks the glowing heart,
With sympathetic love, world-wide, o'erfreighted,
And sends it panting back upon itself,
To murmur in its narrow hermitage.
The boldest hero staggers in thy frown,
And drops his half-formed projects all aghast ;
The poet shrinks before thy phantom glare,
Ere the first echo greets his timid song ;

The startled sage amid the embers hurls
The gathered wisdom of a fruitful life.
O, who may know from what bright pinnacles
The mounting soul might look on coming time,
Had all the marvellous thoughts of genius —
Blasted to nothingness by thy cold sneer —
Burst through the bud and blossomed into fruit?
Benumbing planet, on our system's skirt,
Whirl from thy sphere, and round some lonely sun,
Within whose light no souls their ordeal pass,
Circle and frown amid thy frozen belts;
For I am sick of thee, and stately man
Shrinks to a pigmy in thy fearful stare!

FINALE.

CHORUS OF STARS.

Heir of eternity, mother of souls,
Let not thy knowledge betray thee to folly!
Knowledge is proud, self-sufficient, and lone,
Trusting, unguided, its steps in the darkness.
Thine is the learning that mankind may win,
Gleaned in the pathway between joy and sorrow;
Ours is the wisdom that hallows the child,
Fresh from the touch of his awful Creator,
Dropped, like a star, on thy shadowy realm,
Falling in splendor, but falling to darken.
Ours is the simple religion of faith,
The wisdom of trust in God who o'errules us;
Thine is the complex misgivings of thought,
Wrested to form by imperious reason.
We are forever pursuing the light;
Thou art forever astray in the darkness.
Knowledge is restless, imperfect, and sad;
Faith is serene, and completed, and joyful.
Chide not the planets that rule o'er thy ways;
They are God's creatures; nor, proud in thy reason,
Vaunt that thou knowest His counsels and Him.—
Boaster, though sitting in midst of the glory,
Thou couldst not fathom the least of His thoughts.
Bow in humility, bow thy proud forehead,
Circle thy form in a mantle of clouds,

Hide from the glittering cohorts of evening,
Wheeling in purity, singing in chorus;
Howl in the depths of thy lone, barren mountains,
Restlessly moan on the deserts of ocean,
Wail o'er thy fall in the desolate forests,
Lost star of paradise, straying alone!

July, 1848.

THE VISION OF THE GOBLET.

Evoe Bacche! wine hath seized my soul;
  The fury of the jolly god is on!
Reach me the mighty ancient bowl:
    Fill till the goblet weep,
    Fill till the rushing current sweep
  The dull, cold present to oblivion!
Now swing amain the mystic beaker tall,
  And still to Bacchus breathe the potent spell;
Rouse the red-visaged god from slumbers deep
  In green Arcadian dell!
Swing till the ruby breakers rise and fall,
Swing till the coursing bubbles leap
Above their crystal wall!

What gleams beneath the purple flood,
  Far down upon the nether rim,
Glowing amid the vine's rich blood
  As through a sunset's misty film?
'T is Attica, mild Attica, that sleeps
  Embayed by heaven among her vine-grown hills;
Mantled with flowers and glossy grass she lies,
  Smiling in all her rills;
Palace and temple-crowned she keeps
Her stately slumber 'neath the evening skies;

While Venus, brooding in a feathery cloud,
  As in her nest the silver-breasted dove,
Peeps now and then above her dusky shroud
  Upon the land of love.

Hark! the wine-waves, dashing, splashing,
Seem bacchantian cymbals clashing
    To the rumbling drum,
And the shivering flutes' shrill singing,
And the jingling tabors' ringing;
While, anon, the hurly dying,
Syrinx softly breathes her sighing
    From the warbling reed.
  Caught in the Satyr's wily snare,
What throngs across the valley come;
As whirling in the eddying stream
Of music to the hills they speed,
While upturned Attic foreheads gleam
  Amid their billowing hair!
Reeling, staggering, on they fly,
Wine in the blood and dizzy eye,
Wine in every sinew burning,
Onward still its minions spurning
Over hill, through lushy meadow,
Through the forest's glooming shadow,
Hither, thither, without caring
Where their guideless feet are bearing.

Tossing aloft, with nods of drunken cheer,
Mark old Silenus on his ass appear;
  Plashed is his hoary beard with purple wine,
Daggled his silver locks, his reeking brows
  Crowned with the ivy and the twisted vine.

Mark how the dotard leers,
As through the maids he steers,
And tries to summon love within his filmy eyne!
Thick with the luscious grape
His mumbled words escape,
The barren echoes of his youthful vows.

Lo! full-eyed Bacchus from triumphant war,
Rich with the trophied Orient's boast,
Goads through the crowd his flaming Indian car
Before the Satyr host,
That roaring straggle in their master's rear,
Twirling the ivied thyrsus as they bound,
And dance grotesque, and mingled laugh and jeer,
And cloven foot-falls shake the springing ground.

Around the hairy rout, with streaming hands,
Athena's maidens whirl the dripping urn;
Their floating vestures, loosed from jealous bands,
Half hide, half show, what charms beneath them burn.
There mellow Pan upon the Attic ear,
Framed with a dainty sense for melody,
Pours music from his pipe of knotted reeds,
Lifting the ravished soul to that high sphere
Where joy and pain contend for mastery.

Now tittering glee the grinning Satyr breeds,
Now flings the heart in tearful depths of woe,
Now big-eyed fear the shrinking crowd appalls,
Now to the blithesome dance the music calls;
Then with full power, and long, triumphant flow

Of swelling notes that shake the rooted soul,
And rise and fall with ocean's measured roll,
He lifts to Bacchus his resounding lay;
Tabor and drum confess the potent sway,
  And join their muffled notes.
With nodding heads and brandished arms,
  And flashing eyes, and swelling throats,
  That heave with song's advancing tides,
The crowd obeys the cunning master's charms.
  A murmured hum athwart the listeners glides,
While still the pipes their pealing notes prolong,
  Piercing the heavens with wild exultant shout,
Till, maddened by fierce harmony, the throng
  From end to end in ecstasy bursts out,
And thus to Bacchus pours its choral song.

Joy, joy, with Bacchus and his Satyr train
  In triumph throbs our merry Grecian earth!
Joy, joy, the golden time has come again,
  A god shall bless the vine's illustrious birth!
      Io, io, Bacche!

O breezes, speed across the mellow lands,
  And bear his coming to the joyous vine;
Make all the vineyards wave their leafy hands
  Upon the hills, to greet this pomp divine!
      Io, io, Bacche!

O peaceful triumph, victory without tear,
  Or human cry, or drop of conquered blood,
Save dew-beads bright, that on the vine appear,
  The choral shouts, the trampled grape's red flood!
      Io, io, Bacche!

Shout, Hellas, shout! the lord of joy is come,
  Bearing the mortal Lethe in his hands,
To make the wailing lips of sorrow dumb,
  To bind sad memory's eyes with rosy bands.
      Io, io, Bacche!

Shout, Hellas, shout! he bears the soul of love,
  Within each glowing drop Promethean fire;
The coldest maids beneath its power shall move,
  And bashful youths be bold with hot desire.
      Io, io, Bacche!

Long may the ivy deck thy sculptured brows,
  Long may the goat upon thy altars bleed,
Long may thy temples hear our tuneful vows,
  Chiming accordant to the vocal reed.
      Io, io, Bacche!

Long may the hills and nodding forests move,
  Responsive echoing thy festal drum,
Grief-scattering Bacchus, twice-born son of Jove—
  Our hearts are singing, let our lips be dumb.
      Io, io, Bacche!

ODE TO ENGLAND.

O! DAYS of shame! O! days of woe!
    Of helpless shame, of helpless woe!
The times reveal thy nakedness,
Thy utter weakness, deep distress.
There is no help in all the land;
    Thy eyes may wander to and fro,
Yet find no succor. Every hand
    Has weighed the guinea, poised the gold,
    Chaffered and bargained, bought and sold,
    Until the sinews, framed for war,
    Can grasp the sword and shield no more.
Their trembling palms are stretched to thee;
    Purses are offered, heaping hoards —
The plunder of the land and sea —
Are proffered, all too eagerly,
    But thou must look abroad for swords.

These are the gods ye trusted in;
For these ye crept from sin to sin;
    Made honor cheap, made station dear,
Made wealth a lord, made truth a drudge,
Made venal interest the sole judge
    Of principles as high and clear
        As heaven itself.
        With glittering pelf

Ye gilt the coward, knave, and fool,
Meted the earth out with a rule
Of gold, weighed nations in your golden scales!
    And, surely, this law never fails —
What else may change, this law stands fast —
    "The golden standard is the thing
    To which the beggar, lord, and king,
And all that 's earthly, come at last."
O, mighty gods! O, noble trust!
    They are your all; ye cannot look
    Back to the faith ye once forsook;
The past is dry and worthless dust;
    Gold, gold is all! Ye cannot fill
    Your brains with legends vague and thin;
Hang up your arms amidst their rust:
    These are the gods ye trusted in;
    They can deliver you, and will!

O! bitter waking! mocking dream!
    The gilt has worn away,
    The idols are but clay,
Their pride is overthrown, their glories only seem!
    The land is full of fear,
    Men pale at what they hear,
The widowed matrons sob, the orphaned children
        cry;
There 's desolation everywhere, there 's not one
        comfort nigh!
    The nations stand agaze,
    In dubious amaze,
  To see Britannia's threatening form,
That loomed gigantic mid the splendid haze
    Through which they saw her tower —
    As, at the morning hour,

The spectral figure strides across her misty hills —
  Shrink to a pigmy when the storm
    Rends the delusive cloud,
    And shows her weak and bowed,
A feeble crone that hides for shelter from her ills.

O, mother of our race, can nothing break
    This leaden apathy of thine?
    Think of the long and glorious line
Of heroes who beside the Stygian lake
    Hearken for news from thee!
    Apart their forms I see,
With muffled heads and tristful faces bowed —
Heads once so high, faces so calm and proud!
  The Norman fire burns low
    In William's haughty heart;
    The mirth has passed away
  From Cœur de Lion's ample brow;
    In sorrowful dismay
The warlike Edwards and the Henrys stand,
    Stung with a shameful smart;
While the eighth Harry, with his close-clutched hand,
Smothers the passion in his ireful soul;
    Or his fierce eye-balls roll
Where his bold daughter beats her sharp foot-tip,
    And gnaws her quivering lip.
While the stern, crownless king, who strode between
Father and son, and put them both aside,
    With straight terrific glare,
    As a lion from his lair,
Asks with his eyes such questions keen
As his crowned brothers neither dare
      To answer nor abide.

How shall he make reply,
The shadow that draws nigh,
The latest comer, the great Duke,
Whose patient valor, blow by blow,
Wrought at a Titan's overthrow,
And gave his pride its first and last rebuke?
What shall he say when this heroic band
Catch at his welcome hand,
And trembling, half in fear,
Half in their eagerness to hear,
"What of our England?" ask?
Ah! shameful, shameful task!
To tell to souls like these
Of her languid golden ease,
Of her tame, dull history!
How she frowns upon the free,
How she ogles tyranny;
How with despots she coquets;
How she swears, and then forgets;
How she plays at fast and loose
With right and gross abuse;
How she fawns upon her foes,
And lowers upon her friends;
Growing weaker, day by day,
In her mean and crooked way,
Piling woes upon her woes,
As tottering she goes
Down the path where falsehood ends.
Methinks I see the awful brow
Of Cromwell wrinkle at the tale forlorn,
See the hot flushes on his forehead glow,
Hear his low growl of scorn!
Is this the realm these souls bequeathed to you,

That, with all its many faults,
Its hasty strides and tardy halts,
  To the truth was ever true?
O! shame not the noble dead,
Who through storm and slaughter led,
With toil, and care, and pain,
Winning glory, grain by grain,
Till no land that history knows
With such unutterable splendor glows!

Awake! the spirit yet survives
  To baffle fate and conquer foes!
If not among your lords it lives,
Your chartered governors, if they
Have not the power to lead, away,
  Away with lords! and give the men
Whom nature gives the right to sway,
Who love their country with a fire
That, for her darkness, burns the higher —
  Give these the rule! Abase your ken,
Look downward to your heart for those
In whom your ancient life-blood flows,
  And let their souls aspire!
Somewhere, I trust in God, remain,
Untainted by the golden stain,
  Men worthy of an English sire;
Bold men, who dare, in wrong's despite,
Speak truth, and strike a blow for right;
Men who have ever put their trust
  Neither in rank nor gold,
  Nor aught that 's bought and sold,
But in high aims, and God the just!

Seek through the land,
On every hand,
Rear up the strong, the feeble lop ;
Laugh at the star and civic fur,
The blazoned shield and gartered knee —
The gewgaws of man's infancy ;
And if the search be vain,
Give it not o'er too suddenly —
I swear the soul still lives in thee ! —
Down to thy lowest atoms drop,
Down to the very dregs, and stir
The People to the top !

March, 1855.

THE QUEEN'S TOUCH.

AN INCIDENT IN THE EARLY LIFE OF H. C. M. ISABEL II.

On a Good Friday, as it once befell,
The gentle lady, royal Isabel,
Stepped from her palace with a fair array
Of Spanish nobles. Plumes, and banners gay,
And lines of burnished halberds made a lane,
Through which the sovereign and her glittering train
Swept like a gorgeous cloud across the face
Of some bright sunset. Even was her pace,
And a deep calm dwelt in her steady eyes,
August with queenly power, and counsel wise
To sway a realm; yet round her playful lip
The child still lingered, and a smile would slip,
Like a stray sunbeam o'er a dimpled rose,
When the crowd shouted, or an eager close
Of loyal people broke the martial line,
And stayed her progress. One could scarce incline
Whether to call her queen or child; so bright
And innocent a spirit lit the might
Of awful sovereignty, as on she went
Bearing the diadem of Charles unbent —
Ay, smiling under it, as if the weight
Of empery heaven lightened to the date
Of her few years. For surely heaven may bend
In mercy to the merciful, and lend

Its strength to her who for the weak can feel,
As gracious Isabel. The traitor's steel;
The storms that broke around her princely head,
When they who should have shielded her, instead
Of muttering plots and tempting her with guile,
Turned from her side; the anarchy the while
That rent her kingdom, and made Spain's great throne
Rock as if startled by the earthquake's groan —
All these, and more, she dared, and could withstand,
Because God led her by the trusting hand,
And showed the mercy she has ever shown.

You who look doubtfully, with sighs or sneers,
Citing the history of her after years,
Remember this — and let the thought atone
For many a weakness, many an error done
Out of the lessons of her early days,
When all conspired to lead her evil ways —
Her faults were taught, her virtues are her own.

Across the flower-strewn way she slowly walked,
Wondering at many things; anon, she talked
To the grave minister who moved beside
His youthful mistress with a haughty stride
Of strained decorum. Curiously she asked
Of this and that; and much the lord was tasked
To answer all her questions, which did flow
Like ripples on the shore, — ere one could go
Another leaped above it. For her state
Was new to her, and not a rustic's mate
Among the throng more marvelled at the sight,
Nor drew from it a more sincere delight,

Than royal Isabel. More pleased she seemed
At the hoarse shouts, and at the love that beamed
From the tanned faces of the common crowd,
Than at the courtly whispers, or the proud
Looks of fixed dignity. The beggar's rags
Were dearer to her than the silken flags
That coiled above her; and his *vivas* drowned
The swell of music, and the ringing sound
Of the saluting steel. And once she turned
Full on a lord, while every feature burned
With a new thought; and, pointing unto one
Ill clad, indeed, yet with a face o'errun
With honest love, said, laughing at the close,
"Why wear you purple, and he ragged clothes?"
Much the Don talked about society,
And laws, and customs, and how all agree
To make one world. Although he talked the thing
Clear to himself, and shaped a pretty ring
Of binding words, no answering look he caught
From the Queen's eyes; and when he gravely sought
To draw a word of sympathetic cheer,
Upon her cheek he marked a long, bright tear:
So he passed on in silence, she in thought.

At length the minster's arch above them bent,
And through its gloom the shining courtiers went,
Making strange light within that dusky pile.
And all along the borders of the aisle
Old chiefs and heroes in white grandeur slept
Upon the tombs. Their marble faces kept
A settled quiet, as they upward gazed
Upon their arms and spoils, above them raised,

Along the rafters, each in solemn ward.
Some with their hands upon a sculptured sword,
Some clasped in prayer, and others, full of grace,
Crossed on their breasts. The courtiers' noisy pace
Broke the long silence with a painful jar,
Unmeet and alien. Trophies of old war —
Pennons blood-stained, torn flags, and banners, fell
And rose again, o'er royal Isabel:
As if the soul that fired her ancient strain
Were roused, and all the chivalry of Spain
Breathed in their hollow sepulchres beneath,
And waved the banners with a mighty breath.
Saint George's cross was shaken as with dread;
The lilied silk of France shrank, as when spread
O'er Pavia's bloody field; a second shame
Thrilled the Dutch standards, as if Alva's name
Were heard among them; the horse-tails of the Moor
Streamed to the wind, as when they fled before
The furious Cid; spears glittered, swords were stirred
Within their scabbards; one in fancy heard
The trumpets murmur, and a warlike peal
Through the closed casques — "Saint Jago for Castile!"
If she stepped on more proudly, it was not
That Isabel herself was proud. The spot
Of crimson on her forehead was a gleam
Of the old glory, a reflected beam
Cast from the trophies, that brought back the day
When her sires' sceptre swept the world. A ray
Of keenest sunshine through the aisles shot down,
And blazed amid the jewels of her crown,
Like a saint's aureole, as the Queen drew nigh
The holy altar. With a gentle sigh

The organ whispered through the incense-smoke,
Trilling above her, like a lark awoke
Some misty morning, till she touched the stair
Of the high altar; when, with sudden blare,
In one grand storm of music burst the whole
Torrent of sound o'erhead, and roll on roll
Crashed through the building, from its hundred throats
Of shivering metal thundering forth the notes.
Radiant with sunlight, wrapt in holy sound
And fragrant vapors, that in spirals wound
Up through the pillars of the choir, the Queen
Paused, as in doubt, before a sable screen
Upon the altar, and a courtier led,
By a sweet look, beside her — "Sir," she said,
"Why are those papers on the altar pall?"
"They hold the names, your majesty, of all
Condemned to death by law. The one you touch
Shall surely live. — The ancient rite is such."
Without a pause to weigh it, the great thought
Burst from her nature, as she sprang and caught,
Hither and thither, at each fatal scrawl —
Gathered the whole — and, ere she let them fall,
A gracious look to the rapt court she gave,
And softly said, "See, señors, see, I have
A little hand, but I can touch them all!"

I HAVE a cottage where the sunbeams lurk,
Peeping around its gables all day long,
Brimming the butter-cups until they drip
With molten gold, like o'ercharged crucibles.
Here, wondering why the morning-glories close
Their crumpled edges ere the dew is dry,
Great lilies stand, and stretch their languid buds
In the full blaze of noon, until its heat
Has pierced them to their centres. Here the rose
Is larger, redder, sweeter, longer-lived,
Less thorny, than the rose of other lands.

I have a cottage where the south wind comes,
Cool from the spicy pines, or with a breath
Of the mid ocean salt upon its lips,
And a low, lulling, dreamy sound of waves,
To breathe upon me, as I lie along
On my white violets, marvelling at the bees
That toil but to be plundered, or the mart
Of striving men, whose bells I sometimes hear
When they will toss their brazen throats at heaven,
And howl to vex me. But the town is far;
And all its noises, ere they trouble me,
Must take a convoy of the scented breeze,
And climb the hills, and cross the bloomy dales,
And catch a whisper in the swaying grain,
And bear unfaithful echoes from the wood,

And mix with birds, and streams, and fluttering
leaves,
And an old ballad which the shepherd hums,
Straying in thought behind his browsing flock.

I have a cottage where the wild bee comes
To hug the thyme, and woo its dainties forth;
Where humming-birds, plashed with the rainbow's
dies,
Poise on their whirring wings before the door,
And drain my honeysuckles at a draught.
Ah, giddy sensualist, how thy blazing throat
Flashes and throbs, while thou dost pillage me
Of all my virgin flowers! And then, away —
What eye may follow! But yon constant robin:
Spring, summer, winter, still the same clear song
At morn and eve, still the contented hop,
And low sly whistle, when the crumbs are thrown:
Yet he is jealous of my tawny thrush,
And drives him off, ere a faint symphony
Ushers the carol warming in his breast.

I have a cottage where the winter winds
Wreck their rude passions on the neighboring hills,
And crawl down, shattered by the edgéd rocks,
To hide themselves among the stalactites,
That roof my frosty cave, against midsummer;
Or in the bosom of the stream they creep,
Numbing the gurgling current till it lies
Stark, frozen, lifeless, silent as the moon;
Or wrestle with the cataracts; or glide,
Rustling close down, among the crisp dead grass,

To chase the awkward rabbits from their haunts;
Or beat my roof with its own sheltering boughs; —
Yet never daunt me! For my flaming logs
Pour up the chimney a defiant roar,
While Shakspeare and a flask of southern wine,
Brown with the tan of Spain, or red Bordeaux,
Charm me until the crocus says to me,
In its own way, "Come forth; I've brought the spring!"

I have a cottage where the brook runs by,
Making faint music from the rugged stones
O'er which it slides; and at the height of Prime,
When snows are melting on the misty hills
That front the south, this brook comes stealing up
To wash my door-stone. Oft it bears along,
Sad sight, a funeral of primroses —
Washed from the treacherous bank to which they grew
With too fond faith — all trooping one by one,
With nodding heads in seemly order ranged,
Down its dull current towards the endless sea.
O, brook, bear me, with such a holy calm,
To the vast ocean that awaits for me,
And I know one whose mournful melody
Shall make your name immortal as my love.

I have a cottage in the cloven hills;
Through yonder peaks the flow of sunlight comes,
Dragging its sluggish tide across the path
Of the reluctant stars which silently
Are buried in it. Through yon western gap
Day ebbs away, leaving a margin round,

Of sky and cloud, drowned in its sinking flood,
Till Venus shimmers through the rising blue,
And lights her sisters up. Here lie the moonbeams,
Hour after hour, becalmed in the still trees;
Or on the weltering leaves of the young grass
Rest half asleep, rocked by some errant wind.
Here are more little stars, on winter nights,
Than sages reckon in their heavenly charts;
For the brain wanders, and the dizzy eye
Aches at their sum, and dulls, and winks with them.
The Northern Lights come down to greet me here,
Playing fantastic tricks, above my head,
With their long tongues of fire, that dart and catch,
From point to point, across the firmament,
As if the face of heaven were passing off
In low combustion; or the kindling night
Were slowly flaming to a fatal dawn,
Wide-spread and sunless as the day of doom.

I have a cottage cowering in the trees,
And seeming to shrink lower day by day.
Sometimes I fancy that the growing boughs
Have dwarfed my dwelling; but the solemn oaks,
That hang above my roof so lovingly,
They too have shrunk. I know not how it is:
For when my mother led me by the hand
Around our pale, it seemed a weary walk;
And then, as now, the sharp roof nestled there,
Among the trees, and they propped heaven. Alas!
Who leads me now around the bushy pale?
Who shows the birds' nests in the twilight leaves?
Who catches me within her fair round arms,
When autumn shakes the acorns on our roof

To startle me? I know not how it is:
The house has shrunk, perhaps, as our poor hearts,
When they both broke at parting, and mine closed
Upon a memory, shutting out the world
Like a sad anchorite. — Ah! that gusty morn!
But here she lived, here died, and so will I.

I have a cottage — murmur if ye will,
Ye men whose lips are prison-doors to thoughts
Born, with mysterious struggles, in the heart;
And, maidens, let your store of hoarded smiles
Break from their dimples, like the spreading rings
That skim a lake, when some stray blossom falls
Warm in its bosom. Ah, you cannot tell
Why violets choose not a neighboring bank,
Why cowslips blow upon the self-same bed,
Why year by year the swallow seeks one nest,
Why the brown wren rebuilds her hairy home.
O, sightless cavillers, you do not know
How deep roots strike, nor with what tender care
The soft down lining warms the nest within.
Think as you will, murmur and smile apace —
I have a cottage where my days shall close,
Calm as the setting of a feeble star.

ODE TO A MOUNTAIN OAK.

PROUD mountain giant, whose majestic face,
From thy high watch-tower on the steadfast rock,
Looks calmly o'er the trees that throng thy base,
How long hast thou withstood the tempest's shock?
How long hast thou looked down on yonder vale
Sleeping in sun before thee;
Or bent thy ruffled brow, to let the gale
Steer its white, drifting sails just o'er thee?

Strong link 'twixt vanished ages!
Thou hast a sage and reverend look;
As if life's struggle, through its varied stages,
Were stamped on thee, as in a book.
Thou hast no voice to tell what thou hast seen,
Save a low moaning in thy troubled leaves;
And canst but point thy scars, and shake thy head,
With solemn warning, in the sunbeam's sheen;
And show how Time the mightiest thing bereaves,
By the sere leaves that rot upon thy bed.

Type of long-suffering power!
Even in my gayest hour,
Thou 'dst still my tongue, and send my spirit far,
To wander in a labyrinth of thought;
For thou hast waged with Time unceasing war,
And out of pain hast strength and beauty brought.

Thou amidst storms and tempests hadst thy birth,
Upon these bleak and scantly-sheltering rocks,
Nor much save storm and wrath hast known on earth ;
Yet nobly hast thou bode the fiercest shocks
That Circumstance can pour on patient Worth.

I see thee springing, in the vernal time,
A sapling weak, from out the barren stone,
To dance with May upon the mountain peak ;
Pale leaves put forth to greet the genial clime,
And roots shot down life's sustenance to seek,
While mere existence was a joy alone —
O thou wert happy then !
On Summer's heat thy tinkling leaflets fed,
Each fibre toughened, and a little crown
Of green upon thy modest brow was spread,
To catch the rain, and shake it gently down.
But then came Autumn, when
Thy dry and tattered leaves fell dead ;
And sadly on the gale
Thou drop'dst them one by one —
Drop'dst them, with a low, sad wail,
On the cold, unfeeling stone.
Next Winter seized thee in his iron grasp,
And shook thy bruised and straining form ;
Or locked thee in his icicle's cold clasp,
And piled upon thy head the shorn cloud's snowy fleece.
Wert thou not joyful, in this bitter storm,
That the green honors, which erst decked thy head,
Sage Autumn's slow decay, had mildly shed ?

Else, with their weight, they 'd given thy ills increase,
And dragged thee helpless from thy uptorn bed.

Year after year, in kind or adverse fate,
Thy branches stretched, and thy young twigs put forth,
Nor changed thy nature with the season's date:
Whether thou wrestled'st with the gusty north,
Or beat the driving rain to glittering froth,
Or shook the snow-storm from thy arms of might,
Or drank the balmy dews on summer's night; —
Laughing in sunshine, writhing in the storm,
Yet wert thou still the same!
Summer spread forth thy towering form,
And Winter strengthened thy great frame.
Achieving thy destiny
On went'st thou sturdily,
Shaking thy green flags in triumph and jubilee!

From thy secure and sheltering branch
The wild bird pours her glad and fearless lay,
That, with the sunbeams, falls upon the vale,
Adding fresh brightness to the smile of day.
'Neath those broad boughs the youth has told love's tale;
And thou hast seen his hardy features blanch,
Heard his snared heart beat like a prisoned bird,
Fluttering with fear, before the fowler laid;
While his bold figure shook at every word —
The strong man trembling at a timid maid!
And thou hast smiled upon their children's play;
Seen them grow old, and gray, and pass away.

Heard the low prattle of the thoughtless child,
Age's cold wisdom, and the lessons mild
Which patient mothers to their offspring say;—
  Yet art thou still the same!
    Man may decay;
  Race after race may pass away;
The great may perish, and their very fame
    Rot day by day—
Rot noteless with their once inspired clay:
    Still, as at their birth,
Thou stretchest thy long arms above the earth—
  Type of unbending Will!
Type of majestic, self-sustaining Power!
Elate in sunshine, firm when tempests lower,
May thy calm strength my wavering spirit fill!
    O let me learn from thee,
    Thou proud and steadfast tree,
To bear unmurmuring what stern Time may send;
  Nor 'neath life's ruthless tempests bend:
    But calmly stand like thee,
    Though wrath and storm shake me,
Though vernal hopes in yellow Autumn end,
And, strong in Truth, work out my destiny.
  Type of long-suffering Power!
  Type of unbending Will!
  Strong in the tempest's hour,
  Bright when the storm is still;
Rising from every contest with an unbroken heart,
Strengthened by every struggle, emblem of might thou art!
Sign of what man can compass, spite of an adverse state,
Still, from thy rocky summit, teach us to war with Fate!

THE RIVER AND THE MAIDEN.

From the sunset flows the river,
  Melting all its waves in one;
Not a ripple, not a quiver,
On the flaming water, ever
  Poured from the descending sun.

Seeming like a pathway lately
  Radiant with an angel's tread;
And yon vessel, moving stately,
Is the heavenly one sedately
  Walking with his wings outspread.

What a quiet! Through the branches,
  Silently the orioles skip;
Not again the fish-hawk launches,
Silently his plumes he stanches,
  Silently the sedges drip.

Other sights, and loud commotion,
  Fill this tranquil stream by day;
With a solemn swaying motion,
Wave-worn ships forsake the ocean,
  Bound from countries leagues away;

Odorous with their eastern spices,
  Rich with gems of the Brazils,

Persian silks of quaint devices,
Nameless things of wondrous prices,
  Luscious wines from Spanish hills ;

Furs from the shy ermine riven,
  Ingots of Peruvian mould,
Where the deadly tropic levin
Crashes from the blazing heaven,
  Piercing earth with veins of gold.

But amid the sacred quiet
  Of this gentle evening-time,
Toil and sin have ceased their riot ;
One might judge the awful fiat
  Were removed from Adam's crime.

Holiest eve, thy light discloses
  Holiest things ; for through the shades
Mark I where my love reposes,
Sitting there, amid the roses,
  Like a queen amid her maids.

Through the foliage, green and golden,
  Round her head the sunbeams dart,
Haloing her like some saint olden ;
And a chapel calm is holden
  In the stillness of her heart.

Distant, yet I guess her singing ;
  Haply, some poor lay of mine,
Loud with drum and trumpet ringing,
Or of shameless goblets swinging
  In the tumult of the wine.

Wicked ballad! all unsuited
  To the genial season's calm,
Harsh, discordant, sin-polluted;—
Yet by her sweet voice transmuted
  Almost to a vesper psalm.

See, her steps are hither bending;
  This, our trysting-place, she seeks:
All her wealth is with her wending,
In the lights and shadows blending
  Round the dimples of her cheeks;

In the eyes that melt at sorrow,
  In the wisdom without wiles,
In the faith that will not borrow
From to-day fear of to-morrow,
  In a countless store of smiles;

In the heart that cannot flutter
  For a breath of flattery,
In the mouth that cannot utter
Halting lie or envious mutter—
  In her simple love for me.

Crowd yon river with your barges—
  All the navies of the main—
Till the loaded tide enlarges,
Till it bursts its wonted marges,
  Deluging the pleasant plain;

Freight them with the precious plunder
  Of the lands beyond the sea—
Pearls that make the diver wonder,
All the virgin silver under
  The great hills of Potosi;

All the real and fabled riches
 Of the haughty Persian Khan,
All the gold that so bewitches,
All the gorgeous broidered stitches
 Of the girls of Hindostan;

All the furs, the wines, the treasures,
 Were they at my bidding laid,
Ten times doubled in their measures,
Ten times doubled in their pleasures,
 I would rather have the maid!

VESTIGIA RETRORSUM.

There is a spot I call accursed,
  Because my thoughts forever wing
Back to its gloom, from which they burst,
  And settle on the loathsome thing.

The thick black pool, the waterfall,
  Swart crags that nurture noxious vines;
The long, unbending outer wall
  Made by the solid depth of pines;

The reptile weeds that crawl about
  The rotting shore; the glaring flowers,
Nauseous with odors, that give out
  No grace of heaven's baptizing showers;

The hollow roar that fills the scene —
  A sound caught up, and smothered in,
By the close pines which rise between
  The world and that unholy din.

Long ringéd serpents idly loll,
  With haughty eyes, that never wink,
Upon the oily pool, or roll
  In horrid sports around its brink.

All creatures that abhor the day
  Find harbor in the rocky lair;
And all the foulest birds of prey
  Light slowly down, and settle there.

The moving powers of air bewail
  This blotch upon earth's face allowed —
Moaned by the high o'erpassing gale,
  Wept over by the flying cloud;

Cut by the edgéd hail that pours
  With added wrath here, choked with snow;
Scathed by the thunder-cloud that roars
  Its bolts down, blow reëchoing blow.

Still it arises — rocks and trees,
  Pool, waterfall, and rank-grown sod —
Above my better memories,
  And frowns between me and my God.

This spot had once another look;
  Its sounds were as a choral psalm,
Ere sin's and sorrow's hands I took,
  And walked between them, palm in palm.

Ah! yes, her beauty gave the place
  A wondrous light; and my young rhyme,
Fervid with love's creative grace,
  Brought on the Spring before its time.

Yea, Summer came while May was young,
  And smiled to see the lovers meet,
And all her flowery censers swung
  Their perfumes round our trysting-seat.

Too soon the vernal bloom! too soon
  The year's maturer charms! their dust
Whirled 'twixt us and the harvest moon
  Ere Autumn blew his frosty gust.

She fell — O God! I know not how —
  Fell from her over-trust in me;
The flowers had turned to dust, and now
  Our love had turned to misery.

O fool! the promised fruit I sought
  Was ripening into sweetest use;
I snatched it ere its time, and caught
  Upon my lip but acrid juice.

Nature shrank from me all aghast,
  Men whispered as they passed my door,
The precious lights of life waned fast,
  And heaven seemed further than before.

I would have done her right. We met:
  I owned my crime, I urged her claim;
There was no ebb of love, and yet
  We turned aside with common shame.

We could not get our eyes to meet,
  We could not link our hands again;
I talked, but words had ceased to cheat;
  We parted — 'twas relief from pain.

Priest, vow, and ring, all things arrange —
  Shrewd brokers in our worldly mart —
I tell ye, these are poor exchange
  To offer for a broken heart.

When Winter heaped her grave with snow,
  What right had I to make my moans?
What right to hope a tear would flow,
  Or anger heaven with selfish groans?

The vanished joy, the void of love,
  The heart that nothing fills within,
The fear that dares not look above,
  Are relics of my early sin.

Better beside her shameful tomb
  This aching head for years had lain,
And o'er my mound the Winter's gloom
  Had snowed a mountain from the plain,

Than thus to live — a life in death,
  That courts no peace, and shuns no strife,
A slow, dull drawing of the breath —
  A being you cannot call life.

I wonder not the dell is cursed,
  Upon this world a hideous blot;
I only wonder earth ne'er burst,
  To swallow up that hateful spot.

The pool, the wood, the waterfall,
  The flowers, the cliffs, the gloom — my brain
Whirls with a picture of ye all —
  I rise, and curse ye all again!

A BALLAD OF SIR JOHN FRANKLIN.

The ice was here, the ice was there,
The ice was all around. — COLERIDGE.

O, WHITHER sail you, Sir John Franklin?
Cried a whaler in Baffin's Bay.
To know if between the land and the pole
I may find a broad sea-way.

I charge you back, Sir John Franklin,
As you would live and thrive;
For between the land and the frozen pole
No man may sail alive.

But lightly laughed the stout Sir John,
And spoke unto his men:
Half England is wrong, if he be right;
Bear off to westward then.

O, whither sail you, brave Englishman?
Cried the little Esquimaux.
Between your land and the polar star
My goodly vessels go.

Come down, if you would journey there,
The little Indian said;
And change your cloth for fur clothing,
Your vessel for a sled.

But lightly laughed the stout Sir John,
And the crew laughed with him too: —
A sailor to change from ship to sled,
I ween, were something new!

All through the long, long polar day,
The vessels westward sped;
And wherever the sail of Sir John was blown,
The ice gave way and fled.

Gave way with many a hollow groan,
And with many a surly roar,
But it murmured and threatened on every side,
And closed where he sailed before.

Ho! see ye not, my merry men,
The broad and open sea?
Bethink ye what the whaler said,
Think of the little Indian's sled!
The crew laughed out in glee.

Sir John, Sir John, 't is bitter cold,
The scud drives on the breeze,
The ice comes looming from the north,
The very sunbeams freeze.

Bright summer goes, dark winter comes —
We cannot rule the year;
But long ere summer's sun goes down,
On yonder sea we 'll steer.

The dripping icebergs dipped and rose,
And floundered down the gale;
The ships were staid, the yards were manned,
And furled the useless sail.

The summer's gone, the winter 's come —
We sail not on yonder sea :
Why sail we not, Sir John Franklin ? —
A silent man was he.

The summer goes, the winter comes —
We cannot rule the year :
I ween, we cannot rule the ways,
Sir John, wherein we 'd steer.

The cruel ice came floating on,
And closed beneath the lee,
Till the thickening waters dashed no more ;
'T was ice around, behind, before —
My God ! there is no sea !

What think you of the whaler now ?
What of the Esquimaux ?
A sled were better than a ship,
To cruise through ice and snow.

Down sank the baleful crimson sun,
The northern light came out,
And glared upon the ice-bound ships,
And shook its spears about.

The snow came down, storm breeding storm,
And on the decks was laid,
Till the weary sailor, sick at heart,
Sank down beside his spade.

Sir John, the night is black and long,
The hissing wind is bleak,
The hard, green ice as strong as death : —
I prithee, Captain, speak !

The night is neither bright nor short,
  The singing breeze is cold,
The ice is not so strong as hope —
  The heart of man is bold!

What hope can scale this icy wall,
  High over the main flag-staff?
Above the ridges the wolf and bear
Look down, with a patient, settled stare,
  Look down on us and laugh.

The summer went, the winter came —
  We could not rule the year;
But summer will melt the ice again,
And open a path to the sunny main,
  Whereon our ships shall steer.

The winter went, the summer went,
  The winter came around;
But the hard, green ice was strong as death,
And the voice of hope sank to a breath,
  Yet caught at every sound.

Hark! heard you not the noise of guns? —
  And there, and there, again?
'T is some uneasy iceberg's roar,
  As he turns in the frozen main.

Hurra! hurra! the Esquimaux
  Across the ice-fields steal:
God give them grace for their charity! —
  Ye pray for the silly seal.

Sir John, where are the English fields,
  And where are the English trees,
And where are the little English flowers
  That open in the breeze?

Be still, be still, my brave sailors!
  You shall see the fields again,
And smell the scent of the opening flowers,
  The grass, and the waving grain.

O! when shall I see my orphan child?
  My Mary waits for me.
O! when shall I see my old mother,
  And pray at her trembling knee?

Be still, be still, my brave sailors!
  Think not such thoughts again.
But a tear froze slowly on his cheek;
  He thought of Lady Jane.

Ah! bitter, bitter grows the cold,
  The ice grows more and more;
More settled stare the wolf and bear,
  More patient than before.

O! think you, good Sir John Franklin,
  We'll ever see the land?
'Twas cruel to send us here to starve,
  Without a helping hand.

'Twas cruel, Sir John, to send us here,
  So far from help or home,
To starve and freeze on this lonely sea:
I ween, the Lords of the Admiralty
  Would rather send than come.

O! whether we starve to death alone,
  Or sail to our own country,
We have done what man has never done—
The truth is founded, the secret won—
  We passed the Northern Sea!

THE SIEGE OF CABEZON.

"La justicia del rey Don Pedro."

Don Pedro before Cabezon
  A weary time had lain,
Through summer's heat, through winter's frost,
  Through sunshine and through rain.

Still Trastamara's rebel flag
  Flapped in the mountain gale,
And still the baffled monarch paced
  In ire the tented vale.

"Now, by my crown," Don Pedro swore,
  And clashed his armèd hand,
"I'd give my dearest year of life,
  Upon that rock to stand!

"I'd sprinkle all the path between
  This valley and yon crag,
With my best blood, to lay a hand
  Upon that vaunting flag!"

"As well Don Pedro might besiege
  The eagle's dizzy nest,"
A knight replied; and idly trimmed
  The favors on his crest.

"A train of damsels were as well,
To stare at yonder tower,
As this array of martial men,
Drawn out with useless power."

"Ay," laughed Don Pedro, moodily,
Beneath his lowering brow,
"Arms might be kept for holidays,
If always used as now.

"Yet here I'll lay, hap what will hap,
Till famine drive them out." —
Just then, from the left wing arose
A long, triumphant shout.

"What means that cry?" — "Two men-at-arms,
Flying from Cabezon,
Were by an outpost of your line
Surprised, and seized upon."

"Bring in the prisoners." — Down they knelt
Beneath Don Pedro's eye.
"Ha! traitors, have ye fled your liege,
And come to me to die?"

"To die, Don Pedro, if you will,
Rather than bear the stain
Of those worse traitors unto heaven
Who at their posts remain."

"Speak out: I'll listen. Do not fear
To make your story long:
Gramercy! we have time enough
To tire a woman's tongue!"

Don Pedro yawned, and stretched himself;
But, as the story ran,
I ween, he bounded to his feet.
Thus spake the foremost man:

"We guarded rocky Cabezon —
Unfaltering, nothing loath —
Till faith turned into mutiny,
And guilt sprang up from sloth;

"Till all our lazy garrison
Stood muttering apart,
And framing wicked stratagems,
To vex the Governor's heart.

"And now 't was this, and now 't was that —
Fierce murmurs, huge demands —
Forever closing with the threat
To yield them to your hands.

"The Governor rendered all to them,
Rather than aught to you;
But, day by day, his care-worn face
Paler and paler grew.

"Daily his wife and daughter found
The once so ready smile
Came slower to his lips, and staid
Thereon a shorter while.

"Yet daily, by the old man's side,
They paced around the wall,
Until they saw how with one look
The men pursued them all:

"Until they saw audacious leers
  Upon their persons cast,
Or snatched their skirts from mailéd hands
  That clutched them as they passed.

"Or heard such jests as well might start
  A very wanton's blood,—
Jests that forced modest cheeks to flame
  Beneath the close-drawn hood.

"Then to their bower they fled amain,
  And hid their dangerous charms;
And strove to talk away their tears,
  And lull their wild alarms.

"Bolder and bolder grew the men,
  The Governor grew more wan:
At length, from out a whispering knot,
  Strode one, and thus began:

"Bring us your wife and daughter, fool,
  Or down this flag shall come.—
With a back-handed blow, our chief
  Struck the gross ruffian dumb.

"At once swords flashed, and visors closed,
  And spears gleamed all around;
And, with his dagger in his hand,
  The wretch sprang from the ground.

"We spoke in vain"—"But he—your chief
  Broke in Don Pedro's voice:
Then held his breath, and bent his ear,
  To hear the Governor's choice.

"This said he — Hold that flag secure,
And ere to-morrow's sun
All mine be yours." — "Heavens!" cried the king,
"The like was never done!

"Shall he outdo us? Herald, ho!
And let a parley sound.
Summon the Governor to the wall,
And call my guard around.

"Ho! Governor, send your traitors down,
And, in return again,
I'll send you, man for man, my best,
All belted knights of Spain;

"Who shall be sworn, by book and cross,
To keep you safe from siege
Against all comers, whosoe'er,
Even against their liege."

Low bowed the Governor: "King, fair words
Are barren pay and cold;
Yet God takes up a poor man's debt,
And turns his thanks to gold.

"A thousand times may Heaven o'erpay
The deed you do for me;
And, served I not a better liege,
I'd draw my sword for thee."

The king smiled. "Knights, my future foes,
File through yon rocky arch. —
You, with the love-knots in your crest,
Be you the first to march!"

Up through the gates of Cabezon
Don Pedro's bravest went,
And straggling down the narrow path
The sullen traitors sent.

Around the miscreants silently
The royal soldiers drew.
"Now, *ballesteros*," cried the king,
"Ye know what work to do!

"Stand back, thou ghostly man of God!
Thou shalt not pray nor shrive:
If 't were within my power, to hell
I 'd hurry them alive!"

A hundred maces swang aloft,
A hundred blows were given,
And crushed into one mangled mass
The traitors lay unshriven.

The drawbridge rose, the castle gates
Rolled slowly back; and when
The king looked up, he saw the walls
Glitter with mail-clad men.

Slowly Don Pedro walked, as one
Who turns a purpose o'er,
Plucking the lilies in his path,
Unconscious what he bore:

Slowly Don Pedro towards his camp
Walked through the setting sun;
And patiently next morn he lay
Besieging Cabezon.

COUNT CANDESPINA'S STANDARD.

"The King of Aragon now entered Castile, by the way of Soria and Osma, with a powerful army; and, having been met by the queen's forces, both parties encamped near Sepulveda, and prepared to give battle. This engagement, called, from the field where it took place, *de la Espina*, is one of the most famous of that age. The dastardly Count of Lara fled at the first shock, and joined the queen at Burgos, where she was anxiously awaiting the issue; but the brave Count of Candespina (Gomez Gonzalez) stood his ground to the last, and died on the field of battle. His standard-bearer, a gentleman of the house of Olea, after having his horse killed under him, and both hands cut off by sabre-strokes, fell beside his master, still clasping the standard with his arms, and repeating his war-cry of "Olea!"

MRS. GEORGE'S "ANNALS OF THE QUEENS OF SPAIN."

SCARCE were the splintered lances dropped,
Scarce were the swords drawn out,
Ere recreant Lara, sick with fear,
Had wheeled his steed about.

His courser reared, and plunged, and neighed,
Loathing the fight to yield,
But the coward spurred him to the bone,
And drove him from the field.

Gonzalez in his stirrups rose —
"Turn, turn, thou traitor knight!
Thou bold tongue in a lady's bower,
Thou dastard in a fight!"

But vainly valiant Gomez cried
  Across the waning fray;
Pale Lara and his craven band
  To Burgos scoured away.

"Now, by the God above me, sirs,
  Better we all were dead,
Than a single knight among ye all
  Should ride where Lara led!

"Yet ye who fear to follow me,
  As yon traitor, turn and fly;
For I lead ye not to win a field,
  I lead ye forth to die.

"Olea, plant my standard here,
  Here, on this little mound,
Here raise the war-cry of thy house,
  Make this our rallying-ground.

"Forget not, as thou hop'st for grace,
  The last care I shall have
Will be to hear thy battle-cry,
  And see that standard wave."

Down on the ranks of Aragon
  The bold Gonzalez drove;
And Olea raised his battle-cry,
  And waved the flag above.

Slowly Gonzalez's little band
  Gave ground before the foe;
But not an inch of the field was won
  Without a deadly blow:

And not an inch of the field was won
  That did not draw a tear
From the widowed wives of Aragon,
  That fatal news to hear.

Backward and backward Gomez fought,
  And high o'er the clashing steel,
Plainer and plainer, rose the cry,
  "Olea for Castile!"

Backward fought Gomez, step by step,
  Till the cry was close at hand,
Till his dauntless standard shadowed him,
  And there he made his stand.

Mace, sword, and axe, rang on his mail,
  Yet he moved not where he stood,
Though each gaping joint of armor ran
  A stream of purple blood.

As pierced with countless wounds he fell,
  The standard caught his eye,
And he smiled, like an infant hushed asleep,
  To hear the battle-cry.

Now, one by one, the wearied knights
  Had fallen, or basely flown;
And on the mound, where his post was fixed,
  Olea stood alone.

"Yield up thy banner, gallant knight!
  Thy lord lies on the plain,
Thy duty has been nobly done;
  I would not see thee slain."

"Spare pity, King of Aragon;
  I would not hear thee lie;
My lord is looking down from heaven,
  To see his standard fly."

"Yield, madman, yield! thy horse is down,
  Thou hast nor lance nor shield;
Fly! I will grant thee time."—"This flag
  Can neither fly nor yield!"

They girt the standard round about,
  A wall of flashing steel;
But still they heard the battle-cry,
  "Olea for Castile!"

And there, against all Aragon,
  Full-armed with lance and brand,
Olea fought until the sword
  Snapped in his sturdy hand.

Among the foe, with that high scorn
  Which laughs at earthly fears,
He hurled the broken hilt, and drew
  His dagger on the spears.

They hewed the hauberk from his breast,
  The helmet from his head,
They hewed the hands from off his limbs,—
  From every vein he bled.

Clasping the standard to his heart,
  He raised one dying peal,
That rang as if a trumpet blew—
  "Olea for Castile!"

THE DEATH OF DOÑA URRACA.

Don Pedro rode from Najera
  With fury in his brain ;
He hanged, hacked, burned, and boiled,— blood filled
  The footprints of his train.

Prince Edward's sword had given the land
  Into the tyrant's power,
And Doña Urraca with the rest
  Must bide the dismal hour.

Because her son, Alfonso, fled
  Before the royal court,
That lady fair, of high degree,
  Must make the rabble sport.

Thus, in the strong Alcazar shut,
  She made her piteous moan,
While her maidens gathered round, to hear,
  With many a hopeless groan.

" Make me a robe, my gentle maids,
  And make it light and thin,
That the fire may lap around my heart,
  And quickly creep within.

"So that the bitter death I bear,
If cruel, may yet be brief;
For Don Pedro dooms me to the stake,
And heaven sends no relief.

"The king has sworn to see me burn,
For young Alfonso's sake:
If my son could hear the heavy news,
I ween, his heart would ache.

"Ah! if he knew these tender arms,
That nursed his helpless head,
Must burn to ashes on the breast
Whereat his childhood fed;

"And the breath that fanned his baby brow,
And sang his lullaby,
Must feed the fire of Pedro's wrath,
And shriek with agony; —

"I fear Alfonso's lips would curse
His birth-hour: but, I vow,
I, who would then have died for him,
Am proud to do it now.

"So make me a robe of Moorish stuff,
And let the fire have sway;
For my soul is sick whene'er I think
Of lingering on the way."

"Mistress," said Leonor Davalos,
Whilst the others only wept,
"I'll make thy robe from cloth of wool
Which I so long have kept;

"I 'll make thy robe from Flemish cloth,
Lest, when the fire arise,
Thy garments burn from off thy limbs,
And shame thee in all eyes."

"Be still!" the lady sternly cried,
"And do thy ordered part;
Thou art too coolly provident
To have me much at heart."

Then Leonor in silence bent,
And wrought with little cheer;
For down her cheeks the big drops ran,
With every stitch a tear.

Nathless, the robe was neatly made,
Each seam in proper place;
She bound her lady's girdle on,
And looked into her face.

The lady bade her maids farewell,
She kissed them o'er and o'er,
But not a look of love she cast
On hapless Leonor.

The lady knelt beside the priest,
The holy bread was given,
She made her peace with all the world,
And turned her thoughts on heaven.

The hour is come. The royal guard,
With trampling harsh and loud,
Have led the lady swiftly forth
To face the hooting crowd.

They bound her to the fatal stake
  With iron chains ; and now
The headsman blows his torch aflame
  Beneath his scowling brow.

High into heaven, as if to bear
  Witness against her doom,
The pitchy fagots flashed, then all
  Was silent as the tomb.

Pale with affright, the lady hung
  Upon her chains and wept,
Until a gust of brawling wind
  Across the ramparts swept ;

And drove the flames aslant, and caught
  The lady's fluttering gown,
Stripping her person to the view
  Of every leering clown.

Loud roared the crowd, and laughed, and jeered,
  To see the lady's plight,
Pointing their fingers, nudging those
  Who could not bear the sight.

"O Mary, mother of our Lord,
  I call upon thy name !
Thou who dost know what I endure,
  O hide me from my shame !

"O holy Virgin, take my soul !
  The inward fire I feel
Is crueller than the fire around : —
  I'm bound, or I would kneel !"

Sad Leonor, from where she stood,
  Heard how her lady cried;
She sprang towards the blazing pile,
  And dashed the guard aside.

Right through the smoke and sparkling coals
  She leaped into the flame,
And spread her flowing garments out,
  And hid her lady's shame.

She clasped her body with her arms,
  And straight into the sky, —
High up, as towards some distant spot, —
  The two gazed steadfastly;

Gazed with their wondering lips apart,
  Cheek pressed to pallid cheek,
Heart stilled on heart — no sign they make,
  No stir, no word they speak;

Gazed till their souls were following
  The vision far away,
And the savage fagots blazed around
  A mass of senseless clay.

THE LEGEND OF MARIA CORONEL.

"O, SISTERS of Santa Clara,
  If you'd keep my soul from sin,
Dig me a grave in the convent ground,
  And bury me within.

"Pile the turf loosely o'er my head,
  And closely let me lie,
Till the king hath searched the cloisters through,
  And, haply, passed me by.

"Rather would I lie side by side
  With the foul and grisly dead,
Than loll in wicked luxury
  Upon Don Pedro's bed.

"O, sisters, hasten! Hark! the king
  Is thundering at the grate;
Fierce oaths are thick upon his lips —
  How creaks the bending gate!

"God gave us not this precious time
  To waste in frightened prayer;
We serve him better with our deeds,
  If they be bold and fair.

"He sits in heaven, and smiles serene
  Above each falling bead;
Prayers he but hears, he lends his arm
  To help a noble deed."

"Lady, the king will search the ground,
  And mark the new-turned sod." —
"Ye talk as women talk: I trust
  My chastity to God!"

Scarce could the sexton dig the grave,
  And shoulder up his spade,
With clods of grass, and damp black earth,
  Still clinging to the blade;

Scarce could the lady fall along,
  And hide herself within,
Ere the cloister walls, from end to end,
  Were full of martial din.

Even while the breathless nuns heaped turf
  Above the seeming grave,
Don Pedro's jewelled plumes were seen
  Across the court to wave.

Straight towards the prioress and nuns
  The furious monarch came;
Wrath smouldering in his deadly eyes,
  His cheeks with wrath aflame.

O, wonder! miracle of grace!
  With every step he took
A flower rose lightly from the grave,
  And in the breezes shook.

Lily, and violet, and rose,
Shot up, budded, and bore,
Shedding such odors in the sun
As flowers ne'er shed before.

The alder sank its hollow tubes
Far down into the tomb,
Till all the damp air underneath
Was banished with perfume.

Betwixt the white roots of the flowers
The tender grass peeped out,
While through its spears long creepers trailed,
And coiled their stems about.

So, when the angry monarch's step
Had staid its headlong speed,
A multitude of roses blushed
Between him and his deed.

Naught saw he nigh him to betray
The lady's hiding-place, —
Naught but a little mound that seemed
Flowered o'er by years of grace.

No whisper from the frightened nuns,
No breath, Don Pedro greets,
Save the soft breath of tranquil flowers —
An eloquence of sweets.

I know not if fair sights and scents
May soothe a fiery soul,
And with some subtle, mystic power
Its raging heats control;

But, certes, from that spot the king
  Turned with a calmer air,
Muttering low phrases to himself,
  That sounded like a prayer.

All still, as in a holy trance,
  The blessed lady lay,
Nor knew how heaven had wrought until
  The king was far away.

Nor ye who read, nor I who write,
  Know not how o'er our heads,
When peril frowns, God's tender hand
  Such fragrant bounties spreads.

SONGS AND SONNETS.

SONGS AND SONNETS.

THE ROSE OF GRANADA.

O, THE Rose of Granada was blooming full-blown,
And she laughed at the suitors who thought her their
own,
Till there came from Morocco the Moor, Ala Jaeer,
And he tossed from his spear-head the horse-tails in
air,
Saying, "List to me, lady;
For hither I 've flown,
O Rose of Granada,
To make thee my own."

He sang from his saddle of war and of love,
With a voice that was soft as the houries' above;
And he sang to his gittern of love and of war,
With one foot in his stirrup and one in her door:
Singing, "Look from thy lattice;
I never will rove,
O Rose of Granada,
For war yields to love."

She smiled in his face as she ne'er smiled before,
And the suitors went trooping away from her door;

But they saw from a spear driven deep in the plain,
Where a barb had been tied by his gold-bitted rein,
That the horse-tails were waving,
Now hither, now there ;
For the Rose of Granada
Had fallen in the snare.

The suitors went muttering, by day and by night,
"Our Rose will be stolen away in our sight,"
Till the Moor, Ala Jaeer, from her portal one morn
Stepped, shaking the horse-tails in triumph and scorn :
"O, in, to your lady,
And tend her, I pray,
For the Rose of Granada
Is fading away.

"She is one of a hundred — to tell you 's but fair ;
Who 'll tilt for the lady I 've left in despair ?"
With a scowl on his brow, and a sneer on his mouth,
The horse-tails went dancing away towards the south.
But the suitors were whispering,
Ere daylight was gray,
"O, the rose of Granada
Has faded away !"

There was a gay maiden lived down by the mill —
        Ferry me over the ferry —
Her hair was as bright as the waves of a rill,
When the sun on the brink of his setting stands still,
        Her lips were as full as a cherry.

A stranger came galloping over the hill —
        Ferry me over the ferry —
He gave her broad silver and gold for his will:
She glanced at the stranger, she glanced o'er the sill;
        The maiden was gentle and merry.

"O! what would you give for your virtue again?" —
        Ferry me over the ferry —
"O! silver and gold on your lordship I'd rain,
I'd double your pleasure, I'd double my pain,
        This moment forever to bury."

LIDA.

Lida, lady of the land,
  Called by men "the blue-eyed wonder,"
Hath a lily forehead, fanned
  By locks the sunlight glitters under.
She hath all that 's scattered round
  Through a race of winning creatures;
All, except the beauty found,
  By Johnny Gordon, in my features.

Lida, lady of the land,
  Hath full many goodly houses,
Fields, and parks, on every hand,
  Where your foot the roebuck rouses.
She hath orchards, garden-plots,
  Valleys deep, and mountains swelling;
All, except yon nest of cots,
  Johnny Gordon's humble dwelling.

Lida, lady of the land,
  Hath treasures more than she remembers,
Heaps of dusty gems, that stand
  Like living coals amid the embers.
She hath gold whose touch would bring
  A lordship to a lowly peasant;
All, except this little ring,
  Johnny Gordon's humble present.

Lida, lady of the land,
  Hath a crowd of gallant suitors ;
Squires, who fly at her command,
  Knights, her slightest motion tutors.
She hath barons kneeling mute,
  To hear the fortune of their proffers ;
All, except the honest suit
  Johnny Gordon humbly offers.

Lida, lady of the land,
  Keep your wondrous charms untroubled ;
May your wide domain expand,
  May your gems and gold be doubled !
Keep your lords on bended knee ;
  Take all earth, and leave us lonely ! —
All, except you take from me
  Humble Johnny Gordon only.

Yes, I loved her! Bear me witness,
  Heaven, and sea, and mother earth,
How I felt my own unfitness,
  Matched with her transcendent worth!
How I bent my forehead meekly,
Saying, "I am heart-sick, weakly,
Jaded, worn with many trials, —
  Cursed, unto the last extreme,
With the seven deadly vials!" —
      In a dream.

But, behold, the gentle maiden
  Touched me lightly with her hand;
Saying, "Rise, thou sorrow-laden
  Man of many griefs, and stand!
For I love thee with my youthful
Spirit warm, and pure, and truthful:
Upward, to me, I beseech thee!
  Or, forgetting self-esteem,
I will downward plunge to reach thee!" —
      In a dream.

It has faded from my vision;
  And again I stand alone,
Thrust beyond the gates elysian,
  Listening to my exiled moan.

Hearing her sweet accents never —
Love, joy, hope, all gone together ;
But the pang will ne'er be banished
  Of that bright delusive gleam,
Which has left its sting, and vanished
      In a dream.

When we meet again, shall I behold no shrinking
  Of thy quick eyes, no sidelong glance of pain;
No start, betraying what thy heart is thinking,
          When we meet again?

When we meet again, shall I perceive no trial
  To wake a love already on the wane,
To screen inconstancy by faint denial,
          When we meet again?

When we meet again, shall I hear no bewailing,
  No hollow fiction of a treacherous brain,
Raised to forestall my own true grief's assailing,
          When we meet again?

When we meet again, shall I not know thee playing
  A part whose falsehood is too clearly plain,
That cogs and kisses while it is betraying,
          When we meet again?

When we meet again, O God! shall I not find thee
  As true to me as when thy lips were ta'en,
In the deep calm of love, from lips that then resigned thee
          But to meet again?

THE fever in my blood has died;
  The eager foot, the glancing eye,
  By beauty lured so easily,
No more are moved, or turned aside:
My smiles are gone, my tears are dried.

And if I say I love thee now,
  'T is not because my passions burn —
  Fair as thou art — to ask return
Of love for love, and vow for vow;
Too dear exchanged for such as thou.

I love thee only as he can
  Who knows his heart. I yield, in truth,
  Not the blind, headlong heat of youth,
That pants ere it has run a span,
But the determined love of man.

And if from me you ask more fire
  Than lights my slowly-fading days,—
  The sudden frenzy and the blaze,
The selfish clutch of young desire,—
You point where I cannot aspire.

Yet do not bend thy head to weep,
  Because my love so coldly shows;
  For where the fuel fiercely glows
The flame is brief: in ashes deep
The everlasting embers sleep.

I sit beneath the sunbeams' glow,
Their golden currents round me flow,
Their mellow kisses warm my brow,
But all the world is dreary.
The vernal meadow round me blooms,
And flings to me its faint perfumes ;
Its breath is like an opening tomb's —
I 'm sick of life, I 'm weary !

The mountain brook skips down to me,
Tossing its silver tresses free,
Humming like one in revery ;
But, ah ! the sound is dreary.
The trilling blue-birds o'er me sail,
There 's music in the faint-voiced gale ;
All sound to me a mourner's wail —
I 'm sick of life, I 'm weary.

The night leads forth her starry train,
The glittering moonbeams fall like rain,
There 's not a shadow on the plain ;
Yet all the scene is dreary.
The sunshine is a mockery,
The solemn moon stares moodily ;
Alike is day or night to me —
I 'm sick of life, I 'm weary.

I know to some the world is fair,
For them there 's music in the air,

And shapes of beauty everywhere ;
  But all to me is dreary.
I know in me the sorrows lie
That blunt my ear and dim my eye ;
I cannot weep, I fain would die —
  I 'm sick of life, I 'm weary.

Wheel on thy axle, softly run,
  Dark earth, into the golden day!
Rise from the burnished east, bright sun,
  And chase the scowling night away!

Touch my love's eyelids; gently break
  The tender dream she dreams of me,
With flowery odors; round her shake
  The swallow's morning minstrelsy.

Tell her how, through the lonely dark,
  Her lover sighed with sleepless pain;
And heard the watch-dog's hollow bark,
  And heard the sobbing of the rain.

Tell her he waits, with listening ear,
  Beside the way that skirts her door;
And till her radiant face appear,
  He shall not think the night is o'er.

STREET LYRICS.

I.

THE GROCER'S DAUGHTER.

Stop, stop! and look through the dusty pane. —
  She's gone! —Nay, hist! again I have caught her:
There is the source of my sighs of pain,
  There is my idol, the Grocer's Daughter!

"A child! no woman!" A bud, no flower:
  But think, when a year or more has brought her
Its ripening roundness, how proud a dower
  Of charms will bloom in the Grocer's Daughter!

I have a love for the flower that blows,
  One for the bud that needs sun and water;
The first because it is now a rose,
  The other will be, — like the Grocer's Daughter.

She stood in the door, as I passed to-day,
  And mine and a thousand glances sought her;
Like a star from heaven with equal ray,
  On all alike, shone the Grocer's Daughter.

Mark how the sweetest on earth can smile,
As yon patient drudge, yon coarse-browed porter,
Eases his burdened back, the while
Keeping his eyes on the Grocer's Daughter.

Now, look ye! I who have much to lose —
Rank, wealth, and friends — like the load he brought her,
Would toss them under her little shoes,
To win that smile from the Grocer's Daughter.

II.

A MYSTERY.

Just as the twilight shades turn darker,
  There is a maiden passes me;
Many and many a time I mark her,
  Wondering who that maid can be.

Sometimes she bears her music, fastened
  Scroll-like around with silken twine;
And once — although she blushed and hastened,
  I knew it — she bore a book of mine.

In cold or heat, I never passed her,
  Beneath serene or threatening skies,
That she upon me did not cast her
  Strong, full, and steady hazel eyes.

Eyes of such wondrous inner meaning,
  So filled with light, so deep, so true,
As if her thoughts disclaimed all screening,
  And clustered in them, looking through.

Thus, day by day, we meet; no greeting,
  No sign she makes, no word she says;
Unless our eyes salute at meeting,
  And she says somewhat by her gaze.

Says what? At first her looks were often
As cheering as the sun above;
Next they began to dim and soften,
Like glances from a brooding dove.

Then wonder, then reproach, concealing
A coming anger, I could see:
I passed, but felt her eyes were stealing
Around, and following after me.

Before me once, with firm possession,
She almost paused, and hung upon
The very verge of some confession;
But maiden coyness led her on.

Sometimes I think the maid indulges
An idle fancy by the way;
Sometimes I think her look divulges
A deeper sign — a mind astray.

This eve she met me, wild with laughter,
More sad than weeping would have been —
A pang before, a sorrow after;
Tell me, what can the maiden mean?

III.

THE TWO BIRDS.

Two birds hang from two facing windows :
One on a lady's marble wall ;
The other, a seamstress' sole companion,
Rests on her lattice dark and small.

The one, embowered by rare exotics,
Swings in a curious golden cage ;
The other, beside a lone geranium,
Peeps between wires of rusty age.

The one consumes a dainty seedling,
That, leagues on leagues, in vessels comes ;
The other pecks at the scanty leavings
Strained from his mistress' painful crumbs.

The lady's bird has careful lackeys,
To place him in the cheerful sun ;
Upon her bird the seamstress glances,
Between each stitch, till work is done.

Doubtless the marble wall shines gayly,
And sometimes to the window roam
Guests in their stately silken garments ;
But yon small blind looks more like home.

Doubtless the tropic flowers are dazzling,
  The golden cage is rare to see ;
But sweeter smells the low geranium,
  The mean cage has more liberty.

'T is well to feed upon the fruitage
  Brought from a distant southern grove ;
But better is a homely offering,
  Divided by the hand of love.

The purchased service of a menial
  May, to the letter, fill its part ;
But there 's an overflowing kindness
  Springs from the service of a heart.

Hark ! yonder bird begins to warble :
  Well done, my lady's pretty pet !
Thy song is somewhat faint and straitened,
  Yet sweeter tones I 've seldom met.

And now the seamstress' bird. — O, listen !
  Hear with what power his daring song
Sweeps through its musical divisions,
  With skill assured, with rapture strong !

Hear how he trills ; with what abundance
  He flings his varied stores away ;
Bursting through wood and woven iron
  With the wild freedom of his lay !

Cease, little prisoner to the lady,
  Cease, till the rising of the moon ;
Thy feeble song is all unsuited
  To the full midday glare of June.

Cease, for thy rival's throat is throbbing
  With the fierce splendor of the hour ;
His is the art that grasps a passion,
  To cast it back with ten-fold power.

Cease, until yonder feathered poet
  Through all his wondrous song has run,
And made the heart of wide creation
  Leap in the glory of the sun.

IV.

FLOWERS AT THE WINDOW.

Flowers at the window! tropic blossoms blazing in our wintry air,
On the dark, cold evening looking with a fervid summer glare:
Just a bit of southern landscape prisoned in a northern pane,
Just a hint of how the cactus bristles o'er its native plain;
How the fuchsia hangs its scarlet buds amid the orange bowers,
And the dust of all the valleys rises up at once in flowers.

Yonder room is sick with odors, painful odors, too intense
For the scentless air that nurtured the fresh longings of my sense.
I should swoon among those flowers, their gaudy colors vex my eye,
And their hot oppressive breath upon my whirling brain would lie
Like the poisoned fumes, engendered by the eastern sorcerer's fire,
That rouse the sense to madness, and the heart to horrible desire.

Stay a moment, — through the flaunting stranger flowers, I mark a rose —
One pale native of our forests, standing there in mild repose;
Hanging down its timid head, amid its haughty sisters meek,
From them shrinking back, half-opened, with a blush upon its cheek.
Wait I for the rose to blow, or wait I for the maid who stood
In among the flowers, this morning, blooming into womanhood?

THE AWAKING OF THE POETICAL FACULTY.

All day I heard a humming in my ears,
A buzz of many voices, and a throng
Of swarming numbers, passing with a song
Measured and stately as the rolling spheres'.
I saw the sudden light of lifted spears,
Slanted at once against some monster wrong;
And then a fluttering scarf which might belong
To some sweet maiden in her morn of years.
I felt the chilling damp of sunless glades,
Horrid with gloom; anon, the breath of May
Was blown around me, and the lulling play
Of dripping fountains. Yet the lights and shades,
The waving scarfs, the battle's grand parades,
Seemed but vague shadows of that wondrous lay.

TO ANDREW JACKSON.

Old lion of the Hermitage, again
The times invoke thee, but thou art not here;
Cannot our peril call thee from thy bier?
France vapors, and the puny arm of Spain
Is up to strike us; England gives them cheer,
False to the child that in her hour of fear
Must be her bulwark and her succor, fain
To prop the strength which even now doth wane.
Nor these alone; intestine broils delight
The gaping monarchs, and our liberal shore
Is rife with traitors. Now, while both unite —
Europe and treason — I would see once more
Thy dreadful courage lash itself to might,
Behold thee shake thy mane, and hear thy roar.

1852.

TO LOUIS NAPOLEON.

O, SHAMELESS thief! a nation trusted thee
  With all the wealth her bleeding hands had won,
  Proclaimed thee guardian of her liberty:
  So proud a title never lay upon
Thy uncle's forehead: thou wast linked with one,
  First President of France, whose name shall be
  Fixed in the heavens, like God's eternal sun —
  Second to him alone — to Washington!
Was it for thee to stoop unto a crown?
  Pick up the Bourbon's leavings? yield thy height
  Of simple majesty, and totter down
Full of discovered frailties — sorry sight! —
  One of a mob of kings? or, baser grown,
  Was it for thee to steal it in the night?

TO ENGLAND.

I.

LEAR and Cordelia! 't was an ancient tale
  Before thy Shakspeare gave it deathless fame:
  The times have changed, the moral is the same.
  So like an outcast, dowerless, and pale,
Thy daughter went; and in a foreign gale
  Spread her young banner, till its sway became
  A wonder to the nations. Days of shame
  Are close upon thee: prophets raise their wail.
When the rude Cossack with an outstretched hand
  Points his long spear across the narrow sea, —
  "Lo! there is England!" when thy destiny
Storms on thy straw-crowned head, and thou dost stand
  Weak, helpless, mad, a by-word in the land, —
  God grant thy daughter a Cordelia be!

1852.

II.

STAND, thou great bulwark of man's liberty !
  Thou rock of shelter, rising from the wave,
  Sole refuge to the overwearied brave
  Who planned, arose, and battled to be free,
Fell undeterred, then sadly turned to thee ;—
  Saved the free spirit from their country's grave,
  To rise again, and animate the slave,
  When God shall ripen all things. Britons, ye
Who guard the sacred outpost, not in vain
  Hold your proud peril ! Freemen undefiled,
  Keep watch and ward ! Let battlements be piled
Around your cliffs ; fleets marshalled, till the main
  Sink under them ; and if your courage wane,
  Through force or fraud, look westward to your
      child !

1853.

III.

At length the tempest from the North has burst,
  The threatened storm, by sages seen of old;
  And into jarring anarchy is rolled
  Harmonious peace, so long and fondly nursed
By watchful nations. Tyranny accursed
  Has broken bounds — the wolf makes towards the fold.
  Up! ere your priceless liberties be sold
  Into degrading slavery! The worst
That can befall you is the brunt of war,
  Dealt on a shield that oft has felt the weight
  Of foeman's blows. — Up! ere it be too late!
For God has squandered all his precious store
  Of right and mercy, if the time 's so sore
  That slaves can bring you to their own base state.

1854.

IV.

FAR from the Baltic to the Euxine's strand,
Peals the vast clamor of commencing war;
And we, O England, on another shore,
Like brothers bound, with wistful faces stand —
With shouts of cheer, with wavings of the hand —
With eager throbbings of the heart, to pour
Our warlike files amid the battle's war,
And nerve the terrors of thy lifted brand.
Old wrongs have vanished in thy evil hours;
The blood that fell between us, in the fight,
Has dried away before a heavenly light.
We 'll strew thy paths of victory with flowers,
Weep o'er thy woes, and cry, with all our powers,
Thy cause is God's, because thy cause is right!

1854.

V.

O, MEN of England, with an anxious heart
 We see you arming for the coming fight.
 Pale lips that quiver, in our pride's despite,
 Bid you God speed! Be this our tenderer part.
Yours is the frown of war, the martial start
 That wakes to glory and resistless might,
 When your great standard rises on the sight,
 Blazoned with memories; an awful chart
Of grand adventures done in olden days, —
 At once a pride and terror. Ill bestead
 The soul that shrinks from duty through its dread;
Or seeks another outlet than the ways
 Marked down for you, amid the whole world's praise —
 The noble ways on which your fathers led.

1854.

VI.

ONCE more old England's banner on the gale
Flames like the comet in our western sky;
Beneath its fiery glare are lifted high
Long lines of steel, and clouds of snowy sail.
O, ye who bear it through the eastern vale,
Think how it shone in Cœur de Lion's eye!
Ye who behold it on the waters fly,
Think how it answered Nelson's dauntless hail!
From the Crusader to the Sailor turn,
And mark the lines of glory that appear
Stretched through your chronicles, starred far and near
With names heroical — dread names that burn,
Like deathless lamps, above each funeral urn,
To light you onward in their grand career.

1854.

VII.

FAINT not nor tremble, birthplace of my sires,
  Because the dreadful arm of war is bare,
  And thy sons bleed with many wounds that glare
  In pleading misery on thee. Household fires
Must quench ; there 's trouble in the land. Desires
  For peace, old longings, that with loathful stare
  Take up the sword with such a backward air,
  Must vanish now. I know thy soul aspires
Towards all that 's manly, liberal, and great :
  Therefore, when you behold your children come,
  Gored by the curséd Cossack, wounded home,
Shed not a useless tear ; but edge thy hate
  With double fury ! Sound the mustering drum,
  And fill your ranks up to their wonted state !

1854.

TO AMERICA.

I.

WHAT, cringe to Europe! Band it all in one,
Stilt its decrepit strength, renew its age,
Wipe out its debts, contract a loan to wage
Its venal battles — and, by yon bright sun,
Our God is false, and liberty undone,
If slaves have power to win your heritage!
Look on your country, God's appointed stage,
Where man's vast mind its boundless course shall run:
For that it was your stormy coast He spread —
A fear in winter; girded you about
With granite hills, and made you strong and dread.
Let him who fears before the foemen shout,
Or gives an inch before a vein has bled,
Turn on himself, and let the traitor out!

II.

WHAT though the cities blaze, the ports be sealed,
The fields untilled, the hands of labor still,
Ay, every arm of commerce and of skill
Palsied and broken; shall we therefore yield —
Break up the sword, put by the dintless shield?
Have we no home upon the wooded hill,
That mocks a siege? No patriot ranks to drill?
No nobler labor in the battle-field?
Or grant us beaten. While we gather might,
Is there no comfort in the solemn wood?
No cataracts whose angry roar shall smite
Our hearts with courage? No eternal brood
Of thoughts begotten by the eagle's flight?
No God to strengthen us in solitude?

TO THE MEMORY OF JOHN SERGEANT.

THE world may wait a century to see
  Thy equal mourned. When great men die, we
      say —
  " Just here they missed, or there they went astray:
  Alas! alas! that sweet morality
Locks not her hand with greatness!" But in thee
  Heaven lit a lamp, to show how, day by day,
  The highest flame may shed the purest ray,
  Burning undimmed into eternity.
There 's much of goodness, much of grandeur, gone
  To neighboring slumbers in our ancient earth; —
  Here some bewail a hero, some bemoan
A saintly pilgrim; yet I doubt if worth,
  Religion, greatness, and their active birth,
  Were e'er before so mingled into one.

November 27th, 1852.

TO THE MEMORY OF M. A. R.

With the mild light some unambitious star
  Illumes her pathway through the heavenly blue —
  So unobtrusive that the careless view
  Scarce notes her where her haughtier sisters are —
So ran thy life. Perhaps, from those afar,
  Thy gentle radiance little wonder drew,
  And all their praise was for the brighter few.
  Yet mortal vision is a grievous bar
To weigh true worth. For were the distance riven,
  Our eyes might find that star so faintly shone
  Because it journeyed through a higher zone,
Had more majestic sway and duties given,
  Far loftier station on the heights of heaven,
  Was next to God, and circled round His throne.

TO THE MEMORY OF S. S.

THE world may think I lay this thing to heart:
  I do, indeed, and of my grief am proud;
  Yet would not draw the wonder of the crowd,
  Either to me, or to my rhyming art.
So I will lay thy sacred name apart
  From other griefs that haunt me in the shroud;
  And will not in affliction be too loud,
  Lest men suspect my cunning gives the start
To these true tears. And if nor sigh, nor moan,
  Nor cry of anguish, load my heavy line,
  It is because this holy grief of mine
Is a dear treasure. I am jealous grown,
  To share with men a thing I hold divine,
  Making that common which is all my own.

TO BAYARD TAYLOR.

I.

WHAT changes of our natures have not been,
In the long process of the many days
That passed while we pursued our different ways,
Lost to each other! Fields, that once were green
Beneath our tillage, have been reaped. The scene
Of our young labors has grown old, and lays
Its dust upon us. Things that won our praise,
Are tasteless quite, and only move our spleen.
Experience has nipped the bloom of youth;
The flattering dawn of life has gone; in vain
We look for visions of the morn. Stern truth
Glares over us, and makes our view too plain.
I 'm sick of life's discoveries; in sooth,
I 'd have the falsehoods of our youth again.

II.

The world seems strangely altered to me, friend,
 Since last I pressed my ready hand in thine.
 I feel like one awakening after wine —
 For many yesterdays have had an end
Since we two met — and drowsy tremors send
 A thrill of shame across this heart of mine,
 That I my better feelings could confine
 In easy opiates, make my spirit bend
To slothful rest, — a drunkard, and no more!
 Yet I will rouse me from this lethargy.
 The past is past; the dreaming night is o'er;
Heaven's lamp comes beaming from the East on me,
 Touching my eyelids to reality,
 And all is sunshine that was dark before.

How the fixed gaze of unadmiring time
  Can reconcile us with earth's wondrous sights;
  Win down our fancies from their breathless heights,
  Teaching 't is easier far to crawl than climb!
Age spreads its marvels; but a creeping rime
  Dulls the worn eye; and all the precious lights
  Of early feeling deaden in the blights
  Of care, and avarice, and infectious crime.
O, God! when use has palled my youthful sense—
  When no new wonder daily comes to me
  From hill, or vale, or stream—no joy intense
Breaks with the day, or flows in with the sea,
  Or opens with the flower—O, take me hence,
  Hence, I implore, dear Lord, if not to Thee!

Dear is the fruit of sorrow, priceless store
  Comes from the hand of grief, as sages tell;
  Seeking for comfort in the woes that swell
  Our hearts to bursting; with fore-gathered lore
Lulling the fears that make a gloom before
  Our onward tread. Ah, hollow fraud! As well
  Speak truth, and say — "We healed mishaps that fell
  By their own issue, as with running gore
A wound is healed." — But, lo! the lasting scar!
  We make the best of man's dark destiny
  By self-deceit, while hopes and pleasures flee
Before our vision; till the latest star
  Fades in the dawn of knowledge, and we see
  Earth, like a joyless desert, stretch afar.

Not when the buxom form which nature wears
  Is pregnant with the lusty warmth of Spring;
  Nor when hot Summer, sunk with what she bears,
  Lies panting in her flowery offering;
Nor yet when dusty Autumn sadly fares
  In tattered garb, through which the shrewd winds
      sing,
  To bear her treasures to the griping snares
  Hard Winter set for the poor bankrupt thing;
Not even when Winter, heir of all the year,
  Deals, like a miser, round his niggard board
  The brimming plenty of his luscious hoard;
No, not in nature, change she howsoe'er,
  Can I find perfect type or worthy peer
  Of the fair maid in whom my heart is stored.

Spring, in the gentle look with which she turns
 Her sunny glance on all, indeed I find;
 And ardent Summer in the roses burns
 Of her twin cheeks, and from her gracious mind —
Like rare exotics nursed in precious urns,
 With cultured taste and native grace combined —
 Her teeming thoughts arise: too well she learns
 This summer sweetness! Generous Autumn, bind
A deathless chaplet round her queenly brow;
 For, like thy own, in boundless charity,
 Her heart is filled with motives frank and free,
Her hand with alms. Alas! I see it now;
 From thee, cold Winter, all her fancies flow,
 Who, rich in all, will nothing give to me.

EITHER the sum of this sweet mutiny
  Amongst thy features argues me some harm;
  Or else they practise wicked treachery
  Against themselves, thy heart, and hapless me.
For as I start aside with blank alarm,
  Dreading the glitter which begins to arm
  Thy clouded brows, lo! from thy lips I see
  A smile come stealing, like a loaded bee,
Heavy with sweets and perfumes, all ablaze
  With soft reflections from the flowery wall
  Whereon it pauses. Yet I will not raise
One question more, let smile or frown befall,
  Taxing thy love where I should only praise,
  And asking changes, that might change thee all.

I 'll call thy frown a headsman, passing grim,
  Walking before some wretch foredoomed to death,
  Who counts the pantings of his own hard breath;
  Wondering how heart can beat, or steadfast limb
Bear its sad burden to life's awful brim.
  I 'll call thy smile a priest, who slowly saith
  Soft words of comfort, as the sinner strayeth
  Away in thought; or sings a holy hymn,
Full of rich promise, as he walks behind
  The fatal axe with face of goodly cheer,
  And kind inclinings of his saintly ear.
So, love, thou seest in smiles, or looks unkind,
  Some taste of sweet philosophy I find,
  That seasons all things in our little sphere.

Nay, not to thee, to nature I will tie
The gathered blame of every pettish mood;
And when thou frown'st, I 'll frown upon the wood,
Saying, "How wide its gloomy shadows lie!"
Or, gazing straight into the day's bright eye,
Predict ere night a fatal second flood;
Or vow the poet's sullen solitude
Has changed my vision to a darksome dye.
But when thou smil'st, I will not look above,
To wood or sky; my hand I will not lay
Upon the temple of my sacred love,
To blame its living fires with base decay;
But whisper to thee, as I nearer move,
"Love, thou dost add another light to day."

How canst thou call my modest love impure,
  Being thyself the holy source of all?
  Can ugly darkness from the fair sun fall?
  Or nature's compact be so insecure,
That saucy weeds may sprout up and endure
  Where gentle flowers were sown? The brooks
      that crawl,
  With lazy whispers, through the lilies tall,
  Or rattle o'er the pebbles, will allure
With no feigned sweetness, if their fount be sweet.
  So thou, the sun whence all my light doth flow —
  Thou, sovereign law by which my fancies grow —
Thou, fount of every feeling, slow or fleet —
  Against thyself wouldst aim a treacherous blow,
  Slaying thy honor with thy own conceit.

Why shall I chide the hand of wilful Time
  When he assaults thy wondrous store of charms?
  Why charge the gray-beard with a wanton crime?
  Or strive to daunt him with my shrill alarms?
Or seek to lull him with a silly rhyme:
  So he, forgetful, pause upon his arms,
  And leave thy beauties in their noble prime,
  The sole survivors of his grievous harms?
Alas! my love, though I'll indeed bemoan
  The fatal ruin of thy majesty;
  Yet I'll remember that to Time alone
I owed thy birth, thy charms' maturity,
  Thy crowning love, with which he vested me,
  Nor can reclaim, though all the rest be flown.

Love is that orbit of the restless soul
Whose circle grazes the confines of space,
Bounding within the limits of its race
Utmost extremes ; whose high and topmost poll
Within the very blaze of heaven doth roll ;
Whose nether course is through the darkest place
Eclipsed by hell. What daring hand shall trace
The blended joys and sorrows that control
A heart whose journeys the fixed hand of fate
Points through this pathway ? Who may soar so high —
Behold such glories with unwinking eye ?
Who drop so low beneath his mortal state,
And thence return with careful chart and date,
To mark which way another's course must lie ?

Thou who dost smile upon me, yet unknown,
  Mayst have more cause if thou wilt draw more
    near.
  Now Summer's heat unbinds the golden zone
  Of virgin buds ; then why should chilling fear
Seal up thy heart, and leave thy love unblown,
  While Nature whispers in thy timid ear,
  "Now is the time"? For Summer 's quickly flown,
  And Winter's frost rounds up the flying year.
Lady, I pray thee, take unto thy heart
  The lesson mother Nature reads to thee ;
  Nor act towards me a more ungentle part
Than Summer acts towards every budding tree,
  That feels her influence through its being dart,
  As I would feel thy influence dart through me.

Fear not, dear maid, the love I give to thee
  Shall feel the palsied touch of Time's decay.
  Thou dost confess my love will ever be,
  And only fear its strength may waste away,
Dropping its blossoms as the seasons flee;
  Or like the evening of a boreal day,
  In lingering twilight stretch its sullen ray,
  And on the edge of night hang doubtfully.
Grant love eternal, and thou grantest all;
  Eternity counts not the passing hour,
  Eternity knows naught of wane or fall,
Nor measures days by bloom or fade of flower,
  Nor o'er its splendor casts sad evening's pall;
  To Time belongs this ever-changing power.

WHERE lags my mistress while the drowsy year
  Wakes into Spring? Lo! Winter sweeps away
  His snowy skirts, and leaves the landscape gay
  With early verdure; and there 's merry cheer
Among the violets, where the sun lies clear
  On the south hill-sides; and at break of day
  I heard the blue-bird busy at my ear;
  And swallows shape their nests of matted clay
Along the eaves, or dip their narrow wings
  Into the mists of evening. All the earth
  Stirs with the wonder of a coming birth,
And all the air with feathery music rings.
  Spring, it would crown thee with transcendent worth,
  To bring my love among thy beauteous things.

O! WOULD that Fortune might bestow on me
One hour secluded from the prying world!
So that the crowd through which my heart is hurled,
Like a poor wreck upon a stormy sea,
Might rage afar; and under some kind lea,
Bowered with the creeping woodbine, and impearled
With the fresh gems of morning, I might be
For once alone with Nature and with thee.
For unto Nature's ear I would resign
The struggling secrets which my bosom fill—
The o'erfraught mystery of my own sweet ill,
In loving thee beyond the prudent line
Marked out by selfish philosophic skill—
To Nature's ear, dear lady, and to thine.

YOUR love to me appears in doubtful signs,
Vague words, shy looks, that never touch the heart;
But to the brain a scanty hint impart
As to whose side your dear regard inclines:
Thence, forced by reason through the narrow lines
That mark and limit the logician's art —
Catching from thought to thought — my mind combines
In one idea the mystic things you start,
And coldly utters to my heart — that swells
With tardy rapture — "It is thee she loves!"
Alas! alas! that reason only proves
A fact your cautious action never tells,
That I must reach my joy by slow removes,
And guess at love, as at the oracles.

No gentle touches of your timid hand —
  No shuddering kisses pressed upon my lip,
  'Twixt fear and passion — no bold words that strip
  The feigning garb off in which we two stand,
Acting our parts, at the harsh world's command —
  No deed that offers to our dust a sip
  Of heavenly nectar — no incautious slip,
  To wring a tear, yet calmly bear the brand,
For the great love through which we were betrayed!
  Love flies with us on sorely crippled wings:
  Prudence, and interest, and the bitter stings
Of shrewd distrust, are doled me. I am made
  A beggar on your bounty. Lend me aid:
  My heart starves, lady, on these wretched things.

Doubt is the offspring of a self-distrust,
  The coward mood of a desponding mind,
  The treacherous pathway o'er which fancy, blind
  To love's clear pointings, treads, as o'er the crust
Of a most faithless quicksand ; 'tis the rust
  Upon truth's shield, the blemish that we find
  Upon a mirror, carelessly designed,
  Distorting nature into shapes unjust,
And making all things that within it move,
  Move in confusion, falsely and awry.
  Doubt is the lees of thought, the dregs that lie
Beyond the bounds which reason reigns above,
  Baffling the keenness of his sun-bright eye ; —
  Yea, doubt is anything — but honest love.

As at an altar, love, behold me kneel
  Thus at thy feet. Too solemn for a lie
  My awful action, and thy bended eye,
  Whose searching power I cannot choose but feel.
And here, thus lowly, all that might conceal
  My heart from thee I sunder and cast by;
  Courting thy notice, begging thee to pry
  Through all my nature, till the whole reveal
Itself to thee. Then say if thou dost find
  One hint of falsehood, one poor thought to breed
  Doubt, or doubt's shadow, in thy candid mind?
Ah, no! I love thee; and my sorest need
  Is trust from thee, a patient trust, resigned
  To face all ills, and triumph though it bleed.

I do assure thee, love, each kiss of thine
 Adds to my stature, makes me more a man,
 Lightens my care, and draws the bitter wine
 That I was drugged with, while my nature ran
Its slavish course. For didst not thou untwine
 My cunning fetters? break the odious ban,
 That quite debased me? free this heart of mine,
 And deck my chains with roses? While I can
I 'll chant thy praises, till the world shall ring
 With thy great glory; and the heaping store
 Of future honors, for the songs I sing,
Shall miss thy poet, at thy feet to pour
 A juster tribute, as the gracious spring
 Of my abundance. — Kiss me, then, once more.

To win and lose thee! In one hour to say,
  "Lo! love is mine!" and ere the dazzled mind
  Can know the fulness of its bliss, or find
  Its conscious vision lifted o'er the sway
Of raging passion — while the heart, a prey
  To aching sense, is shrunken and grown blind
  With too much light — to hear from every wind
  Hissed in my ear, "Lo! love has flown away!"
As if some careless angel left apart
  Heaven's golden doors, and I had seen within
  The radiant saints, and heard the holy din
Of choral triumph, ere with jealous start
  The gates shot backward, closing my sad heart,
  With that bright memory, in a world of sin.

Here part we, love, beneath the world's broad eye,
  Yet heart to heart still answers as of old;
  And though fore'er within my breast I hold
  Thy image shut, and ne'er, by look nor sigh,
Betray thy presence to the foes who lie
  Ambushed around us, do not deem me cold.
  For cowering Love's wide pinions only fold
  Closer, to shield him from the storm that's nigh, —
Closer, to warm the fresh and godlike form
  That glows with life beneath the shrinking wings.
  So my deep love around thee darkly flings
This cloud of coldness, that, beneath it, warm
  As the snow-covered currents of the springs,
  Our hearts may beat, safe-sheltered from the storm.

And shall we part without a parting kiss?
  Must all the love I bore thee, all that thou
  Didst swear to me, untrammelled, vow on vow,
  Ebb to this lowness, come at last to this?
A thousand fears have crossed my dream of bliss;
  And in the very blush and early glow
  Of budding passion, I was stricken low
  By boding fancies, lest our love should miss
A happy goal by its too eager start.
  Yet, come what might, I should have boldly sworn
  That if we parted, howsoe'er forlorn
Our future lot, or cruel the present smart,
  Or what wild acts of passion might be born
  From our despair, that thus we would not part.

No hope is mine, no comfort mine ; for I
  Am as an exile, and no pilgrim's grace
  Nerves my despair ; I never can retrace
  The paths I trod, though myriads pass me by,
Journeying, light-hearted, to the happy place
  Whence I am driven. Thou, Nature, on whose face
  I look for aid, dost close thy weary eye
  Against my grief. The moon wanes in the sky,
The flowers dry up and perish, the great sea
  Through all its land-locked arteries ebbs, the dew
  Lies sickening on the blighted branch ; no new
Creation opens with the Spring : to me
  There is no crescent moon, no bud, no view
  Of refluent tides, no fruit,— nor will there be.

Imagine, love, that I bent over thee ;
Imagine, love, I brushed thy eyelids dry,
Hushed in my hands thy oft-recurring sigh,
Warmed thee within my arms, and patiently
Talked down thy sorrows, till thy heart in glee
Leaped up and rapturously laughed ; while I
Stared in blank wonder at the mystery.
Then, with moist lashes, put thy tresses by —
Marvelling in silence at the happy spell
That brought thee comfort — and thy features dyed
With added crimson, as my kisses fell
Warm on thy lips and forehead. In my pride
I fancy thus, and thou canst do as well ;
'T would be no fancy, were I at thy side.

My lady sighs, and I am far away;
  My lady weeps, and I cannot be near
  To still the sigh, or catch the falling tear
  On lips whose office 'tis to own her sway,
And curl in scorn when other maidens play
  Their love-pranks round me. I am lost in fear,
  Haunted with doubts and shadows that appear
  To lengthen ever with declining day.
All things seem dubious; the rise and fall
  Of my own heart, the wild ideas that move
  Like phantoms through my brain, the faith above
My intellectual grasp, do but appall
  By their dim aspects, and I doubt them all;—
  All seem unreal, except alone thy love.

If, by an absence of unnumbered years,
  I could return, and find thy feelings changed;
  If, by the shedding of uncounted tears,
  I could wash out what early sorrow stained;
If by a coldness I could wake thy fears,
  And make thee chary of what love remained;
  Nay, if by hollow pride, and empty sneers—
  Galling to thee, though but by cunning feigned—
I could once more upon thy gentle breast
  Lay my poor head, with all its aching thought,
  And rock my troubled fancies into rest,
Or soothe the sorrows which my cruelty wrought;
  I would endure the grief, or act the jest,—
  Yea, double both, yet hold the price as naught.

HENCE, cold despair! I do believe that they
  Who fold a promise, and within the breast
  Cherish a faith, shall some time know the rest
  Of bliss consummate. This immortal clay
Is tempered in the tears we brush away;
  Made fruitful by our smiles; and every test
  That love o'ercomes adds plumage to his crest,
  And seals the triumph of a future day.
Else would this stormy heart outpour in vain
  Its frequent tears; and its wild bursts of joy,
  And love unutterable, would but annoy,
Not lighten the full spirit of its pain.
  Let us believe these raptures find employ,
  And smooth a pathway that may yet be plain.

ON MY LADY'S LETTER.

THIS slip of paper touched thy gentle hand,
Doubtless was sunned beneath thy radiant eye;
Perhaps had clearer honor, and did lie
Upon thy bosom, or was proudly fanned
Within thy fragrant breath. At my command
A thousand fancies growing, as they fly,
To maddening sweetness, flit my vision by,
And mingle golden vapors with the sand
That times my idle being. Senseless things
Start into dignity beneath thy touch,
Mount from the earth on love's ecstatic wings,
And to my eyes seem sacred. If from such
I draw such rapture, who may say how much,
Wert thou the theme of my imaginings!

THE ghostly midnight settles on my heart,
  The winter rain against my window beats,
  The flaring lights along the level streets
  Look through a misty halo; torn apart
By every gust, the fog-wreaths twist and start
  In wild disorder. Not a passer meets
  My straining eye; no song nor whistle greets
  My listening ear. This thronged and feverish mart
Sleeps through the night, and Nature rules supreme.
  What thoughts are mine? what visions come to me,
  Drifting alone amid this tideless sea,
When e'en thy eyes are closed above a dream
  In which, perhaps, no trace of me may seem, —
  What can I do but dream and dream of thee?

In this deep hush and quiet of my soul,
  When life runs low, and all my senses stay
  Their daily riot; when my wearied clay
  Resigns its functions, and, without control
Of selfish passion, my essential whole
  Rises in purity, to make survey
  Of those poor deeds that wear my days away;
  When in my ear I hear the distant toll
Of bells that murmur of my coming knell,
  And all things seem a show and mockery —
  Life, and life's actions, noise and vanity;
I ask my mournful heart if it can tell
  If all be truth which I protest to thee:
  And my heart answers, solemnly, "'T is well!"

I HAVE been mounted on life's topmost wave,
  Until my forehead kissed the dazzling cloud;
  I have been dashed beneath the murky shroud
  That yawns between the watery crests. I rave,
Sometimes, liked cursed Orestes; sometimes lave
  My limbs in dews of asphodel; or, bowed
  With torrid heat, I moan to heaven aloud,
  Or shrink with Winter in his icy cave.
Now peace broods over me; now savage rage
  Spurns me across the world. Nor am I free
  From nightly visions, when the pictured page
Of sleep unfolds its varied leaves to me,
  Changing as often as the mimic stage;—
And all this, lady, through my love for thee!

AH! would to heaven that this dear misery,
  Which day by day within my heart I nurse,
  Shaping the issue of the direful curse,
  Against myself, with sad fatality —
This snare of love, which so entangles me,
  Might be unknit. For in my dark reverse
  Of hopeless passion, I must suffer worse
  Than the dull wretch who, ignorant, yet free,
Plods through his daily round of easy cares,
  Nor knows the shuddering depths and trembling
    heights
  Of my deep sorrows and supreme delights;
The dizzy summits which my spirit dares,
  Winging towards thee, in its audacious flights,
  Its gloomy falls to fathomless despairs.

Sometimes, in bitter fancy, I bewail
  This spell of love, and wish the cause removed;
  Wish I had never seen, or, seeing, not loved
  So utterly that passion should prevail
O'er self-regard, and thoughts of thee assail
  Those inmost barriers which so long have proved
  Unconquerable, when such defence behoved.
  But, ah! my treacherous heart doth ever fail
To ratify the sentence of my mind;
  For when conviction strikes me to the core,
  I swear I love thee fondlier than before;
And were I now all free and unconfined,
  Loose as the action of the shoreless wind,
  My slavish heart would sigh for bonds once more.

To-night the tempest rages. All without
  Is darkness, terror, and tremendous wails
  From the mad winds. Fierce rains and savage hails
  Dash on my window; and the branches shout,
To see their luckless blossoms strewn about,
  Like frantic mourners. God, this night she sails
  O'er the chaotic ocean! Fear prevails
  Above my cowering spirit; and a rout
Of dark forebodings makes this pitchy night
  One solid gloom. Hark, how the rushing air
  Clashes my casement! Ah! what heart shall dare
Stand between her and danger, as I might,
  Cheering her courage with love's steady light?
God, I am absent, wilt not Thou be there?

Another shriek like that, O furious wind,
  Will madden me! Is there no hand to check
  Thy wild career? no power whose awful beck
  May lull thy frenzied wrath? For thou art blind
With loosened passion; and, thus unconfined,
  Thou dost abuse thy license, to the wreck
  Of all creation. Now, how reels the deck
  Above my helpless love! How every mind,
Pent in that groaning vessel, paints its thought
  Of shameless fear upon each pallid face!
  How the infectious passion spreads! till, base
With selfish terror, man is worse than naught,
  And manhood but a name. If prayers are aught,
  God, stand me near her, in some coward's place!

Again the tireless winds are rushing past,
  Heavy with blinding vapors ; and again
  The streaming willows lash my window-pane,
  Dotting the glass with yellow leaves that fast
Cling to their dripping hold, like wretches cast
  Upon my charity. Across the main
  My love still sails ; and forth, through storm and rain,
  My heart goes out to seek her. Ruthless blast,
Chill northern mist, and cutting hail, are ye
  Fit comrades for a being who has known
  No harsher sounds than the close whispered tone
Of my affection ? — cold to no degree
  More than my arms clasped round her tenderly ? —
  No crueller wounds than from my eyes were thrown ?

THANK Heaven, a lull — a lull in the long roar
  Of the spent hurricane ; and, lo ! afar,
  Through the fast-scudding rack, one splendid star —
  Brighter to me than star e'er shone before —
Looks downward, like the mystic light that bore
  Peace and good will to mortals. Ye that are
  The seaman's joy, soft western gales, debar
  Your breath no longer ; waft her gently o'er
The calming sea : then, if ye will, return
  In stormy fleetness, hissing from the East,
  With your old rage a thousand-fold increased ;
For though the universal ether burn
  With your hot flight, too soon I cannot learn
  That all the perils of my love have ceased.

WHAT fancy, or what flight of wingéd thought,
  O lady of my heart, hast thou to chime
  Accordant with the flow of my poor rhyme?
  Have my strange songs a dearer solace brought
Than those remembered lays thy childhood caught,
  And treasured safely through disloyal time —
  Lays of a sweeter tongue and fairer clime;
  Pure as thy dreams, before our passion sought
And won the shadowy realm, and steeped thy sleep
  In fiery visions and terrific throes
  Of self-consuming love? My songs are foes
To peace and thee; yet thou dost bid me sweep
  The torturing strings, although thy eyelids weep:
Find'st thou a pleasure in thy very woes?

I KNOW art hardens what my love would speak,
  And bounds my feelings with a rigid line
  Of measured rhymes, whose narrow laws confine
  My forward passions, making cold and weak
The warm rich currents that forever seek
  An outlet from my heart. The loss is thine —
  To taste but water where you hoped for wine;
  But mine the shameful burning of the cheek —
Mine the cruel sorrow o'er a fruitless deed,
  Who boasted nobly how sublime a thing
  Should bloom from love, and decorate the Spring
With beauties suited aptly to the seed
  From whence it grew; — but grew a sightless weed,
  Shaming the hand that makes the offering.

Yet, love, forgive thy Poet if his lays
  Faint with a burden which they cannot bear;
  And vain regret, and miserable despair,
  Are the sole offsprings of my weak essays.
To paint a passion that so strongly sways
  My lowly heart, I should be master where
  I feel myself but slave, and scarcely dare
  Lift up my eyes to what my hand portrays.
Forgive my feeble efforts: and believe
  Feeling o'ermasters art; and conquered art,
  Like a true slave, works on with heavy heart,
Slighting its ordered task. Then, do not grieve
  At my cold words; but say my words deceive,
  Reaching at that which words cannot impart.

O! for some spirit, some magnetic spark,
That used nor word, nor rhyme, nor balanced pause
Of doubtful phrase, which so supinely draws
My barren verse, and blurs love's shining mark
With misty fancies! — O! to burst the dark
Of smothered feeling with some new-found laws,
Hidden in nature, that might bridge the flaws
Between two beings, end this endless cark,
And make hearts know what lips have never said!
O! for some spell, by which one soul might move
With echoes from another, and dispread
Contagious music through its chords, above
The touch of mimic art: that thou might tread
Beneath thy feet this wordy show of love!

There is a sorrow underlays mere grief,
  A gnawing woe beyond the source of tears,
  A weary pain with neither hopes nor fears,
  A dull, dead load that cannot find relief
In running eyes, whose passions are as brief
  As their o'erflowings. For each tear-drop clears
  The heart from which it issues, and oft cheers
  With sunny dew the gloomiest cypress-leaf.
But, ah! my care sticks ever at the heart,
  Haunts every thought, and deadens every sense;
  Sighs are in vain, tears come not, and the tense
Cords of existence strain, yet will not part
  Their stubborn hold on earth. O! bitter smart,
  To call thee mine, who must be ever hence.

To love thee absent were sufficient pain,
  Even though that pain might not outlast a day;
  And with to-morrow's sunset I could say,
  "Lo! moonrise comes, and love shines out again!"
Or stretch the term a week; I might restrain
  This heart until the Sabbath morn should lay
  Its peace upon it. Months might glide away;
  And I could count the sunshine and the rain,
And sum them up in flowers, to prophesy
  Thy fragrant coming. Though a year would be
  A weary time, I could wait patiently
To hear Christ's birthday clamored through the sky
  By the rejoicing bells: but who shall try
  To fix time's measures on eternity?

Why should I cheat my heart with open lies,
  Summoned by Fancy from her teeming store?—
  Why call thee mine alone forevermore,
  Yet know what distance parts, what fate defies
Our mutual love? True, we are joined by ties
  That girdle earth, and bind fate's functions o'er
  To sovereign love: but shall I not deplore
  That I no longer look into thy eyes—
Bask in thy presence—fill my aching soul
  With love's sweet calm?—Or all my senses thrill
  With kisses gathered here and there at will,
As flowers in spring-time, till we touch the goal
  Of more than mortal ecstasy, and roll
  In joys that make the wondering gods stand still?

Ah! let me live on memories of old, —
  The precious relics I have set aside
  From life's poor venture; things that yet abide
  My ill-paid labor, shining, like pure gold,
Amid the dross of cheated hopes whose hold
  Dropped at the touch of action. Let me glide
  Down the smooth past, review that day of pride
  When each to each our mutual passion told —
When love grew frenzy in thy blazing eye,
  Fear shone heroic, caution quailed before
  My hot, resistless kisses — when we bore
Time, conscience, destiny, down, down for aye,
  Beneath victorious love, and thou didst cry,
  "Strike, God! life's cup is running o'er and o'er!"

In vain to thee I stretch imploring arms
  Across the hollow waste of barren night;
  In vain I task my jaded eyes for sight
  Of some fair vision, whose imagined charms
May mimic thine. My bitter knowledge warms
  Against my fancy. Love draws no delight
  From self-delusion; and a hateful flight
  Of stinging truths around my senses swarms,
Forcing thy absence on me. Idle dreams
  Trouble my slumbers; but when any ray
  Of thy bright presence through the darkness beams,
I start and wake, as though the height of day
  Flamed on my eyelids: for it only seems
  That I must love, and thou be far away.

Time shall not dry thy ever-falling tears
For me, thou lone one! sorrowing o'er the ill
That tortures thee, and can do aught but kill.
I will pursue thee through the bitter years,
A loathful shadow, following thee still,
Dragged after thee against my better will;
Struck by the burning hand which God uprears
Against our sin; and doomed o'er vale and hill
To dog thy feet, to trail my blackness o'er
Thy brightest path, to make the flowers assume
A dull, sick look, to wrap in horrid gloom
All things around thee, till the awful store
Of vengeance on our crime be poured no more,
And we together sink into the tomb.

I do not sorrow that thy love was cast
On one unworthy of thy purer thought;
Nor that the promise of thy youth was brought
To barren issue by the deadly blast
That plagued the heart to which thy heart held fast,
And in the rarest gift of nature wrought
A noxious canker, mocking thee who sought
To find a sweetness in it. If the past
Were passed indeed; and thou, away from me,
Couldst gather bloom, and for the future nurse
Thy withered youth to beauty; or rehearse,
Some day, the moral of thy grief, and be
From the infection of my influence free, —
'T were well, but I pursue thee like a curse.

I HEARD a voice that through the midnight cried,
"Thy peace is gone, thy sweet content is fled!
Never again," the phantom prophet said,
"Shalt thou taste joy; for love to thee has died,
And naught of love remaineth, now, beside
His ashes and thy sorrow. Where is sped
The shaft you shot? Has not your bosom bled,
By your own hand transpierced?" O! thou hast lied —
O! viewless phantom, thou hast lied to me!
Love is immortal as this crown of bay,
Which from my brow upon his tomb I lay —
Love is immortal in my memory!
And I will watch his relics, weep and pray,
And from my heart sing his sad elegy.

LIKE old King Hamlet sleeping in the flowers,
O'er-arched with woodbine and the clustering rose,
I lay supine in odorous repose,
Safe, as I thought, amid my garden bowers:
While with light footsteps tripped the smiling hours,
And my heart fluttered with the rapturous throes
Of such a dream of joy as, haply, flows
Past the closed eyelids of the musing powers
Who rest in Eden — with a dream of thee.
Anon upon me, with accursèd bane,
Fate stole on tiptoe, and through ear and brain
Poured his foul poison. Wild with agony,
I shriek, I wake, I would but cannot flee;
Then helpless fall, no more to dream again.

No forward step in all my history,
  Through the wide region of my coming life,
  But shall resound, above the din and strife
  Of every action, with the fame of thee.
No lyric song, no stately tragedy,
  No cry of joy nor pain, but shall be rife
  With thy sweet self. More close than man to wife
  Shall we be joined through all futurity.
Doubt not the issue. While my melody
  Shall move the world, in each applauded lay
  Men shall behold my love's undimmed display;
And when the troubles of our life shall be
  Laid in the dust, the sorrows of to-day
  Shall be the glory of thy memory.

I WILL not blazon forth thy sacred name,
  Holding thee up for wonder to the mood
  Of those poor fools whose darts of malice strewed
  Thy path of life, and might thy grave defame;
I will but hint it dimly. Love's pure flame
  Will shine as brightly, though the spicy wood
  Whereon it feeds be little understood;
  For, to all light man's reverence is the same.
And if, in coming time, some lover weep
  Over the sorrows of my mournful line —
  Some wretch whose fortune has been sad as mine—
Wondering, meanwhile, what gentle name may sleep
  Under my phrase, the homage shall be thine,
  Though my sealed lips thy mystic title keep.

As a sad hermit in his cloistered cell,
  With the lone image of his martyred Lord,
  The last, best treasure of a wasted hoard,
  Do I alone with thy dear image dwell.
To thee alone my sinking heart shall swell,
  To thee alone my scalding tears be poured ;
  And to such vows as thou didst once accord
  I 'll shape my faith to thee invisible.
And when Death's hand within my own be pressed —
  Welcome as friendship's cordial pressure — I
  Will grasp his icy fingers, doubly blest ;
And down to happy dreams of thee will lie,
  With thy sweet promise cradled in my breast,
  With thy sweet image beaming in my eye.

Only through this, this precious gift of song,
  Can I hold converse with my lady now.
  For many a threat, and many a lowering brow,
  Are raised between us; and the ruthless thong
Of slander hisses through the air, to wrong
  Her tender nature. To the storm I bow;
  But, like a reed, the fiercer tempests grow,
  The clearer is my singing. Ah! the throng
Of heedless men, who in my music hear
  Only the echoes of their hearts, and see
  Their petty loves reflected back from me,
Know not that every tone is meant to cheer
  The dismal fortune of thy history, —
  Know not, dear heart, I 'm whispering in thy ear.

Fate, of all seasons, chose the happy time
  When the bud swells, the golden grasses spring,
  The loosened brooks for their new freedom sing,
  The blue-bird carols, and the poet's rhyme
Renews its wasted nature ; when, sublime
  With his own power, day's rich and generous king
  Wheels on in state, and all the land doth fling
  The flowery tributes of its loyal clime
Before the light of his triumphant smile : —
  Ah ! then the hand of fell intruding Fate
  Struck me the blow that made me desolate ;
Nor yet content, with unrelenting guile,
  He chose this time, to wreak his fury vile,
  And with fair Spring bemocked my fallen state.

I SHALL be faithful, though the weary years
  Spread out before me like a mountain chain,
  Rugged and steep, ascending from the plain,
  Without a path ; though where the cliff uprears
Its sternest front, and echoes in my ears
  My own deep sobs of solitary pain,
  It is my fate to scale ; though all in vain
  I spend my labor, and my idle tears
Torture but me : I know, despite my ill,
  That with each step a little wastes away —
  A little of this life wastes day by day ;
And far beyond the desert which I fill
  With my vast sorrow, I have faith to say
  That we shall meet ; so I press onward still.

I HAVE not turned for sympathy to friends;
I have not told the story of my wrong,
Nor all the falsehoods that to thee belong, —
That shallow-hearted fickleness which sends
A pang through all my nature, and oft ends
In dreary tears the proudest dream of song.
I have not burst the knitted fetters, strong
With my own truth, because thy flight offends.
What man can say he heard me sigh or groan,
Quail at the sound of thy oft-mentioned name,
Sneer at thy faith, or stain thy taintless fame
With the least breath of slander? No, alone
I've borne the dreadful secret of thy shame,
Hiding thy guilt as if it were my own.

Across the waters, through the void of night,
My spirit sends its last despairing cry.
One moment poised, as in the act to fly,
With arms outstretched, and heart that yearns for flight,
I bend towards thee. O! hear me, ere the bright
And happy impulse fades beneath the eye
Of outraged pride, and self-love sullenly
Resumes his sceptre! Hear me, ere the blight,
With which thy falsehood cankered me, shall fall,
Like God's dread judgment, and the clinging stain
Add to my sorrow, — pain begot on pain!
O, faithless Love! O, perjured heart! O, all
Unworthy, yet all loved! if vain my call,
Rest, dream, forget! — I shall not call again.

HERE let the motions of the world be still! —
  Here let Time's fleet and tireless pinions stay
  Their endless flight! — or to the present day
  Bind my Love's life and mine. I have my fill
Of earthly bliss: to move, is to meet ill.
  Though lavish Fortune in my path might lay
  Fame, power, and wealth,—the toys that make the play
  Of earth's grown children, — I would rather till
The stubborn furrows of an arid land,
  Toil with the brute, bear famine and disease,
  Drink bitter bondage to the very lees,
Than break our union by love's tender band,
  Or drop its glittering shackles from my hand,
  To grasp at empty glories such as these.

All the world's malice, all the spite of fate,
Cannot undo the rapture of the past.
I, like a victor, hold these glories fast;
And here defy the envious powers, that wait
Upon the crumbling fortunes of our state,
To snatch this myrtle chaplet, or to blast
Its smallest leaf. Thus to the wind I cast
The poet's laurel, and before their date
Summon the direst terrors of my doom.
For, with this myrtle symbol of my love,
I reign exultant, and am fixed above
The petty fates that other joys consume.
As on a flowery path, through life I 'll move, —
As through an arch of triumph, pass the tomb.

www.ingramcontent.com/pod-product-compliance
Lightning Source LLC
LaVergne TN
LVHW021121110826
845150LV00005B/910